XSLT Developer's Guide

About the Authors

Chris von See is a senior technical director at eFORCE, a systems integration company specializing in the development of enterprise-class Java 2 Enterprise Edition applications. Chris has been in the computer software business since 1983 and has spent time in product development and management at a number of major computer software companies. Chris and his wife Sharon are also the founders of TechAdapt, Inc., a company that provides technology and services to assist in the production of electronic materials for the blind and visually impaired.

Chris lives in Dallas, Texas, with his wife, two children, and three dogs. When he's not working, he enjoys traveling and reading adventure and mystery novels.

Nitin Keskar, Ph.D., is a senior technical director at eFORCE. He has been programming since 1989 and has worked for the software giant Oracle as well as the premier e-business consulting firm Sapient. In his career, Nitin has had a variety of responsibilities including product development, management, and consulting.

Nitin lives in Dallas, Texas, with his wife Rupa and his daughter Reesa. Among other things, Nitin enjoys camping and traveling, reading, and listening to music from a variety of genres.

XSLT Developer's Guide

Chris von See
Nitin Keskar

McGraw-Hill/Osborne

New York   Chicago   San Francisco
Lisbon   London   Madrid   Mexico City
Milan   New Delhi   San Juan
Seoul   Singapore   Sydney   Toronto

McGraw-Hill/Osborne
2600 Tenth Street
Berkeley, California 94710
U.S.A.

To arrange bulk purchase discounts for sales promotions, premiums, or fund-raisers, please contact **McGraw-Hill/**Osborne at the above address. For information on translations or book distributors outside the U.S.A., please see the International Contact Information page immediately following the index of this book.

XSLT Developer's Guide

1234567890 CUS CUS 0198765432

ISBN 0-07-219408-1

Publisher	Brandon A. Nordin
Vice President & Associate Publisher	Scott Rogers
Acquisitions Editor	Jim Schachterle
Project Editors	Janet Walden, Jennifer Malnick
Acquisitions Coordinator	Timothy Madrid
Technical Editor	David Gulbransen
Copy Editor	Judy Ziajka
Proofreader	Pat Mannion
Indexer	David Heiret
Computer Designers	Lucie Ericksen, Michelle Galicia, John Patrus
Illustrators	Michael Mueller, Lyssa Wald
Series Design	Roberta Steele
Cover Design	Greg Scott
Cover Illustration	Eliot Bergman

This book was composed with Corel VENTURA ™ Publisher.

Contents at a Glance

Contents

Acknowledgments

If this endeavor has taught us nothing else, it's taught us that it's incredibly easy to let the demands of a career (or two), family and personal needs, and life in general push you off the path to your final goal. For keeping us (gently) on track with this book, special thanks go out to our editor, Jim Schachterle, and our acquisitions coordinator, Tim Madrid; both have been great to work with and extremely helpful when inspiration and imagination ran low. We would also like to thank our project editor, Janet Walden, and our technical reviewer, David Gulbransen.

Thanks also go to our friends at eFORCE, who contributed comments and support throughout the writing process. In particular, we'd like to acknowledge the contributions of Vince Cross, Glenn Kimball, and Vasundhara Andolu for their technical comments, personal guidance, and overall support.

Introduction

Looking back at the meteoric rise in the popularity of XML, it's amazing to see the broad applicability and far-reaching impact on the computer software, database/data management, and business-to-business communications worlds of such a seemingly simple technology. Those in the document management industry who saw XML's evolution from SGML knew the power that an extensible tag-based markup language could have; by providing a way to structure data in a highly configurable and easy-to-process way, such a language makes it possible to store information about the *meaning* of data, and not just an indistinguishable stream of bits and bytes.

After XML's initial release in February of 1998, a whole range of related standards sprang up, each with its own twist on the XML name: XLink, XPath, XPointer, XSL, XML Query, XFragment, XML Information Set, and many others. Some, such as XPath (the XML Path Language), proved to be extremely useful by themselves or as components of other technologies and standards; others still have not reached their full potential and may never do so.

So now we have the Extensible Stylesheet Language for Transformations, or XSLT, a spin-off of the Extensible Stylesheet Language (XSL), which focuses on the transformation of one XML document into another, different structure. XSLT has, in its first release, proven itself to be extremely useful for certain applications and yet somewhat difficult to understand and use effectively. Is XSLT a niche technology, to be relegated to only certain types of applications? What is XSLT capable of, and what's the best way to use it? How can XSLT be integrated with other applications to create larger systems?

Who Should Read This Book

This book is intended for application developers, system architects, and IT managers who want to learn what XSLT is, what it is capable of doing, and how to use it to solve business problems. Although the more technical topics presume a high-level familiarity with XML concepts, HTML, and/or programming using Java or C++, it is not at all difficult to gain a general understanding of XSLT even if you have never touched XML before. If you are not familiar with XML, we hope that Chapter 1 will provide you with enough background information about it to get started with XSLT programming.

What's in This Book

Given the close relationship between XML and XSLT, it is crucial to know the basics of XML before learning XSLT programming. To provide the reader with a foundation for understanding the rest of the book, Chapter 1, "An XML Primer," introduces the key fundamentals of XML, describing this powerful technology in straightforward terms. Building on this background, Chapter 2, "An Introduction to XSLT," introduces XSLT by providing insights into its history and why it was created, discussing how XSLT works, and identifying the key features that make it a powerful tool in today's software arsenal.

Chapter 3, "XML and XSLT Applications," delves into the application of XSLT in more detail. In particular, this chapter discusses the types of enterprise applications that XML is best suited for and how XSLT can complement XML and streamline application development in many of these applications. It also provides some real-life examples of how XSLT is used today; by the end of this chapter, you should be prepared to tackle the more technical aspects of the tool and learn to develop your own XSLT applications.

The structure of an XSLT stylesheet is discussed in Chapter 4, "The Structure of an XSLT Stylesheet." Unlike conventional programming tools, XSLT does not use a procedural language; rather, it depends on constructs called templates to indicate how portions of an XML document are to be processed. Understanding how to construct a stylesheet and how templates are used by XSLT is critical to successful use of this tool.

Chapter 5, "Expressions," introduces the powerful XML Path Language (XPath), which is a key part of the XML standards suite and is the language XSLT uses to select nodes in the input XML document for processing by templates. XPath is extremely powerful, but that power comes at the cost of a certain amount of complexity. We walk through this pathing language step-by-step, and at the end of this chapter, you should have a good understanding of how to use XPath expressions in XSLT stylesheet templates.

In Chapter 6, "Template Rules," we talk about some of the rules that influence the way that XSLT templates work. Some of these rules are built into XSLT itself, while others depend heavily on the relationships among templates in the stylesheet. By using (and manipulating) these rules effectively, you can perform all sorts of interesting and useful XSLT tricks.

By the time you reach Chapter 7, "Creating the XSLT Result Tree," you will have learned much about how to read an input XML document and drive portions of your stylesheet to process certain elements in that input document. This chapter introduces you to the facilities that XSLT provides for generating static and dynamic output from your stylesheet, using data from your input document to determine what kinds of output should be generated, and controlling the flow of control inside your template. Using these facilities, it's possible to carry out some very powerful transformations on input XML documents, performing extensive restructuring, and data manipulation using a combination of XSLT and XPath functions.

Chapter 8, "Variables and Parameters," introduces the concept of XSLT variables and parameters. Variables and parameters can help you develop generic stylesheets whose processing can be customized by providing additional information when the stylesheet is invoked, and they complement other XSLT capabilities by allowing data to be shared among templates. This chapter also outlines how the concepts of variables and parameters in XSLT differ from those in many other programming languages that you may be familiar with.

Chapter 9, "Creating Stylesheet Output," revisits XSLT output with a discussion of the finer points of the generation of XML, HTML, and text output from your XSLT stylesheet. XSLT's built-in functions make it easier to control characteristics of your output document, such as document encoding, and provide tools to automatically generate numbering and error messages.

To facilitate development of more complex applications, XSLT provides tools for sorting data, cross-referencing elements by their attributes and data, processing multiple documents in a single stylesheet, and so on. Chapter 10, "XSL/XSLT Power Programming," discusses these features and more in detail to help you understand when and how to make the most of these advanced functions.

Tying it all together, Chapter 11, "Practical XSLT Examples," gives you some real-life examples of how XSLT is used, complete with working code examples.

This chapter pulls from all of the other chapters in this book and shows you how to use different XSLT features together to perform powerful transformations on your XML documents, generate stylesheets from other stylesheets, and so on.

Because of XML's broad applicability in enterprise applications, we thought it important to discuss XSLT's relevance in that same context. Chapter 12, "XSLT in the Enterprise," does just that, with more detailed explanations of how and why XSLT is used in enterprise-class applications. This chapter also discusses key issues related to real-life XSLT deployment, and provides a checklist of questions to go over before undertaking a complex XSLT project.

Chapter 13, "Programming Tools and Technologies," discusses the currently available XSLT tools. Although many commercial vendors support XML, the most popular XSLT tools are open source or in the public domain. This chapter not only points out the most popular tools, but also discusses how these tools are used in cooperation with applications written in Java, C++, and Perl and points you to resources where you can find more information on these and other programming languages.

Since XSLT 1.0 is the current W3C specification, the examples discussed in this book relate to the same. However, Working Drafts for versions 2.0 of XSLT and XPath have been recently released, and we expect the specification to be finalized soon. With this in mind, Appendix A provides a brief overview of XSLT2 and XPath2.

Appendix B provides an overview of W3C's Working Groups (WG) that develop the specifications and recommendations for interrelated web technologies such as XSL/XSLT, XML Protocol, HTML, DOM, HTTP, Encryption, and several others.

Appendix C lists key resources to find out more about XSL and XSLT. These resources include books as well as web sites that you will find useful.

Finally, the Glossary provides definitions of technical terms related to XSLT and XML.

How to Read This Book

This book assumes that you are at least somewhat familiar with XML, but have little or no knowledge of XSLT. If you are not familiar with XML or feel you need a refresher before starting on XSLT, we suggest you read the introduction to XML in Chapter 1 before tackling the more technical material in this book.

Because the technical material in later chapters builds extensively on that in prior chapters, you will be best served by reading this book in a linear fashion, although jumping into a chapter emphasizing the tools and techniques you need for your current interest should be fruitful as well. If you are a beginner in the world of XSLT, consider starting with the introduction to XSLT in Chapter 2 and proceeding through the descriptions of XSLT tools in Chapter 13. If you already have a general understanding of XSLT and are looking for more specifics on the functionality that XSLT offers, you can focus more on Chapters 2 through 7 and then skip to Chapter 11 for the detailed examples. If you are interested in finding out what XML and XSLT can do for you before learning the XSLT syntax, discussions in Chapter 1 and 12 should be helpful.

An XML Primer

In this chapter, we discuss the background of the XSLT language, which is a standard set by the World Wide Web Consortium (W3C). XSLT, which stands for Extensible Stylesheet Language for Transformations, is designed to *transform* XML source trees into practically any document format you need. In fact, an XSLT stylesheet itself is required to be a well-formed XML document. Hence, it's only appropriate that we begin our discussion with an overview of the history of XML and other developments related to the World Wide Web (WWW). We will then explore the structure of XML documents, discuss the concepts of well-formed and valid XML documents and then move on to a short discussion of the related W3C standards.

A Brief History of XML

The roots of XML can be traced back to the domain of electronic publishing. In the late 1960s, IBM researchers were working on defining a language that would be useful in managing large amounts of electronic documents. In 1969, Charles Goldfarb, along with Ed Losher and Ray Lorie, invented the General Markup Language (GML), which is the granddaddy of XML. GML aided editing, formatting, and document publishing and worked well with text search subsystems. Goldfarb then continued his work and invented the much-improved, much more powerful Standard Generalized Markup Language (SGML), in 1974. The first working draft of SGML was then created by the American National Standards Institute (ANSI) committee in 1980.

These developments were followed by the release of the initial standard in 1983 and the acceptance of the first draft standard, in 1985, by the European community. SGML was further legitimized when it was established as an ISO standard (ISO 8879:1986) in 1986.

An interesting tidbit: the final SGML standard was published using SGML itself. The system used for this publishing was developed by Anders Berglund at the respected high-energy nuclear physics laboratory Conseil Européen pour la Recherche Nucléaire (CERN), now known as the European Particle Physics Laboratory.

SGML proved to be a robust and powerful information standard for electronic publishing and was widely adopted by key United States government organizations such the Department of Defense and the Internal Revenue Service (IRS), as well as by large companies in the automotive, telecommunications, and aerospace sectors, and of course, IBM. Needless to say, IBM continues to support and use SGML and XML. The common thread among all these organizations is their large size, and therefore, the vast resources that they can muster to use SGML. Smaller companies have generally stayed away from this versatile but relatively complex language.

While SGML provided a very powerful and versatile means of marking up electronic documents, its complexity was its downside, and hence it attracted a relatively small and specialized technical user base. For wider adoption, what was needed was a language that was a lot simpler to read as well as to code. This need gave rise to the creation of Hypertext Markup Language (HTML), which was invented by Tim Berners-Lee and Robert Cailliau, who were then working at CERN.

CERN, a premier research organization, had thousands of scientists working on a large number of projects and used hundreds of complex computer systems that hosted a wide variety of programs. Berners-Lee, then a consultant to CERN, developed his first hypertext system, Enquire, in 1980 to manage the internal data about the people, projects, and programs within CERN. Berners-Lee joined CERN full-time in 1984 and continued his work related to hypertext. In March 1989, he submitted a proposal to develop a hypertext-based system that would have an open architecture and that would be distributed over a communications network. Cailliau, who was independently working on a hypertext system himself, joined forces with Berners-Lee and helped rewrite the original proposal. To begin, a simplified tag-based language based on SGML was developed. This precursor to HTML had a small user base, consisting primarily of European scientists, who used it to author and share electronic documents over the EUNet, which was also linked the ARPANet.

Out of the collaboration between Berners-Lee and Cailliau was born the first web browser, WorldWideWeb, which was developed on a NeXT computer, and then the first web server, at info.cern.ch, in December 1990. Berners-Lee graciously shared the web server with the global computing community in August 1991. This was followed by the development and release of another browser for Unix, ViolaWWW, by Pei Wei at the University of California at Berkeley in May 1992. ViolaWWW provided advanced capabilities such as support for graphics and applets.

Joseph Hardin and Dave Thompson, working at the National Center for Supercomputing Applications (NCSA) of the University of Illinois, Urbana-Champaign (UIUC), downloaded the ViolaWWW browser and demonstrated it to NCSA's Software Design Group in 1992. This demonstration of the use of the web inspired two students from that group, Marc Andreessen and Eric Bina, who began working on a web browser for XWindows in February 1993, which they shared with the computing community at large. Andreessen diligently monitored the usegroups to gather feedback about this infant browser and ensured that bug fixes and code enhancements were handled promptly. Andreessen then led a software team at NCSA that developed the free, publicly available web browser Mosaic. Mosaic built on the foundation of Berners-Lee's original browser and provided support for graphics, sound, and video. In 1994, NCSA assigned the commercial rights for Mosaic to Spyglass, which, in turn, licensed its technology to Netscape and Microsoft.

Jim Clark, the founder of SGI, joined forces with Mark Andreessen and other developers from the original Mosaic team to start Mosaic Communications, which developed a commercial web browser in May 1994. The name of this company was later changed to Netscape as a part of settlement of a lawsuit filed by UIUC.

In a parallel development, the first standard of HTML as we know it was agreed upon in May 1994 at the first World Wide Web (WWW) conference. This, together with the launch of Netscape, led to a landmark historic event: Netscape released version 1.0 of its first commercial web browser, Mozilla, in December 1994.

Mozilla gained overnight popularity, and Netscape responded promptly to the needs of its user community by incorporating support for e-mail and newsgroups within the browser. After its initial version aimed at Unix systems, Netscape quickly ported the browser to other popular operating systems such as Windows and Macintosh OS. Around this time, HTML, given its fixed tag set and easy-to-read syntax, was perceived to be simple and approachable by even the neophyte programmers, and it quickly rose to become a standard for web publishing.

HTML, despite its simplicity, has been a wonderful tool for web developers and has performed beyond anyone's wildest imagination, thanks to Berners-Lee's ingenious architecture. Innumerable web sites using this static tool have been developed and launched almost overnight.

Over the years, however, the limitations of HTML have become clear to the ever-demanding, ever-innovative computing community. HTML is not extensible—that is, if developers need tags beyond what is provided in the standard toolset, they cannot create any.

HTML is primarily aimed at managing presentations on a thin client—that is, a browser—and so is not especially reusable. One major consequence of this limitation is that HTML web sites are not very scalable and cannot meet future demands made on that web site. In short, managing complex, dynamic web sites using just HTML is a webmaster's nightmare. Finally, HTML by itself can provide only one way of displaying content or data and thus violates one of the prime directives of the electronic publishing industry: separation of data from presentation. These deficiencies, among other factors, gave rise to the need to develop an open standard that was extensible, yet as portable (if not more so) as HTML. SGML, by design, meets all of these demands. Alas, its complexity does not make it suitable for use by anyone other than SGML experts. A combination of these factors created the perfect atmosphere for the genesis of XML and related standards.

Beginning in early 1996, Dan Connolly at the W3C foresaw the need for a standard related to SGML, although W3C did not have the necessary resources to pursue this work. Jon Bosak, then at Sun, had been in communication with W3C about such an open standard since his days at Novell. In May 1996, Connolly convinced Bosak to organize and lead a W3C working group to put SGML on the web, using some of Sun's resources. This approach was different from that for W3C's other working groups, which were organized and run by W3C's own staff. Bosak agreed to the proposal and talked to the world's foremost SGML experts at WWW, SGML, and ISO conferences that he attended over the next few weeks. The follow-up work was titled "Web SGML Activity," although James Clark, an SGML/DSSSL veteran, came up with the name Extensible Markup Language (XML). As an aside, you might note that although it is fashionable to write Extensible as *eXtensible*, the former is the correct word to use in XML's complete name as it appears in the W3C specifications.

The basic design was started in earnest in August 1996 under the guidance of Tim Bray, Jean Paoli, and C. M. Sperberg-McQueen and was completed at a rapid pace in just 11 weeks. The first draft of the specification was presented at the SGML'96 conference in November 1996. The W3C working draft that resulted from this work was published in November 1996 and called XML "an extremely simplified dialect of SGML." The Proposed Recommendation for XML was published about a year later in December 1997 and finalized as a Technical Recommendation for version 1.0 in February 1998. Thereafter, XML became a buzzword in record time, and its momentum shows no signs of slowing down.

XML now enjoys wide support from key players in the software industry such as Sun, Oracle, Microsoft, SAP, IBM, and Adobe. It has become the de facto standard for describing data and content on the web. As you will see in the next section, XML is straightforward to read and code, it is a great tool for describing hierarchical data that is machine readable, and it is useful in building web applications involving a diverse range of technologies, including RDBMS, Java, HTML, XSL, and XSLT.

Anatomy of an XML Document

In this section we will discuss the structure of XML documents, and their fundamental components. The best way to dissect an XML document is to look at the components of a sample document and discuss them as we go along. So consider the following XML document, `auth.xml`, which outputs a list of authors:

```
<?xml version="1.0"?>

<!-- data specifications begin-->
<All_authors>
  <Author AuthID="77">
  <Name>
```

```
      <First_name>Samuel</First_name>
      <Last_name>Clemens</Last_name>
   </Name>
   <Address>
     <Address_line1>111 Mansion Boulevard</Address_line1>
     <Address_line2>Suite 100</Address_line2>
     <City>Chicago</City>
     <State>IL</State>
     <ZIP>31313</ZIP>
   </Address>
   </Author>

   <Author AuthID="88">
...
   </Author>
</All_authors>
<!-- data specifications end -->
```

The following sections discuss the components of the XML document.

The XML Declaration

The preamble to the document, `<?xml version="1.0"?>`, simply indicates that this is an XML document following the 1.0 specification of the W3C. You can optionally add the detail about the exact ISO specification that XML follows, as shown in the following line of code:

```
<?xml version="1.0" encoding="iso-8859-1"?>
```

Comments

Any comments that you want to enter in the XML document can be entered between the tags `<!--` and `-->`.

Tags

Just like HTML, XML tags such as `<All_authors>` are enclosed within the delimiters `<` and `>`. There are a few differences, however: whereas HTML uses a fixed set of tags, you have the freedom to make up any name for a tag as long as you don't use special characters such as single or double quotation marks. The second difference is that the tags in XML are case sensitive. The third major difference is that an end marker is required in XML for every tag. In the following example, the end tag </First_name> is the end marker:

```
<First_name>Samuel</First_name>
```

Elements

An element consists of a start tag, an end tag, and everything between the tags (commonly referred to as "element content"). The following code shows a complete Name element, which contains a number of other elements:

```
<Name>
  <First_name>
    Samuel
  </First_name>
  <Last_name>
    Clemens
  </Last_name>
</Name>
```

Every XML document is required to have one and only one document element that contains the rest of the data. This is the first, or the outermost, element in the data specification and is called the *document* or *root* element. In the XML file auth.xml, <All_authors> is the document element.

All elements are required to be nested properly—that is, each element except the document element must be contained wholly inside another element. For example, since the start tag for an element, First_name, is contained within another element, Name, there must be a corresponding end tag, </Name>. The following code is illegal:

```
<Name>
  <First_name>
    Samuel
  <Last_name>
    Clemens
  </First_name>
  </Last_name>
</Name>
```

A word of caution about tags and elements: you cannot use the HTML tags in an XML document and expect the parser to treat them as they would be in HTML. This is because the XML parser makes no assumptions about what a tag may mean; that responsibility lies completely with you, the programmer. For example, if you use the

<B></B> tags in an XML document, the parser will not know that you intend the element contained within these tags to be boldface in the output.

Attributes

In an XML document, you can optionally declare any number of attributes to associate name-value pairs with any given element. For example, AuthID is an attribute of the Author element in the following code, and 77 is the value of the AuthID attribute. Note that the value of an attribute must be enclosed within double quotation marks. An attribute is a part of an element's definition, so it is included with the element name between the element's starting and ending brackets.

```
<!-- data specifications begin-->
<All_authors>
  <Author AuthID="77">
  <Name>
...
  </Author>
</All_authors>
<!-- data specifications end -->
```

Here the attribute AuthID gives additional information about the author. In this instance, you might guess the an ID is specified for an author record so the desired record can be searched for using the ID. Or perhaps it is specified so the author list can be sorted by the ID. Or perhaps AuthID is a key exported along with the rest of the information from a database and has no specific meaning since it is automatically generated by the database. Your guess is as good as anyone else's; the fact is that the purpose of the attribute is determined by the developer who wrote (or designed) the document.

An attribute may point to an external resource such as an URI. Such usage is illustrated in the following example, in which the author's home page is specified using the attribute homePageURI:

```
<!-- data specifications begin-->
<All_authors>
  <Author AuthID="77" homePageURI="http://www.greathomepage.com/~clemens">
  ...
  </Author>
</All_authors>
<!-- data specifications end -->
```

Attributes may be specified only within start-tags or empty-element tags. In all the previous examples, we have shown attributes being used in start-tags. In the following example, we show how an attribute may be specified in an empty-element tag:

```
...
<Author AuthID="77"/>
...
```

One word of caution: attributes in XML serve a different purpose than their HTML counterparts. In HTML, you may be used to using attributes to specify elements of formatting such as the font type, size, color, and so on. Since the XML processor pays no special attention to HTML attributes, any attempts to use them as such will lead to unexpected results.

Entities

Unless you are already familiar with XML, you are probably wondering how you can output special characters such as <, >, quotation marks, and the like. For this purpose, you use XML entities. XML entities are represented by simple text strings. There are five predefined XML entities that you can use:

`&amp;`	for the ampersand symbol &
`&lt;`	for the less-than sign <
`&gt;`	for the greater-than sign <
`&quot;`	for the opening or closing double quotation mark " or "
`&apos;`	(short for apostrophe) for the opening or closing single quotation mark ' or '

All of these are called *internal* entities. Note that each entity definition begins with an ampersand (&) and ends with a semicolon (;).

In addition to representing special characters, entities can also be used to point to MIME types such as audio or video files, static graphic files, or any binary files that you want to use. An example of such usage is shown here:

```
<!ENTITY graphic-files
        PUBLIC "../pictures/gifs/index.gif"
        NDATA gif >
```

Well-Formed and Valid XML Documents

As you will have noticed in the preceding discussion, there is a set of basic rules that an XML document has to follow. An XML document that conforms to all these rules is considered a *well-formed* document. An XML parser is required to throw an exception if any of the basic rules of well-formedness are violated. You might want to specify additional rules to be followed by a certain set of XML documents using a DTD or an XML Schema that we will discuss shortly. An XML document that follows these user-specified rules in addition to the basic rules is considered a *valid* document. A valid XML document is necessarily a well-formed document, although the converse is not true.

Internationalization Using XML

Since XML is used to represent information in a structured fashion, with no attention paid to the presentation of the data itself, users can write their own stylesheets to display it in any manner they see fit. This property of XML also provides great impetus to international use: for example, to facilitate data interchange or for electronic publishing. Additionally, the data representation itself supports multiple Asian and European languages by the use of Unicode character sets in UTF-8 or UTF-16 encoding. In fact, if you do not explicitly specify the encoding in an XML document, the processor will generally default to UTF-8 encoding.

XML As a Meta-Language

So far, we have discussed XML in connection with representation of structured data. However, XML is much more than that. It is not a stand-alone markup language like HTML, but it is much more powerful in its abilities. One of the core strengths of XML is that, just like SGML, it can be used as a meta-language: that is, XML can be used to define markup languages with a restricted vocabulary of your choice. One of the reasons for using XML in such a way is so that the markup language thus defined is suitable for a particular purpose. For example, if a particular industry has a certain format a purchase order must follow, you can define a set of rules that every company in that industry must follow if it is to facilitate data interchange based on that particular *vocabulary* or *dialect* of XML. Such a dialect specification may be provided in the form of a Document Type Definition (DTD) designed for the industry in question.

XML Dialects and Markup Languages Derived from XML

Developing a standard dialect for a given industry can potentially facilitate B2B applications in that industry. This is because every company in that industry can then follow that standard to export the XML data to another organization, or use data in the format that another company within that industry follows. Thus facilitated, the data exchange can bring significant efficiencies to the value chain of that industry. With this in mind, several industry-specific XML dialects have been developed. Here is a list of some of those dialects:

SML	Steel Markup Language
FRXML	For general accounting reporting
FinXML	For data interchange for capital markets
NTM	For risk management and derivatives, from Infinity
XML/EDI	For general electronic data interchange

XHTML

Since HTML first came into being, programmers of varying backgrounds and skill levels have embraced it. No doubt HTML is straightforward to learn and allows developers to build simple, static web pages very quickly. However, as already noted, it has major limitations. These limitations, at least in part, provided the momentum for the development of XML in the first place. We are now at a point where the developer community will greatly benefit from a new language that provides the simplicity of HTML and the power of XML. With this in mind, W3C came up with Extensible HyperText Markup Language, or simply XHTML.

The XHTML 1.0 Recommendation draws on the previous versions of HTML, including the latest version, 4.01. In a way, you can view XHTML as the next version of HTML, after the 4.01 specification was finalized in December 1997. Given the existing base of millions of HTML web pages, W3C provides an open-source tool called HTML Tidy. This tool turns existing HTML pages into XHTML pages by correcting markup errors (yes, HTML, by design, is quite forgiving of these), removing clutter, and generally tidying up the code by providing indentation and so on.

Depending on your background, the existing web applications that you have, and the rigor to which you want to subject your web site, you can choose from among three flavors of XHTML that W3C provides. Your choice will tell the XHTML parser the level of scrutiny your web pages must be subjected to when validating them. The three flavors are as follows:

► **XHTML 1.0 Strict**   As the name suggests, use this when you want a clean markup that excludes any tags that specify the layout of the document. Remember that W3C provides the Cascading Style Sheet (CSS) language to take care of presentation-related needs such as font type, size, color, and layout.

► **XHTML 1.0 Transitional**   When your user base is likely to be using older browsers that do not support stylesheets, this may be your best option. It allows you to use XHTML features by making incremental modifications to your web site until your users catch up with newer browsers (and, of course, your programmers catch up with XHTML in its full glory!).

► **XHTML 1.0 Frameset**   You can use this option if you want to continue using frames in building your web pages.

Subject-Area Standards: CML, MathML, MusicML

In addition to the industry-specific dialects just mentioned, there are subject-area standards you can use. The major ones are the Chemical Markup Language (CML), Mathematics Markup Language (MathML), and Music Markup Language (MusicML). These are briefly described here.

► CML is designed to represent information about chemicals on the web: for example, molecular properties. You can think of it as a mixture of HTML with a chemistry twist to it.

► MathML 2.0 Recommendation was published by the W3C in February 2001. It supports mathematical notation as well as the content to be exchanged over the web. MathML provides about 150 fixed tags to specify mathematical expressions and includes a toolkit of 30 tags reserved for more abstract notation.

► MusicXML is designed to represent musical compositions. At this point, it primarily supports the standard western notation that has been in use for about four centuries. It can be used to facilitate the exchange of musical scores and their analysis, retrieval, and rendering.

W3C Standards Related to XML

The W3C sets standards for numerous technologies that are closely related to the XML specification that we have been discussing thus far in this chapter. This section provides brief overviews of each of the key technologies that fall under the XML umbrella at the time of this writing. We are sure that W3C will continue adding names to this ever-growing list.

DTDs

As a user, you have complete freedom to define and use any sets of tags in your XML documents. When you create an XML document by using tags within it, they impart *implicit* meaning and structure to your data. However, let us say that you want to explicitly create rules that other users, or software applications, must conform to, while creating XML documents that you, or a software application of your choice, will use. Toward this end, XML provides a mechanism called Document Type Definition (DTD). You can define your own tags in a DTD. These definitions can be fluid and can change as your programming requirements change. Thus, the DTD allows you to separate rules that the data must follow from the data itself.

For example, consider the following constraints that you can choose to place on an XML document:

▶ The document must have the element `All_authors` as the root element.

▶ The root element must contain only `Author` elements as children.

▶ Each `Author` element must have the attribute `AuthID`.

▶ Each author must have a name and an address: that is, `Name` and `Address` must be children of the `Author` element.

▶ Each author's name must consist of `First_name` and `Last_name`.

▶ The address of each author must allow two lines for the street address and a way to specify the city, state, and zip code.

▶ Although the first line of the street address is a mandatory field, the second line is optional. Similarly, each author must have a first name, but need not have a last name.

The preceding list is a verbose description of the rules that our original XML document, `auth.xml`, followed. Now let us take a look at the DTD in which all of the rules are codified. Note the use of CDATA, which stands for character data, and PCDATA, which represents *parsed* character data.

```
<?xml version="1.0" encoding="UTF-8"?>

<!ELEMENT All_authors (Author)*>

<!ATTLIST Author AuthID CDATA #REQUIRED>

<!ELEMENT Author (Name, Address)>

<!ELEMENT Name (First_name, Last_name)>

<!ELEMENT First_name (#PCDATA)>

<!ELEMENT Last_name (#PCDATA)>

<!ELEMENT Address(Address_line1, Address_line2, City, State, ZIP)>

<!ELEMENT Address_line1 (#PCDATA)>

<!ELEMENT Address_line2 (#PCDATA)>

<!ELEMENT City (#PCDATA)>

<!ELEMENT State (#PCDATA)>

<!ELEMENT ZIP (#PCDATA)>
]>
```

XML Schema

We just saw how DTDs may be used to specify the constraints that an XML document must follow. XML Schemas may also be used for the same purpose. In a nutshell, you can use the XML Schema definition language to create a schema that defines a *class* of XML documents. Conceptually, the word *class* has a meaning similar to its meaning in object-oriented programming: that is, an XML document that conforms to the schema in question is considered an *instance* of that schema.

A schema is an XML document itself. Let us consider an example XML Schema that is equivalent to the DTD we discussed earlier:

```xml
<?xml version="1.0" encoding="UTF-8"?>
<xsd:schema
 xmlns:xsd="http://www.w3.org/2000/10/XMLSchema">

 <element name="All_authors">
  <complexType>
   <sequence>
    <element ref="xsd:Author"/>
   </sequence>
  </complexType>
 </element>

 <element name="Author">
  <complexType>
   <sequence>
    <element ref="xsd:Name"/>
    <element ref="xsd:Address"/>
   </sequence>
   <attribute name="AuthID" type="xsd:string" use="required"/>
  </complexType>
 </element>

 <element name="Name">
  <complexType>
   <sequence>
    <element ref="xsd:First_name"/>
    <element ref="xsd:Last_name"/>
   </sequence>
  </complexType>
 </element>

 <element name="First_name" type="xsd:string"/>
 <element name="Last_name" type="xsd:string"/>

 <element name="Address">
  <complexType>
   <sequence>
    <element ref="xsd:Address_line1"/>
```

```
    <element ref="xsd:Address_line2"/>
    <element ref="xsd:City"/>
    <element ref="xsd:State"/>
    <element ref="xsd:ZIP"/>
   </sequence>
  </complexType>
</element>

<element name="Address_line1" type="xsd:string"/>
<element name="Address_line2" type="xsd:string"/>
<element name="City" type="xsd:string"/>
<element name="State" type="xsd:string"/>
<element name="ZIP" type="xsd:integer"/>

</xsd:schema>
```

Although XML Schemas and DTDs may both be used to specify the constraints that an XML document must follow, they differ in the following key respects:

DTDs	XML Schemas
DTDs use a nonXML syntax. Separate DTD authoring tools must be used.	Schemas are XML documents themselves. Hence, XML authoring tools can be used to manipulate schemas. Tools are also available to generate documentation from schemas.
DTDs provide no support for namespaces.	Being XML documents, Schemas provide full support for the use of namespaces. This enables co-existence of multiple schemas without any name conflicts between them.
DTDs allow only rudimentary data-typing. For example, support is provided for simple strings, although no support exists for more complex data-types such as dates, numbers, and currency values.	Schemas provide extensive support for a far richer collection of built-in data-types. For example, URIs, dates and times, currency, Boolean, integers, real numbers, and so on.
No support for user-defined datatypes.	User can define custom data-types of arbitrary complexity.
No support for attribute grouping.	Common attributes for all elements in a schema may be grouped together and reused.
Suport for parsed entities.	Parsed entities can not be declared in schemas.

From the preceding comparison between the key features of DTDs and XML Schemas you can see that schemas generally have advantages over DTDs. So if you are currently using DTDs and would like to start using schemas instead, you can use tools to convert existing DTDs to schemas.

Namespaces

XML namespaces are a mechanism for avoiding ambiguity between elements with identical names, but which are defined at multiple URIs, including those of the W3C, a software vendor, or perhaps ones that you custom defined. We will discuss namespaces in detail in Chapter 2.

XLink

Since XML documents contain hierarchical, structured data, a mechanism is needed for specifying and describing the relationships, or links, between different parts of the source tree. The XML Linking Language, known as XLink, provides such a mechanism and allows you to insert elements into XML documents, associate metadata (data about data) with links, and separate the location for link storage from location of the linked resources. At a simplistic level, you can think of such links as hyperlinks in HTML documents, although XLink supports far more sophisticated links. The XLink 1.0 Recommendation was published in June 2001.

XPointer

XPointer (XML Pointer Language) is based on XPath (Extensible Path Language), another XML-related standard we will describe shortly. XPointer is a mechanism that allows you to identify, or point to, individual entities or fragments within an XML tree using XPath expressions. XPointer works very closely with XLink, described in the previous section, and allows you to locate resources of three MIME types: `text/xml`, `application/xml`, and `text/xml-external-parsed-entity`.

XML Query

As of the end of 2001, XML Query was still at the W3C Working Draft stage. However, the formal Recommendation is likely to be finalized soon. Therefore, we discuss this important technology here.

As we have seen, XML provides a way to represent hierarchical, structured information. XML Query is being designed to use the structure of XML documents in an intelligent manner. It will define a data model for XML documents, the necessary query operators (like the operators provided by SQL), and a query language called XQuery. You will be able to use XQuery to write queries across multiple sources of data, including XML documents (single or multiple documents), and create a result tree document as output. XML Query will perhaps even be useful when the data source is something traditional such as a database and when XML is used as an intermediary form. At present, the XML Query specifications address certain types of data a lot better than certain other types, although this weakness should be rectified by the time the final Recommendation is released to the public.

XPath

XSLT works very closely with the Extensible Path Language (XPath), another W3C standard. You can use XPath expressions in your XSLT stylesheets to associate templates with objects (such as elements, attributes, processing instructions, comments, and text strings) in source XML documents. When an object in the source tree matches the specified XPath expression, the template associated with that object is instantiated, filled in with data from the source document, and written to the output document. XPath expressions can also represent data types such as numbers and Boolean operators. Hence, XPath can also be used to perform simple computations. We discuss XPath in detail in later chapters. It is interesting to note that, despite its close association with XML and XSLT, XPath itself is a non-XML language. XPath is discussed in detail in Chapter 5.

XSL and XSLT

XSLT is, of course, the main topic of this book. At first, W3C aimed at creating a stylesheet language called Extensible Stylesheet Language (XSL). It quickly became apparent that the stylesheet language that would operate on XML source trees needed two major sets of capabilities: namely, those related to presentation and additional ones to transform the data to a certain type of result tree. Later, the part of the XSL language that addressed the presentation, or formatting aspects, came to be known as XSL for Formatting Objects, or simply XSL-FO. Data transformations are handled by XSL for Transformations, that is, XSLT. On a development project of reasonable size and complexity, you will generally end up using both XSL-FO and XSLT.

Summary

Since XSLT is primarily meant to be used with XML documents, we began our book with an overview of XML. We began with a history of XML to provide answers to any of the *why* questions that you may have. We also discussed the structure of XML documents: this is important for you to understand since an XSLT stylesheet itself is an XML document. We then discussed a range of technologies that are closely related to, and frequently used with, XML. We described how XML works as a meta-language in defining an application-specific vocabulary and went over some commonly known XML dialects. Armed with this knowledge, we will now move on to discuss the main topic at hand: XSLT.

An Introduction to XSLT

IN THIS CHAPTER:

To make sure that we build a solid foundation for our understanding of XSLT, this chapter will look at the basics of this important tool—what it is, when and why it came into being, and what problems it was designed to solve. You'll also get a general idea of how XSLT works and what capabilities it provides, gain an understanding of structured documents and why document structure is important, and discover the features of XSLT. Later chapters will address each aspect of the tool in depth.

What Is XSLT?

In August 1997, a team of authors from Inso Corporation, Microsoft, ArborText, and the University of Edinburgh, joined by James Clark, presented a proposal to the World Wide Web Consortium (W3C) for a new stylesheet language they called the Extensible Style Language, or XSL. This new language, which was based on work done with the Standard Generalized Markup Language (SGML), Document Style Semantics and Specification Language (DSSSL) and targeted specifically at Web development, was intended to facilitate the creation of electronic documents from the Extensible Markup Language (XML) by providing powerful facilities for the formatting and reordering of XML documents. XSL included two major components: a set of *formatting objects* that could be used to describe the format and content of material presented on a display, in print, or in other media, and a *transformation language* that described how one XML document could be rearranged into a new, completely different form. XSL, which differed from the popular Cascading Style Sheets (CSS) in that it was better suited to heavy-duty transformation of highly structured data, was seen as an extremely valuable tool for automating many complex publishing tasks, such as the creation of tables of contents, indexing, and so on.

In the course of developing the XSL specification, the W3C team came to realize the value of XSL's transformation capabilities beyond their use with document formatting objects. In July 1999, the W3C formally split the XSL specification into two parts, one dealing with the use of formatting objects to style XML documents (which continued to be called XSL) and one dealing with transformation of one document into another (which we now know as the Extensible Stylesheet Language for Transformations, or XSLT). While primarily intended to be used with XSL, XSLT gained prominence not only for its ability to transform one XML document into another, but because it provided a relatively simple, straightforward way to generate HTML and other presentation languages, such as Wireless Markup

Language (WML), from an XML document without requiring the use of the complex and sometimes confusing formatting objects provided by XSL. Presentation of the same content on HTML and WML formats is discussed in Chapter 12.

XSLT provides the ability to create *templates* of portions of the transformation output and to associate those templates with objects in source XML documents (whether they be elements, attributes, processing instructions, comments, or text) through expressions coded in the Extensible Path Language (XPath). For each object in a source document that matches the XPath selection criteria for a given template, that template is instantiated, filled in with data from the source document, and written to the output document. XSLT is particularly powerful in that it can process not only the object that invoked the template, but it can pull data from anywhere in the source document, apply conditional logic, accept runtime parameters to change its behavior, and link multiple documents together. The combination of XSLT and XPath can create extremely complex output that rearranges the source data, provides cross-references among related elements, indexes documents, and performs other labor-intensive tasks.

In the current XSLT W3C recommendation, version 1.0, XSLT provides facilities to:

▶ Associate transformation operations with certain specific objects in an XML document, using the Extensible Path Language (XPath) as the addressing mechanism.

▶ Create XML elements, attributes, text, processing instructions, and comments from content in the source document, or embed literal content in the result document.

▶ Reuse stylesheet logic by including or importing stylesheet fragments.

▶ Perform conditional processing based on document content or relative position.

▶ Define variables and parameters that can be passed to an XSLT processor from the invoking program.

▶ Generate explicit links between implicitly related portions of a document.

▶ Perform limited string, number, and Boolean processing.

Miscellaneous other facilities in addition to those just mentioned make XSLT an excellent tool for performing many different types of XML document processing. An overview of each of these facilities is provided later in this chapter. The details of how each of these operations is accomplished, along with strategies for their effective use, are covered in the chapters that follow.

The Search for Structure and Meaning

To gain a clear understanding of XSLT and how it can enhance your ability to process and present XML documents, it's important to have some fundamental concepts under your belt. One of the most significant is the concept of XML document structure: how the XML markup you use to impart meaning to your data translates into a structure that XSLT and other processing applications can use to navigate your document and find information. An effective document structure helps convert raw data into usable information that can be processed quickly and efficiently; a poor structure can make it difficult and time consuming to interpret data programmatically.

Why Structure Documents at All?

If you have a background in computer programming, the idea of structured data probably isn't new. Many programming languages and data storage mechanisms support the concept of nested structures, which can be used to assign meaning to data, group related information, and allow the reuse of logical data structures. More often than not, programmers think of structured data as being organized in records or rows, such as are found in relational databases, as shown in Figure 2-1.

However, there are other types of data, such as text, for which it can be difficult to assign structure and meaning. For example, take a look at the following item:

```
At 1:10 PM today, an earthquake struck the city of Mexico City, Mexico,
causing widespread panic among the citizens there.
```

As it is, this item would be difficult to process programmatically, because there is no mechanism for determining what the text represents or whether the words or spaces inside have any meaning. The lack of such a mechanism makes it difficult to develop format and content standards for similar documents, such as technical manuals; because programs can't determine what the structure of the document is or what the content represents, there is no way to enforce a required structure or detect deviations.

The need for such a mechanism gave rise to markup languages such as IBM's Generalized Markup Language (GML), which was one of the predecessors of the widely used SGML, the parent of both Hypertext Markup Language (HTML) and XML. In particular, the concept of a Document Type Definition (DTD), available in SGML, HTML/XHTML, and XML, allowed users the ability to develop and enforce

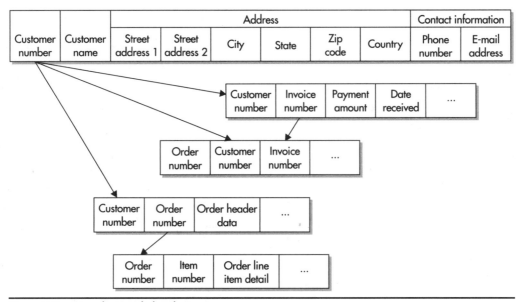

Figure 2-1   *A relational database structure*

standards for document format and separate a document's structure and meaning from its presentation. Using markup languages, it finally became possible to logically organize and intelligently process unstructured, textual data:

```
<article>At <time><hour>1</hour><minute>10</minute><second>
</second><ampm>PM</ampm></time> <date>today</date>, an
<naturalEvent>earthquake</naturalEvent> struck the city of
 <location><city>Mexico City</city>, <country>Mexico</country>
</location>, causing widespread panic among the citizens
there.</article>
```

Fortunately, the same mechanism that allows us to create structure for unstructured data also allows us to structure data traditionally stored in rows and tables:

```
<Customer>
   <CustomerID>121-232004</CustomerID>
   <PersonalName>
     <FirstName>John</FirstName>
     <MiddleInitial>A</MiddleInitial>
```

```
      <LastName>Doe</LastName>
   </PersonalName>
   <Address>
      <StreetAddress1>123 Main Street</StreetAddress1>
      <StreetAddress2>Apartment 23</StreetAddress2>
      <City>Anytown</City>
      <State>California</State>
      <ZipCode>12345</ZipCode>
      <Country>United States</Country>
   </Address>
   <ContactInformation>
      <HomePhone>111-555-1212</HomePhone>
      <BusinessPhone>111-555-2323</BusinessPhone>
      <FaxNumber>111-555-4545</FaxNumber>
      <EmailAddress>jdoe@theinternet.com</EmailAddress>
   </ContactInformation>
</Customer>
```

This ability, fundamental as it may seem, gives rise to a whole new range of capabilities and services that were either previously unavailable or considerably more difficult to achieve. For instance:

▶ Structural and validation information about data, formerly locked up in a company's database schema and enterprise applications, can now be externalized and shared with trading partners and other companies in the same or similar industries. This capability gave rise to standards such as RosettaNet, cXML, and ebXML, which provide vocabularies to facilitate the automated exchange of business documents. An important aspect of this capability is that the definition of the document's structure is embedded in or explicitly associated with the document itself; once companies agree on these definitions, document identification and processing becomes a snap.

▶ Document designers now have the ability to identify the meaning of portions of a document or data object, creating new opportunities for contextual processing, explicit cross-referencing, and other applications. For example, it is now possible to design software that can process appropriately structured documents to answer questions such as "Give me a list of all the natural disasters that have occurred in cities in the state of Texas."

▶ The same document or data object can store multiple representations of a given item, and the appropriate item for a given presentation method can be selected at runtime. Error messages, for example, can be stored in multiple languages in the same document, and the correct version can be selected based on the end user's language preference. Having these items grouped together facilitates document creation, editing, and access.

Of course, new tools sprung up to enable all of these new applications, and one of the most powerful of those tools is XSLT.

The XML Document Hierarchy

When you mark up a document using XML, you're assigning structure and meaning to portions of the document, based on your particular needs. For XSLT (or any other XML processor, for that matter) to be able to process the structure that you've provided, the structure has to be converted into a form that allows easy navigation of the structure and facilitates quick retrieval of information.

Let's take a look at a simple example: a basic customer list containing the following information:

```
Customer number: 001
Name: The Boat Masters, Inc.
Address1: 123 Riverside Street
Address2: Suite 100
City: Chicago
State: Illinois
Zip code: 60604

Customer number: 002
Name: North Side Marine
Address1: 123 Main Street
Address2:
City: Dallas
State: Texas
Zip code: 75001
```

Some of the structure we might impose on this data is obvious. We can, for example, group a customer's address information into an Address object, making it easier to treat addresses as a unit rather than as the discrete elements address1, address2, city, state, and zipcode. Likewise, we can treat each set of customer information as a unit, imposing a second grouping level that contains the customer's number and name, as well as the `Address` object we created earlier. With the addition of this second grouping level, it becomes obvious which data items belong to what customer:

```
<Customer>
    <CustomerNumber>001</CustomerNumber>
    <CustomerName>The Boat Masters, Inc.</CustomerName>
    <CustomerAddress>
        <StreetAddress1>123 Riverside Street</StreetAddress1>
        <StreetAddress2>Suite 100</StreetAddress2>
        <City>Chicago</City>
        <State>Illinois</State>
        <ZipCode>60604</ZipCode>
    </CustomerAddress>
</Customer>
```

If we were to graph this structured data, it would look like Figure 2-2.

Looked at in this way, you can see that we've created a *document hierarchy* containing the information about our customer, with each structural group creating a new level in the hierarchy. If desired, we could continue along this same path, creating new logical groups of information (such as a `CustomerList` group for all our customers) in the same way. It's important to note that not all of the levels in this hierarchy must have textual data associated with them—our `CustomerAddress` element, for example, has only other elements as its content, and no text of its own.

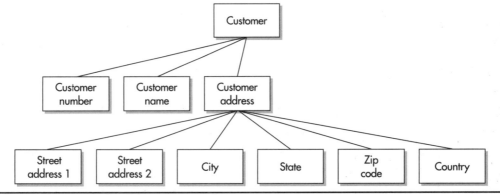

Figure 2-2   *A graph of the customer data*

Although the hierarchy might be less obvious, textual information can be treated in much the same way. Articles such as the one that follows can be marked up with XML elements that allow them to be effectively indexed and searched.

```
Boaters Rejoice After Recent Rains

by Charles Williams
Staff Writer

Dallas, Texas (07/04/2001) - In every cloud, there's a
silver lining.

Although some flooded neighborhoods are still recovering
from the highest monthly rain total in recent history,
Metroplex boaters are overjoyed at the rise in the water
levels of area lakes. On many lakes, areas that were
formerly off-limits due to submerged trees and other
obstructions are now wide-open for sailboats, jet skis and
other watercraft.
```

Depending on the needs of the applications used to process this article, it may be appropriate to structure the article into title, byline, location, date, and paragraphs, with other markup added to enhance processing:

```
<Article>
   <Title>Boaters Rejoice After Recent Rains</Title>
   <Byline>
      <AuthorName>Charles Williams</AuthorName>
      <AuthorPosition>Staff Writer</AuthorPosition>
   </Byline>
   <Body>
      <Location>
         <City>Dallas</City>
         <State>Texas</State>
      </Location>
      <Date>07/04/2001</Date>
      <Paragraph>In every cloud, there's a silver
      lining</Paragraph>
      <Paragraph>Although some flooded neighborhoods are
      still recovering from the highest monthly rain total
      in recent history, Metroplex boaters are overjoyed at
      the rise in the water levels of area lakes. On many
```

```
    lakes, areas that were formerly off-limits due to
    submerged trees and other obstructions are now wide-
    open for sailboats, jet skis and other watercraft.
    </Paragraph>
  </Body>
</Article>
```

Figure 2-3 shows a graphical view of the document hierarchy for this article.

Trees and Nodes

Now that you understand how the way you use XML to assign structure and meaning to data can create a hierarchy of logical groupings inside the data, let's take a look at how that hierarchy is viewed from an XSLT processor's perspective.

XSLT and most other XML processors (which also view documents as hierarchies) see each item in the document hierarchy as a generic object called a *node*. Nodes have various relationships to each other, as defined by the hierarchy:

▶ Nodes that are at the same level in the hierarchy are called *siblings*.

▶ Nodes directly below a given node in the hierarchy are considered to be *children* of that node, and that node is considered to be the *parent* of its children.

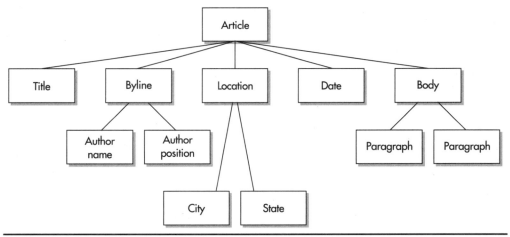

Figure 2-3   *The article document hierarchy*

▶ All nodes below a given node in the hierarchy—not only the child nodes, but their children, their children's children, and so on—are called *descendants* of that node. From the descendant's perspective, all nodes higher in the subtree (parents and above) are called *ancestors*.

▶ The topmost node in the hierarchy (the parent of all the other nodes) is called the *root node*.

▶ The entire hierarchy is referred to as a *document tree*. In this book, you'll see multiple references to *source trees* (that is, the node hierarchy of an XML document used as input to an XSLT processor) and *result trees* (the hierarchy resulting from the operations performed by an XSLT processor).

▶ The term *document order* refers to the order in which you would encounter nodes in a document by performing a depth-first traversal of the tree. In other words, a program that is processing nodes in document order would see the first node and its children and descendants before seeing that node's siblings.

▶ Nodes at the very ends of each branch of the document hierarchy are called *leaf nodes*.

Figure 2-4 illustrates the order in which nodes are visited in a document-order traversal of a document tree.

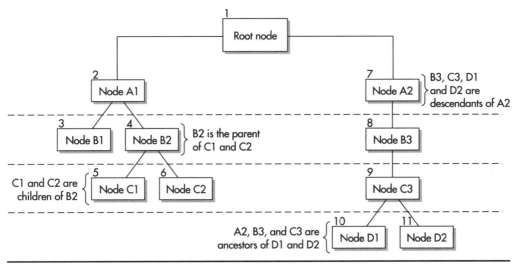

Figure 2-4   *A document hierarchy, with numbers illustrating the order in which the nodes are visited during a document-order traversal*

While there are several different valid entity types in XML, only a subset of these can be processed by XSLT. These include the following:

Node Type	Meaning
Element	A collection of other content, including text and other elements. These other elements are stored as children of the element; the rules governing the types of children an element can have are defined in the XML document's DTD.
Attribute	A name-value pair associated with an element. While some possible element attributes are explicitly defined in the XML specification (id and idref, for example), the majority of the attributes found in XML documents are user defined.
Text	The text associated with an element node. Text nodes are generally stored as children of their respective element nodes.
Processing Instruction	A processing instruction (PI) is a special type of XML node that can contain instructions for applications processing the document containing the PI.
Comment	Comment nodes store information deemed relevant by the creator of the XML document.

These XML entities are considered to be *subtypes* of the generic node object—that is, an XSLT processor can treat these entities both as nodes and as their concrete entity type. Usually, however, these entities will be treated by XSLT as what they actually are; the only circumstance in which an element, for example, might be treated as a node is when the XPath node() function is used to select nodes to be processed by a template.

Names and Namespaces

Let's say that two men named Joe Smith work in your company: one in the purchasing department and one in the sales department. If both of them come to you and say, "The price of widgets is $4.95 each," how can you tell whether they're talking about the price for buying a widget or for selling one? The answer, of course, is context—based on the department that Joe Smith works in and the other content of your conversation, you can determine which price is which.

But how can you make this distinction clear to your XML processing programs? Because it's quite possible that we might construct an XML document that includes both a purchase price and a sales price (and also quite possible that the purchasing and sales software development teams will both use the XML element or attribute name price), we need some other mechanism to let our programs unambiguously identify these concepts and handle them correctly. Of course, we could use different XML element names to distinguish between the two types of price, but if we had to do this for every similar situation, we'd run out of meaningful element names (or end up generating some really long or very strange names) fairly quickly. This is the problem that XML namespaces were designed to solve.

Simply put, an *XML namespace* is a mechanism that allows users to avoid element and attribute name collisions and to accurately recognize the meaning of a given element. By developing an XML DTD (or XML Schema) with the elements we want to use to represent various concepts in a given context (the price concept in purchasing, for example) and making the DTD available for use as an XML namespace, we can then refer to elements of the same name and use the namespace to identify and process them unambiguously. This modular approach to markup definition also facilitates reuse of XML vocabularies and allows different organizations to exchange documents and, as long as they both recognize and agree on the meaning of namespaces used in the documents, process the exchanged information correctly.

There are two key pieces of information that makes the namespace scheme work. The first is the namespace's Uniform Resource Identifier, or URI, which is used to unambiguously identify a namespace. Although the URI specification (RFC 2396) allows substantial latitude when defining these globally unique identifiers, more often than not the names used are Uniform Resource Locators (URLs), the familiar subset of URIs that we typically used to access resources on the Web.

The other key piece of information used in a namespace is the namespace prefix. Because URIs and URLs are often long and unwieldy, namespace prefixes are used as a shortened version of a URI which, when combined with the XML element name (often referred to as the local part of a namespace-qualified name), allows programs to unambiguously identify an element. Namespace prefixes are mapped to their corresponding URIs using special namespace attributes, which can be attached to a document's root element or to any other element in the document. Namespace prefixes are not globally unique, but they do have to be unique within a given XML document.

To give you a more concrete idea of how namespaces work, let's go back to our price example. Let's say that the purchasing software development team has created a namespace with the URI http://www.mycompany.com/namespaces/purchasing/, and the sales department has created a namespace

with the URI http://www.mycompany.com/namespaces/sales. Both of these
namespaces have an element called price, and we want to use both price elements
in the same XML document. Our XML document might look like this:

```
<?xml version="1.0" ?>
<transactions
    xmlns:purch="http://www.mycompany.com/namespaces/purchasing"
    xmlns:sales="http://www.mycompany.com/namespaces/sales" >
  <transaction type="purchase">
    <itemName>widget</itemName>
    <purch:price currency="usd">4.95</purch:price>
  </transaction>
  <transaction type="sale">
    <itemName>widget</itemName>
    <sales:price currency="usd">4.95</sales:price>
  </transaction>
</transactions>
```

The root element of our document, `transactions`, contains two attributes
called `xmlns`, each of which is further qualified with the namespace prefix we want
to use (`purch` and `sales`) and points to the appropriate namespace identifier.
When we want to distinguish between the two different `price` elements, we prefix
the element name (or local part) with the appropriate namespace prefix, resulting in
a fully qualified, unambiguous name. If we were to process this document using an
XSLT stylesheet, we could declare the namespace in our stylesheet (using the same
mechanism we used in the document earlier) and qualify the elements we wanted to
process using the appropriate namespace prefix, just as we did earlier.

For more information on XML namespaces, see the W3C recommendation,
"Namespaces in XML," which can be found at http://www.w3.org/TR/
1999/REC-xml-names/.

XSLT Feature Overview

This section provides an overview of XSLT's major capabilities and points you to
the chapters that provide detailed information. We highly recommend that you focus
your initial efforts on gaining a clear understanding of the XPath expression
language and of general template structure; once you've mastered these topics,
you should find that the rest of XSLT is fairly straightforward.

Finding Your Data: The XPath Language

XSLT uses the XML Path Language, also known as XPath, to address parts of an XML document. XPath was developed by W3C as a mechanism for providing absolute and relative addressing of portions of XML documents, and it serves as a core technology for both XSLT and the XML Pointer Language (XPointer). Later versions of XPath will also incorporate much of the functionality of the W3C's XML Query facilities.

XPath uses a construct known as an *expression* to identify nodes to be processed. Expressions can contain a combination of literals, numbers, calls to intrinsic functions, and other expressions. The result of the evaluation of an expression can be a reference to one or more nodes in the XML document, a Boolean value, a number, or a string. These values can, in turn, be used to locate specific portions of the document, resolve conditional expressions, assign values to variables, and so on.

The flexibility of XPath, combined with XSLT's ability to use it to not only find certain nodes in an XML document but to generate comparison operators, variable values, and other handy items, makes it an extremely critical piece of XSLT's functional arsenal. XPath's expression syntax and the rules for expression evaluation are covered in depth in Chapter 5.

Transforming Your Data: XSLT Templates

Virtually all of the processing in an XSLT stylesheet takes place within blocks of XSLT statements and content called *templates*. As mentioned previously, templates are aptly named: literally, they constitute a skeleton for portions of transformed output that can be filled with content from nodes, literal values, and even content from other documents.

Templates contain two major parts: an XPath pattern that is used to determine the nodes in an XML document to which the template applies, and a body containing XSLT instructions or elements (conditional logic, for example) or literals. When nodes are found in the source tree that match the pattern specified in the template, the body of the template is instantiated, content from the selected node is (optionally) combined with content from the template body, and the template's output is written to the result tree. Any portion of the selected node, or of any other node in the source tree, can be extracted from the source tree and inserted into the template.

Here's an example of a simple template:

```
<xsl:template match="CustomerName" >
   <p><xsl:value-of select="." /></p>
</xsl:template>
```

This template, when applied to the Customer XML document used earlier in this chapter, selects all of the CustomerName elements in the document and writes their content into an HTML p element.

Templates and rules for template processing are covered in Chapter 6.

Creating XML Elements, Attributes, and Other Objects

There are several ways to create nodes in the output tree using an XSLT stylesheet. The easiest is to embed literal elements in the XSLT template. If these literal elements do not belong to the XSLT namespace or are not extension elements, they are instantiated as nodes and added to the result tree. Content for these elements can be expressed as literals or can be generated from portions of the XML source tree.

Here is an example of this that you'll likely see quite often:

```
<xsl:template match="/">
   <html>
   <head><title>Summary of document</title></head>
   <body>
      <xsl:apply-templates />
   </body>
   </html>
</xsl:template>
```

This sample matches on the root node of the source tree and generates the starting and ending elements of an HTML document. The xsl:apply-templates element inside body tells XSLT to process the descendants of the root element and insert the output at the point in the result tree immediately after body.

Another method is to use the xsl:element, xsl:attribute and xsl:attribute-set elements. These are particularly valuable when creating elements or attributes with names that come from the XML source tree or are computed as a result of processing on the source tree. As with literal elements, content for elements and attributes created in this way can be extracted from the XML source tree. The same example just shown could be coded (somewhat more verbosely) as follows:

```
<xsl:template match="/">
   <xsl:element name="html">
      <xsl:element name="head">
         <xsl:element name="title">Summary of document
         </xsl:element>
      </xsl:element>
      <xsl:element name="body">
```

```
        <xsl:apply-templates />
      </xsl:element>
    </xsl:element>
  </xsl:template>
```

Text elements in the result tree can be created using `xsl:text` elements. One major benefit of using `xsl:text` is that it provides the option of automatically escaping characters as needed (for example, conversion of "<" to "<"); of course, this option can be disabled if needed.

If, in our simple example, the title of the document could be derived from the name of the root element, we could code an `xsl:text` element to generate that title as follows:

```
<xsl:text>Summary of document:
  <xsl:value-of select="name(.)" />
</xsl:text>
```

Processing instructions can be created using the `xsl:processing-instruction` element, and comments can be created using the `xsl:comment` element. The method for using both of these elements is essentially the same as for `xsl:text`.

All of these methods of creating nodes in the result tree are covered in Chapter 7.

Reusing Stylesheet Logic

Given that many applications have the opportunity to reuse data elements and/or their associated structures, it seems reasonable that XSLT users would want to reuse those portions of their stylesheets that apply such structures. XSLT has two features that facilitate this reuse: `xsl:import` and `xsl:include`.

The `xsl:include` element allows stylesheet designers to import another stylesheet, including its templates, into the target stylesheet without overlaying any existing templates. This approach allows XML document designers to create stylesheets specifically for their documents, and for content distribution mechanisms to include only those stylesheets and templates that process data appropriately for the distribution mechanism used (HTML/XHTML, plain text, and so on).

Importing a stylesheet using `xsl:import` works in much the same fashion as including a stylesheet, but with one major difference. When a template is imported, templates that already exist in the destination stylesheet that match the same elements take precedence over templates imported into another stylesheet. This differs significantly from the behavior of included templates; in this case, the determination of which template to use for a given element follows the template conflict rules defined in the XSLT specification.

Importing and embedding stylesheets is discussed in detail in Chapter 4.

Performing Conditional and Repetitive Processing

XSLT has conditional and repetitive processing instructions that, when combined with the ability to use XPath to generate Boolean, numeric, and string values, gives stylesheet designers good flexibility in customizing their processing to the specific structure and content of the document.

The `xsl:if` instruction allows actions to be taken depending on the result of an XPath expression evaluation. The expression's result is converted to a Boolean value, which then determines the path of processing to be taken.

Here is a simple example:

```
<xsl:if test="position() = 1">
   <xsl:text><xsl:value-of select="." /></xsl:text>
</xsl:if>
```

Unfortunately, `xsl:if` does not provide what similar constructs in most programming languages do: a path to be taken when the conditional expression is false (usually implemented as an `else` clause). In this case, or when more powerful conditional processing is needed, the stylesheet designer can use the `xsl:choose`, `xsl:when`, and `xsl:otherwise` statements. These function much like the `switch` statement found in many popular programming languages, except that each condition to be tested does not have to be evaluated against the same variable. Each `xsl:when` instruction has its own XPath expression, which is evaluated to determine whether the processing associated with the `xsl:when` instruction should be executed. For situations where no `xsl:when` instruction's expression is true, the `xsl:otherwise` instruction's processing is executed.

```
<xsl:choose>
   <xsl:when test="contains(., 'abc')">
      <!-- perform some processing -->
   </xsl:when>
   <xsl:when test="contains(., 'def')">
      <!-- perform some processing -->
   </xsl:when>
   <xsl:otherwise>
      <!-- perform some error processing -->
   </xsl:otherwise>
</xsl:choose>
```

The preceding example checks the value of the current node to see if it contains either abc or def; if it contains neither, error processing is performed (perhaps `xsl:message terminate="yes"` or something similar).

Repetitive processing can be performed using the `xsl:for-each` instruction. When this instruction is used, each node in the context that matches the instruction's XPath expression is processed using the instructions contained with the `xsl:for-each` clause; the exact nodes to be processed depend on the current context (the nodes selected by the template containing the `xsl:for-each` instruction). If, for example, we had a document with a single `CustomerList` element containing multiple `Customer` elements, we could print a message for each customer by using the following:

```
<xsl:template match="/">
   <xsl:for-each select="CustomerList/Customer">
      <xsl:text>We love <xsl:value of select="." /></xsl:text>
   </xsl:for-each>
</xsl:template>
```

Conditional and repetitive instructions are covered in Chapter 7.

Defining Variables and Parameters

The ability to define variables and assign values to them is a fundamental capability of all programming languages. Although XSLT isn't a true programming language and doesn't provide nearly the same functionality, it does provide the ability to assign a name to a value and to use that name/value pair in XPath expressions and XSLT instructions and as part of the content of the result tree. Variables are implemented using the `xsl:variable` instruction, which accepts both literal values and the results of XPath expressions as values.

Parameters in XSLT, which are implemented using the `xsl:param` element, function in much the same way as variables, with one substantial additional benefit: their values can be passed in from programs invoking the transformation engine or provided on a command line, allowing stylesheet designers to modify the behavior of stylesheets based on external criteria.

Variables and parameters are discussed in Chapter 8.

Creating Keys to Link Portions of a Document

One particularly interesting feature of XSLT is its ability to define and reference implicit relationships among nodes in the source tree. Using the `xsl:key` element and corresponding `key()` intrinsic function, XSLT can assign key values to nodes in the source tree, using a key name and some portion of the data from the node (such as an attribute value) as the value of the key. Using the key name and a specific value, stylesheet templates can then gain access to the node(s) with the specified values, using information in those nodes to include data in the template's output. This capability is extremely valuable for generating intradocument HTML hyperlinks.

Keys and their uses are discussed in detail in Chapter 10.

Performing String, Number, and Boolean Processing

While XSLT itself does not provide substantial functionality for processing string, numeric, and Boolean values, XPath provides some robust capabilities that are very helpful when generating nodes in an XSLT result tree. These capabilities include functions for data type conversion, robust tools for string manipulation, concatenation and substring creation, and some mathematical functions. These are complemented by XSLT's own functions for number-to-string conversion and number formatting.

The XPath functions for string, number, and Boolean processing are covered in Chapter 5.

How XSLT Works

There are, of course, many different XSLT processors available, each with its own level and style of support for the XSLT specification, its own application programming interfaces, and its own processing peculiarities. If we step back from the details of a particular XSLT processor implementation, however, we can generalize what XSLT does into three major areas: template processing, expression processing, and result tree generation.

Keep in mind that the descriptions provided here are meant to give you a general understanding of how XSLT processors work. The XSLT specification does require that processors adhere to certain rules, but it also gives processors some leeway when it comes to their actual implementation.

Template Processing

The processing of a stylesheet starts with a depth-first (or document-order) navigation of the source tree. As the source tree is traversed, each node is evaluated to determine whether the stylesheet contains templates whose node selection criteria match that node. Since XSLT specifies that multiple templates can match a node but only one template can process the node, the best template to process the node is considered to be the one whose match expression most closely matches the node. XSLT has a range of rules for resolving conflicts among templates; these are discussed in depth in Chapter 6.

When the correct template to process the node is selected and instantiated, it (along with the node that caused it to be instantiated, which becomes that template's *current node*) becomes the source of information for a portion of the result tree. Templates can generate that output themselves (using literal or generated elements), defer the creation of output to other templates by redirecting the flow of processing using `xsl:apply-templates` or `xsl:call-template`, or perform some combination of the two. A call to `xsl:apply-templates` or `xsl:call-template`, in turn, can select additional nodes from the tree, and the process of matching, processing, and selecting starts all over again.

Let's take another look at one of our customer examples from earlier in this chapter:

```
<Customer>
    <CustomerID>121-232004</CustomerID>
    <PersonalName>
        <FirstName>John</FirstName>
        <MiddleInitial>A</MiddleInitial>
        <LastName>Doe</LastName>
    </PersonalName>
    <Address>
        <StreetAddress1>123 Main Street</StreetAddress1>
        <StreetAddress2>Apartment 23</StreetAddress2>
        <City>Anytown</City>
        <State>California</State>
        <ZipCode>12345</ZipCode>
        <Country>United States</Country>
    </Address>
    <ContactInformation>
        <HomePhone>111-555-1212</HomePhone>
        <BusinessPhone>111-555-2323</BusinessPhone>
        <FaxNumber>111-555-4545</FaxNumber>
        <EmailAddress>jdoe@theinternet.com</EmailAddress>
    </ContactInformation>
</Customer>
```

If we wanted to code a stylesheet to display this customer's information as HTML, one possible approach might be as follows:

```
<xsl:stylesheet version="1.0"
      xmlns:xsl="http://www.w3.org/1999/XSL/Transform" >
   <!--
      Write HTML header and trailer information
   -->
   <xsl:template match="/" >
      <html>
      <head><title>Customer information</title></head>
      <body>
      <xsl:apply-templates />
      </body>
      </html>
   </xsl:template>
   <!--
      Select the customer
   -->
   <xsl:template match="Customer" >
      <h1>Customer Identification</h1>
      <xsl:apply-templates />
   </xsl:template>
   <!--
      Select the customer and write the customer ID
   -->
   <xsl:template match="CustomerID" >
      <p>Customer ID: <xsl:value-of select="." /></p>
   </xsl:template>
   <!--
      Write personal identification information
   -->
   <xsl:template match="PersonalName" >
      <h1>Personal Information</h1>
      <p>First name: <xsl:value-of select="FirstName" /><br />
      Middle initial: <xsl:value-of select="MiddleInitial" /><br />
      Last name: <xsl:value-of select="LastName" /></p>
   </xsl:template>
   <!--
      Write address information
   -->
   <xsl:template match="Address" >
      <h1>Address</h1>
      <p>Street address 1: <xsl:value-of select="StreetAddress1" /><br />
      Street address 2: <xsl:value-of select="StreetAddress2" /><br />
      City: <xsl:value-of select="City" /><br />
```

```
        State: <xsl:value-of select="State" /><br />
        Zip code: <xsl:value-of select="ZipCode" /><br />
        Country: <xsl:value-of select="Country" /></p>
    </xsl:template>
    <!--
        Write contact information
    -->
    <xsl:template match="ContactInformation" >
        <h1>Contact information</h1>
        <p>Home phone: <xsl:value-of select="HomePhone" /><br />
        Business phone: <xsl:value-of select="BusinessPhone" /><br />
        Fax number: <xsl:value-of select="FaxNumber" /><br />
        Email address: <xsl:value-of select="EmailAddress" /></p>
    </xsl:template>
</xsl:stylesheet>
```

This spreadsheet combines all of the basic concepts in template processing:

▶ By selecting the root node of the document (using the template with match="/"
specified), we can write our HTML header and trailer information. Note that
the output from all of the other templates is inserted at the point where the
xsl:apply-templates element occurs in this template (that is, between
<body> and </body>).

▶ Templates are supplied for each section of the document we want to write to our
HTML page. Each one combines literal content (the headings and line titles) with
the use of xsl:value-of to extract information from subordinate elements.

▶ The template with match="Customer" illustrates the use of xsl:apply-
templates to process the high-level subordinate elements (CustomerID,
Address, and ContactInformation).

The final output of this stylesheet looks like Figure 2-5.

Expression Processing

Expressions coded in the XPath language are widely used in XSLT as a mechanism
both for locating nodes with certain characteristics and for computing values to be
used in comparisons or as output of the transformation process. The dominant use
for expressions is in the match attribute of a template, where it is used to determine
which nodes the template is to process. Expressions also appear as criteria in
conditional and repetitive statements, in assignment statements, and in computation
of transformation output.

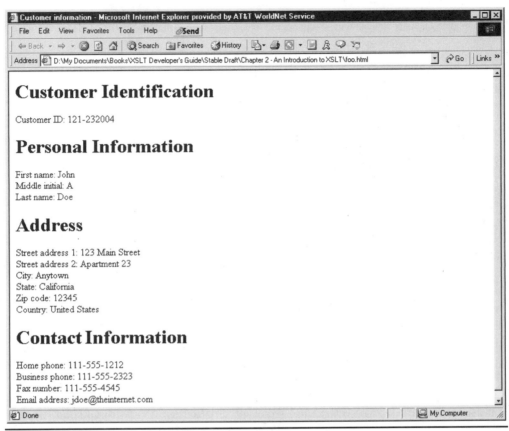

Figure 2-5 *Customer information, formatted in HTML*

Result Tree Generation

When a template processes a node, the results are written to a *result tree*, which is a hierarchy of nodes that correspond to the various output segments written by templates in the stylesheet. The output from the template (literal values or values generated using xsl:element) is converted to XML elements and stored at the appropriate location in the result tree (which is relative to output written by other templates). For example, if a template writes output and then passes control to other templates using xsl:apply-templates, the output of the called template is written as XML elements at the point where the xsl:apply-templates element appears in the template.

Output can be written by the XSLT processor as one of three types: XML, HTML, or text. The style of output is controlled by the `xsl:output` element which, in addition to indicating the type of output required, also provides various information that controls the generation of the `?xml?` element, indicates which public or private DTDs are in use, and so on.

Summary

At this point, you should have a reasonably good idea of what XSLT is, what it does, and how its use with structured documents can improve your ability to both present and use information effectively. The next chapter describes XSLT applications in more detail and shows how XSLT can fit into an overall software application architecture.

XML and XSLT Applications

IN THIS CHAPTER:

The Power of XML

Extending XML: The Extensible Stylesheet Language for Transformations

The Structure of an XML/XSLT Application

Summary

The concept behind structured markup languages such as SGML and XML is very simple: provide structure to data—and thereby convey additional information about the *meaning* of that data—by identifying each component of the data in a way that is recognizable both by humans and by programs. Although markup languages have been around for a number of years, it's only recently that they've achieved any prominence beyond the application that gave them birth: document development and processing. This is in part because early markup languages, and in particular the venerable Standard Generalized Markup Language (SGML), were very complex and had idiosyncrasies that made them difficult to use. In addition, tool support for markup languages was slow in coming, and the market was dominated by relatively small companies with niche products, by open-source products, or in the case of SGML, by individuals (James Clark, one of the fathers of XML, was also the creator of many of the most popular SGML tools).

Fortunately for us, there were visionaries in the SGML crowd who saw the value of a simplified markup language for a much wider range of industries and applications. Their creation, XML, is still very relevant to document processing, but thanks to its simplicity and extensibility, it has won supporters in other application realms and now enjoys widespread use.

The Power of XML

Understanding XSLT's ability to solve problems in enterprise application development first requires an understanding of the types of applications for which XML itself is best suited. In Chapter 2, we discussed how XML can bring structure to both totally unstructured data (such as text documents) and data that has a logical, but not physical, structure (such as records in a file, where all the fields are distinguishable only by programs that know the record layout). We'll examine this capability in more detail now and look at two concrete examples that illustrate the power of XML in real-world scenarios.

XML in Document Development and Processing

Contrary to what some enterprise application developers may think, document development and processing can be an extremely challenging endeavor. Structuring a very large amount of material, created by a number of content providers working as a team to provide maximum usability, requires an understanding of how the material will be used, the specific needs of the intended audience, and no small amount of attention to detail. XML and SGML give content developers a tool to not only broadly structure documents (into parts, units, chapters, sections, and so on) but also to facilitate the rapid development of material, improve access to important information, and enable search of content based not only on word matches but on *concepts* as well.

In addition to fundamentally changing the way that documents are structured, XML also changes the way that they can be presented to end users. Where once it was necessary to prepare a document for a particular presentation medium, it's now possible to present the same master document in a range of different media.

Rapid Document Development

Using XML to structure document content enables many content authors to accelerate the development of content through standardized document structure; component reuse; automatic construction of tables of contents, indexes, and other cross-references; and improved management of document content. Developers of technical manuals in particular have leveraged markup languages for these purposes for many years, and the tools that enable them to do so have become highly sophisticated.

The fact that XML and SGML provide the ability to explicitly define the rules that govern a document's structure and content has been a substantial benefit to organizations that demand consistent treatment of published material. Using an XML DTD or XML schema, it is possible to impose rules on content such as:

▶ Explicit identification of the *parts* of a given document. An XML DTD can, for example, indicate that a document conforming to the DTD should be composed of one or more organizational units called parts, each of which is composed of one or more units. Each unit, in turn, must be composed of one or more chapters, which may contain zero or more sections.

▶ The creation of new *types of data* and the structure of a given type of data. It becomes possible to create new types of data, identifying a word or phrase as a *key concept* data type or *indexable* data item. It's also possible to impose rules on the structure of data such as dates, geographic locations, names of individuals, or even the way that the parts of a machine are listed.

▶ *Relationships* among different data items. Organizations can require content developers to explicitly identify relationships that control document structure (between a picture and its caption, for example, or between form labels and the data entry fields they identify), conceptual relationships (for example, identifying that both sparrows and eagles are *birds*), or simply man-made relationships (as in the relationship among the parts within a certain mechanical component).

Because certain types of data can now be explicitly identified and grouped in some logical order, it is also possible to use these logical groupings meaningfully as a single unit in multiple documents. Boilerplate items, such as a company's description or logo graphics, can be stored external to the documents that reference them and referred to by a logical name; when the external item changes, all documents that use that item automatically reflect the change. Similarly, explicit identification of the meaning of data allows the rapid creation of tables of contents, indexes, and other cross-references that once required tedious, time-consuming manual work.

Improved Access to Information

Arguably, one of the most important benefits to come out of the World Wide Web is the ability to establish and navigate relationships among similar pieces of widely separated data using hyperlinks. While hyperlinking on the World Wide Web is often arbitrary, there's no denying that the technique can improve the use and understanding of data by tying together data that shares some concept or relationship, even if that relationship exists only in the mind of the data's creator.

Thanks to its ability to structure data and to attributes such as ID and IDREF, XML provides the ability to define implicit and explicit relationships among data as well. Data can be related structurally by the fact that items share a common parent element or are part of the same logical concept. Using explicit identifiers, a single piece of data can be referred to by multiple points in a document (as might be the case when words in a document refer back to a definition in the document's glossary). Using external entities, XML documents can also refer to resources outside the document itself, making it possible to link multiple documents either as a network of related resources or through the use of a catalog or master document.

Two additional W3C standards developed after the initial XML specification extend XML's linking capabilities even further. The XML Linking Language (XLink) provides the ability to insert elements into an XML document that identify and describe links between resources, and the XML Pointer Language (XPointer) provides a mechanism for identifying any node, data, or selection in an XML document.

Concept- and Context-Based Searches

All of the features of XML we've described up to this point enable one particularly powerful capability: the ability to search a collection of resources not only for explicit words, but for concepts as well—and to do this within a particular context. Without XML's ability to identify types of data and to assign relationships and structural meaning, searching for the answers to certain types of questions becomes extremely difficult, if not impossible. For example, consider the following query:

Show all the years in which cities in Mexico experienced a natural disaster.

To answer this query meaningfully, a search engine would have to know:

▶ How to identify a "year" (without resorting to arbitrary range-based techniques)

▶ How to identify a city name and determine if the city is in Mexico

▶ How to identify a natural disaster

The intelligent use of XML tags in the documents to be searched can make satisfying this query a relatively simple task:

▶ Identifying date formats and explicitly tagging the parts of a date (as in `<date><month>12</month><day>1</day><year>2000</year></date>`) makes recognition of each date component simple. Further, using the rules in an XML DTD allows each individual part of a date to stand alone (to allow `<year>2000</year>` to be used as part of a sentence, for example).

▶ Similarly, city names and their geographic location can be tagged for easy identification (as in `<geographicLocation><city>Mexico City</city><country>Mexico</country></geographicLocation>`). In situations where a city name is used without the country name, a linking element can be provided to a section later in the document that provides the name of the country.

▶ Natural disasters can be tagged both with their names and with other descriptive information. For example, an earthquake could be identified as `<NaturalDisaster severity="high">earthquake</NaturalDisaster>`.

Multiple Presentation Styles

Content creators and publishers often find it advantageous to provide the same content in several different presentation formats, such as HTML, WML, and text. Perhaps the reason is to provide additional avenues for content sales, or to improve accessibility for visually handicapped individuals, or simply to repurpose the content. Regardless of the reason, using XML to structure the content makes creating multiple presentation formats much easier.

The key to supporting multiple presentation formats is to completely separate any aspects of presentation from the content of the document itself. It's often tempting to use boldface, italics, or changes in font size and color to highlight words or passages of particular meaning; however, doing so not only does not impart clear meaning to your content, but it interferes with your ability to repurpose the content effectively. Some users cannot distinguish color; others require large print; and yet others need access from a mobile device with a small, monochromatic display. Satisfying all of these users requires uniformly structured, nonpresentation-oriented content.

XML's ability to support multiple character encodings—and, in particular, to support the Unicode standard—is an additional benefit to content publishers. Using current XML tools and the ubiquitous Unicode standard, it's possible to read, write, and store any character set—from English to Cyrillic—using a single set of tools. Using XML can also facilitate language translation: presentation developers can separate all language-specific strings into a separate XML document and then send only that document to a translation house for conversion into any language required.

XML in Electronic Commerce

Many would argue that XML has changed the face of electronic commerce forever. XML has already seen action in several areas related to e-commerce—particularly in standards for the exchange of business data among trading partners and, most recently, in the development of networks of web services.

Business-to-Business Document Exchange

Although XML is not the first major technology to be brought to bear on the problem of exchanging business data between companies, it is almost certainly the most successful due to its flexibility, its low cost of implementation, and the advent of complementary technologies and standards.

Most organizations have proprietary internal data structures for their key business objects, such as purchase orders, shipping notifications, bids, and so on. Traditionally, these documents have been exchanged between companies in formats that are easily readable only by humans, such as fax or e-mail; sometimes these documents can be processed automatically, but more often exchanging this information across corporate boundaries means extensive rekeying, which creates errors that cause problems when the data is processed. The most successful solutions to date are the Electronic Data

Interchange (EDI) standards, such as ANSI X.12 and EDIFACT. Even though these standards define a common mechanism for encoding information to be exchanged between business partners, they are extremely expensive to implement and leave so much to subjective interpretation that implementers are forced to establish data transformation rules (EDI maps) for each individual company with which an organization does business.

Within the past few years, more companies have turned to XML as a tool to facilitate data exchange among business partners. Many standards have arisen that define common business objects using an XML-based vocabulary; while many of these standards are still not quite robust enough to force consistent content format across all users, the use of XML as an encoding standard has allowed many companies to save substantial amounts of time and money either by leveraging one of the many inter-enterprise application integration tools on the market or, for smaller organizations, by using freely available XML tools to accept these business documents and convert them to the appropriate internal format.

Now that it is possible to assign meaning to data, constructs such as

```
<PONumber>121914</PONumber>
```

or

```
<ShippingAddress>
   <Street1>123 Anyplace Drive</Street1>
   <Street2></Street2>
   <City>Anytown</City>
   <State>Maryland</State>
   <ZipCode>12345-6789</ZipCode>
</ShippingAddress>
```

can have a specific, *consistent* business meaning attached to them by the parties at both ends of a transaction. Further, by using XML Schema to define business documents, enterprises can dictate both the structure of the document and the data types that are used for each field.

Web Services

Web services are the latest in the evolving line of technologies designed to allow businesses, consumers, and other organizations to interact at a very low level—much lower than would be possible with the business object-oriented approach described in the preceding section. The web services concept is actually very simple: an organization registers itself with one of a number of directories as a provider of services, and other companies needing that service can find a provider in the directory and request its services. Some of the key mechanisms that allow entities to interact are—you guessed it—based on XML.

There are three key technologies that work together to make this possible. Two of these are based on XML:

▶ The **Simple Object Access Protocol (SOAP)** provides the specification for expressing a service request in XML, including the detailed contents of a request envelope and headers and the way to encode application data types. Using SOAP, an application can make a procedural request of a web service by encoding its request and any required parameters in an XML document, wrapping that document in XML-based headers and an envelope that provides routing information, and sending the package to the web service using whatever protocol is supported by that service. The web service removes the envelope and headers, decodes the request, executes it, encodes the result in XML, wraps it in a return envelope and headers, and returns it to the sender.

▶ The **Web Services Description Language (WSDL)** is used to describe the services provided. This service description, which is XML based, provides abstract, protocol-independent information on the messages exchanged between the service provider and service consumer as well as a description of the specific protocols that can be used to invoke the service.

▶ In addition, the **Universal Description Discovery and Integration (UDDI)** specifications provide definition of the mechanisms for publishing and discovering web services.

What makes XML such a perfect choice for SOAP and WSDL is its flexibility in expressing the structure and meaning of messages between producer and consumer. There is no data type, either simple or complex, that cannot be expressed in some way using a combination of XML elements and attributes. Further, because XML is extremely easy for applications to process and tools for doing so are widely available, developing a web services system is a fairly straightforward process—this enhances the appeal of the technology and drops the price point for participation in the web services network.

Extending XML: The Extensible Stylesheet Language for Transformations

The key to understanding XSLT's potential benefits to XML lies in its name: the Extensible Stylesheet Language *for Transformations*. Fundamentally, XSLT can do only one thing well, and that's transform data from one format or structure to another. Its power comes from its ability to perform these transformations in an extremely flexible way, by leveraging the combination of a unique processing model and the powerful XPath language to rearchitect data into whatever form you need. Although the World Wide Web Consortium (W3C) XSLT specification emphasizes transformation of one XML document to another, the potential uses of XSLT don't stop with simply converting between XML structures; it's possible—and even fairly easy—to not only fundamentally restructure an XML document by following the implicit or explicit links within the data, but to convert that data to almost any text-based format, such as HTML, WML, or plain text. XSLT even provides the abilities to combine XML documents and to use data in one document as an index into the content of another.

XSLT is not a "silver bullet," however, and it can't help with every XML processing problem you'll run into—not even all of the ones described in this chapter. Let's take a look at a couple of examples that illustrate the range of applications for which XSLT *is* suited.

Generating Presentation Formats

When most people think of using XSLT with XML, they think of using it to convert data into some presentation format, usually HTML. This is easily the most popular application of XSLT, and the one most closely tied to XSLT's origins as the transformation language for XSL—and it's the application you'll see most often in the examples in this book.

Typically, when web designers put together a page, they think in terms of visual presentation elements. Using tables, images, text, JavaScript, and other web components, they produce pages that capture the casual surfer or intuitively direct the more focused visitor. HTML is a great tool for putting together crisp presentation of data; however, doing so programmatically can be difficult at best, and a maintenance headache at worst. Writing applications that generate HTML or other presentation markup from data is not only tedious and time consuming, but it makes code difficult to read and maintain, precludes the use of advanced authoring tools, lengthens testing and review cycles, and limits your ability to change the presentation in response to your ongoing needs. Let the marketing department change a few logos or make wholesale changes to the official corporate color scheme, and you'll spend weeks reworking and reverifying the presentation you so lovingly crafted in code.

However, by separating the data you want to present from the graphical elements you use to present it, you make it much easier on your applications programmers and yourself by eliminating all that tedious coding work. Programmers familiar with the Model-View-Controller (MVC) design pattern will recognize this as one of the basic concepts of many Java 2 Enterprise Edition (J2EE) applications. With data and presentation separated, it becomes much simpler to change the look of your site without changing your applications, making it easy to keep up with the Marketing department or simply to tweak your site to keep it interesting and fresh.

The XML/XSLT approach to this problem is for your applications or content developers to generate XML documents containing the data to be presented, and for your web designer to produce XSLT stylesheets that contain the instructions for converting that information into its final presentation format. XML is a perfect tool for this because it can carry not only textual content but information about the meaning of that content as well—which can be translated into more visually interesting presentation on your web site. XSLT can easily read these XML documents and generate the appropriate presentation, and as you'll see during your progress through this book, changing an XSLT stylesheet is much easier that writing code. Separating presentation from data also makes it easier to separate responsibilities in an organization; content and applications people do what they're good at, and the web designer makes the most of the data they produce on your web site.

Chapter 11 provides some concrete examples of how presentation generation can be performed.

XML Document Restructuring

Not all applications need the same data, and it's often not appropriate to give applications access to data they don't need—especially if those applications reside on someone else's system. If your organization is currently using XML as the storage medium for business objects, documents, or other data, then you've almost certainly run into situations where you need to restructure, modify, or augment that data in order to pass it on to another application or business partner, or convert it to a presentation format for customer consumption.

XSLT provides a very powerful facility for extracting data from a combination of other XML documents, performing extensive restructuring, cross-linking and editing, and then writing the data as a new XML, HTML, or text document. Applications such as those for indexing documents, converting to and from standardized business object formats, extracting a subset of document data, and creating internal document relationships (using XML's ID and IDREF attributes, or XLink and XPointer links and references) are perfect candidates for XSLT applications.

To make the work of these applications as easy as possible, your input XML documents should contain some sort of information that allows your XSLT stylesheet to make programmatic decisions about what goes where and how items are to be related; this can be done using the contents of the input document's elements and attributes, or it can be done by providing a separate editing rules file that tells the stylesheet how to do its work. Again, Chapter 11 provides some examples of techniques you can use to restructure data for your application.

The Structure of an XML/XSLT Application

When considering the use of a new technology, it often helps to take a step back and consider how the technology fits into the bigger strategy for solving the problem at hand. Before you can use XSLT effectively, you need to understand what's required to use it and how it fits into new and preexisting system architectures in your organization. The sections that follow attempt to help you understand what's required to use XSLT so you can decide for yourself where it fits.

XML and XSLT Processing Tools

You may have a grand plan for your data stretched out before you; you see information flowing through the organization, transformed by the magic of your applications, bringing the power of knowledge to your business partners. But before you code that first XSLT stylesheet to make all of this happen, you need to know what to do with it, and to do that you need to understand the tools required to do the job.

At a minimum, every XSLT application needs two tools. Because the input to the XSLT transformation process (both the input data and the XSLT stylesheet itself) is XML, your transformation process will need an *XML parser* to allow you to read that input. There are many fine XML parsers on the market, including those from Apache, IBM, Sun, Microsoft, and other vendors; the vast majority of these are freely downloadable from the Web and come under licenses that allow their use for internal, nonredistributable applications. Your choice of parser depends on several factors: what language your applications are written in, what operating system the transformations will run on, whether you'll use the parser only with XSLT or for other applications, and whether you want the (relative) comfort of a vendor product or are willing to use an open-source tool. Chapter 13 examines several tools and provides more information to help you make this decision.

The second tool (and, of course, the more important one for our purposes) is the *XSLT stylesheet processor*. This is the tool that actually reads the XSLT stylesheet and interprets it into a set of executable instructions, which it then uses to process your input document. Many XSLT stylesheet processors, such as the one from the Apache Group, come bundled with an XML parser that they can use to read the input document and the XSLT stylesheet, and most give you the option of substituting your own XML parser, if, for example, your company has standardized on a given software package. If you're using the XSLT processor in stand-alone mode (from the command line, for example), then you should find everything you need in the processor's installation bundle; if you're invoking it from your application programs, you may, depending on your particular needs, be required to read the input XML document separately using an XML parser before running it through the stylesheet processor.

Chapter 13 goes into more detail on the various types of XSLT stylesheet processors and describes how you can invoke these processors from your application programs.

Single-Tier Application Architectures

We use the term *single-tier applications* to describe XSLT applications whose component programs reside in a single layer and are not spread out across a network (as you might find in a client-server system, for example). A single-tier application is composed of some number of steps, each of which is performed by an XSLT stylesheet processor, a custom-developed application program, or a packaged tool.

The simplest single-tier application is one in which only one step executes an XSLT stylesheet processor. An example of this might be a command-line invocation of the processor, where you specify arguments to tell the processor where to find your input XML document and your stylesheet, as well as where to place the output of the transformation process. This is most appropriate when no pre- or post-processing of the transformation input or output is required; many transformation needs can be satisfied in just this way.

A slightly more complex example is the situation where the application contains a single step that executes custom application code, and this code invokes the stylesheet processor dynamically. In this case, the application has the ability to handle the input and output of the transformation process, and yet the processing is still contained in a single step. You might consider using this strategy if, for example, there's a need to filter the input document in some way before sending it through the transformation process, or when timing or performance requirements do not allow the overhead of writing the output of the transformation to storage before it is processed by a subsequent operation.

Multistep single-tier applications are perfect for situations where the total application requires several distinct operations to accomplish its goal. One or more of these steps can be XSLT transformations; the remainder can be custom code, packaged applications, or a combination of the two. There are many problems for which this approach is appropriate; as powerful as XSLT is, it can't do everything, and the multistep approach allows you to use different tools in ways that leverage each one's particular strengths.

N-Tier Application Architectures

Applications that segregate functionality into layers are called *n-tier* applications. Client-server applications are an example of an n-tier application composed of two tiers: one for the client (typically a user interface) and one for the server (where the bulk of the work gets done). Java 2 Enterprise Edition (J2EE) applications are generally composed of three tiers: one for the client (browser or application), one for the business logic (the J2EE application server), and one for the database.

Typically, XSLT stylesheet processors fit into the server layer in a two-tier configuration or in the business logic layer in a three-tier configuration. Technically, there's really nothing to keep you from using a stylesheet processor in the client layer as well, but there are some browser compatibility issues you'll need to be aware of before you do so (more information on this is provided in Chapter 12). Using the HTML generation example described earlier, it's very reasonable to have server-side applications that generate XML data that is then transformed into HTML using XSLT before being sent to the client. Likewise, business-to-business data exchange systems will perform the transformation between the internal data format and external data format using XSLT before sending business documents to partner applications.

In an n-tier application, the steps we discussed for single-tier applications become components of the server or business logic layer. In a J2EE application, for example, several objects (JSP pages, servlets, Java beans, session beans, or entity beans) work together to perform a specific operation; entity beans could use XSLT when they read and write data, or stateless session beans could perform transformations on behalf of other components of the application. When using XSLT for HTML generation, the stylesheet processor is usually invoked by a JSP page, a servlet, or a Java Bean; the choice of which is appropriate depends on the needs of your application.

Summary

At this point, you should have a reasonably good idea of what XSLT is, what it does, and how its use with structured documents can improve your ability to both present and use information effectively. The next chapter describes XSLT applications in more detail and shows how XSLT can fit into an overall software application architecture.

CHAPTER

4

The Structure of an XSLT Stylesheet

IN THIS CHAPTER:

A compilation of XSLT instructions should more appropriately be called a transformation sheet, rather than a stylesheet. However, for historical reasons, we will continue calling it a stylesheet. Such a stylesheet contains a set of template rules and serves to transform the source tree into a result tree. While the source and result trees are hierarchical structures represented by XML documents, the output does not necessarily have to be XML. In this chapter, we will review the structure of a stylesheet and its key components. We will see that `xsl:stylesheet` is the outermost element in an XSLT stylesheet and learn the syntax and usage of top-level XSLT elements. We will also learn about the forwards-compatible mode. We will discuss `xsl:stylesheet`, along with its child elements, in this chapter, deferring the treatment of the rest of the elements until later in the book.

Some real-life situations will likely require complex transformations for which a stand-alone stylesheet may not be an appropriate solution. In such circumstances, it may be better to break the work across several stylesheets. Such a modular approach has multiple advantages. Each stylesheet then becomes easier to develop, debug, and maintain. Moreover, the "modules" may be reused across multiple development projects. This chapter will also deal with combining multiple stylesheets to achieve the desired result using the `xsl:import` and `xsl:include` facilities of XSLT. Although you would typically separate the XML data source from the XSLT stylesheet, there is a way to embed the stylesheet within the data document, as you will see in this chapter.

General Stylesheet Structure

As in any other programming language, XSLT stylesheets may become quite complicated when you set out to solve real-life problems. In such circumstances, you would want to split the transformations across multiple stylesheets. This is discussed later in the chapter. We will start by discussing the structure of a simple stylesheet. By simple, we mean a self-contained stylesheet that is used to achieve the goal of carrying out the requisite transformations. This is best done by showing code samples for the source XML tree, the XSLT stylesheet that is going to operate on the source tree, and the HTML output resulting from this operation:

Here is the XML source tree auth.xml:

```
<?xml version="1.0"?>
  <!-- data specifications begin -->
<All_authors>
  <Author>
  <Name>
```

```
      <First_name>Chris</First_name>
      <Last_name>von See</Last_name>
    </Name>
    <Address>
      <Address_line1>111 Mansion Boulevard</Address_line1>
      <Address_line2>Suite 100</Address_line2>
      <City>Chicago</City>
      <State>IL</State>
      <ZIP>31313</ZIP>
    </Address>
    </Author>
    <Author>
      <Name>
      <First_name>Nitin</First_name>
      <Last_name>Keskar</Last_name>
      </Name>
    <Address>
      <Address_line1>222 Metropolis Street</Address_line1>
      <Address_line2>P.O. Box 500</Address_line2>
      <City>Minneapolis</City>
      <State>MN</State>
      <ZIP>55455</ZIP>
    </Address>
    </Author>
</All_authors>
<!-- data specifications end -->
```

Here is the XSLT stylesheet auth.xsl:

```
<?xml version="1.0"?>

<!-- stylesheet specifications begin -->
<xsl:stylesheet version="1.0"
    xmlns:xsl="http://www.w3.org/1999/XSL/Transform">

  <xsl:template match="/">
    <html>
      <head>
        <title>Information about OMH authors</title>
      </head>
      <body>
        <xsl:apply-templates select="All_authors"/>
      </body>
    </html>
  </xsl:template>
```

```
<xsl:template match="Name">
  <B>
    <xsl:value-of select="."/>
  </B>
</xsl:template>

<xsl:template match="Address">
  <I>
    <P>
      <xsl:apply-templates/>
    </P>
  </I>
</xsl:template>
</xsl:stylesheet>
<!-- stylesheet specifications end -->
```

The HTML output (auth.htm) that was generated as a result of this transformation is shown next. Instant SAXON (v6.4.4) written by Michael Kay was used to generate the output, although we took the liberty of removing the blank lines from the output.

```
<html>
  <head>
    <title>Information about OMH authors</title>
  </head>
  <body>
    <B>
      Chris
      von See
    </B>
    <I>
      <P>
        111 Mansion Boulevard
        Suite 100
        Chicago
        IL
        31313
      </P></I>
    <B>
      Nitin
      Keskar
    </B>
    <I>
```

```
      <P>
         222 Metropolis Street
         P.O. Box 500
         Minneapolis
         MN
         55455
      </P></I>
   </body>
</html>
```

Figure 4-1 shows the HTML output rendered in Internet Explorer 5.5.

In the XSLT stylesheet, the preamble shown here indicates that an XSLT document is essentially an XML document, and the current version 1.0 is also indicated therein:

```
<?xml version="1.0" ?>
```

If you intend to use a specific encoding, such as ANSI (officially known as iso-8859-1), it may be specified in the same line as follows:

```
<?xml version="1.0" encoding="iso-8859-1"?>
```

As in any other XML document, the comments are enclosed within `<!--` and `-->`. The rest of the document is enclosed between the outermost matching tags `<xsl:stylesheet>` and `</xsl:stylesheet>`. These tags identify this

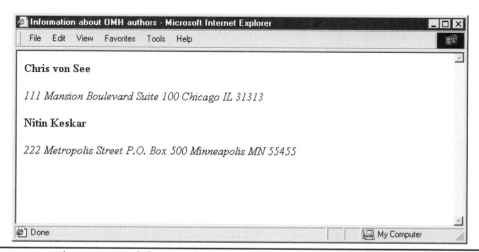

Figure 4-1   *The output auth.htm resulting from the application of auth.xsl to auth.xml rendered in IE 5.5*

document as an XSLT stylesheet. Note that the element names /xsl:stylesheet and /xsl:transform are synonymous and may be used interchangeably. The attribute xmlns:xsl is a standard XML namespace declaration. The URI http://www.w3c.org/1999/XSL/Transform shows the location of the specification of this namespace. You must use this URI as a namespace prefix for all XSLT documents. You may use multiple namespaces, including custom-defined ones as described in Chapter 2. This allows you to avoid conflicts between element and attribute names. This element xsl:stylesheet of the stylesheet is required to have a version attribute. Since the current version of XSLT is 1.0, that is what is indicated here.

As an aside, the use of xsl in the namespace declaration, and in the rest of the document, is purely a matter of habit. You can call it anything else—for instance, foo, as shown here:

```
<foo:stylesheet id="stylesheet"
                version="1.0"
                xmlns:foo="http://www.w3.org/1999/XSL/Transform">

    <foo:template match="/">
      <html>
        <head>
          <title>Information about OMH authors</title>
        </head>
        <body>
          <foo:apply-templates select="All_authors"/>
        </body>
      </html>
    </foo:template>
...
```

Although using foo is perfectly legal, we will use the standard phrase xsl since the use of anything less familiar may hamper the readability of the code.

The rest of this stylesheet provides instructions for which elements to look for, and what kind of transformations to carry out for those elements. Note that you can use the standard HTML tags in the stylesheet to format the output according to your needs. Let us take a look at the template rules one by one.

The first template rule shown here is applied when it finds a match for the root template denoted by "/" and outputs the HTML tags as instructed by the stylesheet:

```
<xsl:template match="/">
  <html>
    <head>
      <title>Information about OMH authors</title>
    </head>
```

```
      <body>
        <xsl:apply-templates select="All_authors"/>
      </body>
    </html>
  </xsl:template>
...
```

The element `xsl:apply-templates` is instrumental in traversing the XML tree in a recursive fashion, starting at a specified node, which is `All_authors` in this example. Thus, all child elements of `All_authors` will be processed according to any template rules that you may care to specify later in the stylesheet, and they all will be placed between the `<body></body>` tags.

The next template rule is encountered for the node `Name` whereby the element `xsl:value-of` computes the value of the current node (specified by the character ".") and places it between the `<B>` and `</B>` tags.

```
  <xsl:template match="Name">
    <B>
      <xsl:value-of select="."/>
    </B>
  </xsl:template>
...
```

The next template rule applies to `Address`, as shown here:

```
...
  <xsl:template match="Address">
    <I>
      <P>
        <xsl:apply-templates/>
      </P>
    </I>
  </xsl:template>
...
```

In this case, we are putting HTML tags for italics and paragraph breaks before and after the value of the `Address` node is output. When the element `xsl:apply-templates` is used without specifying an attribute as we did before, the rule will be applied recursively to the rest of the tree starting at the `Address` node, and the HTML markup will be applied to the value of that node. The value of the node is simply the character string that is obtained by removing the XML tags (such as `<Address_line1>`, `<Address_line2>`, and so on for the `Address` node). Thus, in this particular case, replacing `<xsl:apply-templates/>` with `<xsl:value-of select="."/>` will result in the same output.

In Figure 4-1, there are no paragraph breaks between the descendant nodes of `Address`. If you want to process the XML tree recursively and put paragraph breaks between individual descendant nodes (indicated by `/*` in XSLT), you could make the following simple change in the code:

```
...
   <xsl:template match="Address/*">
     <I>
       <P>
         <xsl:apply-templates/>
       </P>
     </I>
   </xsl:template>
...
```

This would result in the rendered output shown in Figure 4-2.

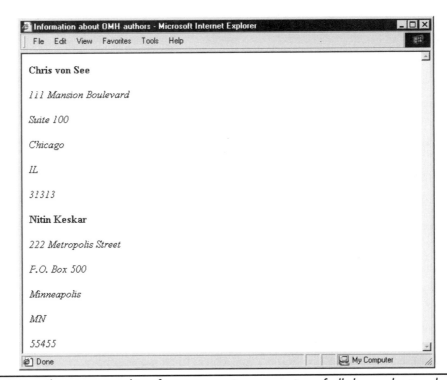

Figure 4-2   *The output resulting from a recursive processing of all descendant nodes of* Address

This, in a nutshell, gives you an idea of the structure of an XSLT stylesheet. In the rest of the chapter, we will discuss a few more nuances of writing a stylesheet and address the top-level elements that you may use in writing one.

XSLT Version and Forwards-Compatible Mode

In general, when the version attribute of the stylesheet element is higher than the current implemented version of XSLT, a forwards-compatible mode is enabled for the current element and all its descendants. Since XSLT 1.0 is the only version available for now, you may not have an immediate use for an in-depth knowledge of this mode. However, future XSLT specifications are in the works, and you should be familiar with the programmatic constructs to use when multiple XSLT versions do become available.

The rules for forwards-compatible mode depend of the level at which the element occurs and the kind of attributes that it has, as explained here.

Top-Level Elements

If the element is a top-level element that is disallowed in the current version of XSLT, the XSLT processor will ignore it completely. For example, if you changed the version of your stylesheet to 1.1 and tried to use `xsl:new-top-level-element-in-v1.1`, which your XSLT 1.0 processor does not implement, the XSLT processor will not generate an error. Thus, if you changed the original code in the following manner (changes are highlighted in **bold**), it will work just fine, and the XSLT processor will generate the same output as before:

```
<?xml version="1.0"?>

<!-- stylesheet specifications begin -->
<xsl:stylesheet id="stylesheet"
                version="1.1"
                xmlns:xsl="http://www.w3.org/1999/XSL/Transform">

<xsl:new-top-level-element-in-v1.1/>

    <xsl:template match="/">
...
```

Attribute Undefined in Version 1.0

If you attempt to use an attribute that the current XSLT processor does not understand, it will be ignored. For example, if you change the original code to the following, which uses `new_attribute_in_v1.1`, you will get the same output as before:

```
...
<xsl:stylesheet id="stylesheet"
                version="1.1"
                xmlns:xsl="http://www.w3.org/1999/XSL/Transform">
...
<body>
  <xsl:apply-templates select="All_authors" new_attribute_in_v1.1="."/>
</body>
...
```

Element Occurring in a Template

If you use a currently unsupported element `xsl:new-element-in-v1.1` within a template, how it will get processed depends on whether the element is instantiated or not. For example, the following code sample shows the use of `xsl:new-element-in-v1.1` in the template for the root node:

```
<xsl:stylesheet version="1.1"
    xmlns:xsl="http://www.w3.org/1999/XSL/Transform">

<!-- stylesheet template processing begins -->
    <xsl:template match="/">
      <xsl:new-element-in-v1.1/>
      <html>
        <head>
          <title>Information about OMH authors</title>
        </head>
...
```

In this case, the `Name` node does get instantiated, and the XSLT processor is required to signal an error when it encounters the unknown element within this template.

If you want to work around such a problem, you may conditionally process `xsl:new-element-in-v1.1`, depending on whether the current implemented version supports this feature or not. This is shown in the following code sample. Although this example uses XSLT elements that we will discuss later in the book, the use of when ... otherwise is similar to the if ... then structure from other programming languages that you may be familiar with.

```
. . .
    <xsl:template match="Name">
      <B>
        <xsl:choose>

          <xsl:when test="system-property('xsl:version') >= 1.1">
            <xsl:new-element-in-v1.1/>
          </xsl:when>

          <xsl:otherwise>
            <xsl:value-of select="."/>
          </xsl:otherwise>

        </xsl:choose>
      </B>
    </xsl:template>
. . .
```

Such conditional processing will ensure that the stylesheet is interpreted without error by the current XSLT processors supporting version 1.0 since xsl:new-element-in-v1.1 is not reached in this case.

Top-Level Stylesheet Elements

Although xsl:template is the only child element of the outermost xsl:stylesheet element that is shown in the previous examples, xsl:stylesheet may additionally contain (but does not have to) the following types of child elements that are known as the *top-level* elements:

- ▶ xsl:import
- ▶ xsl:include
- ▶ xsl:strip-space
- ▶ xsl:preserve-space
- ▶ xsl:output
- ▶ xsl:key

- ▶ xsl:decimal-format
- ▶ xsl:namespace-alias
- ▶ xsl:attribute-set
- ▶ xsl:variable
- ▶ xsl:param
- ▶ xsl:template

In the rest of this section, we will discuss each of these elements individually.

xsl:import and xsl:include

The elements xsl:import and xsl:include let you combine multiple stylesheets so that complex transformations may be modularized into manageable units. The syntax for both is very similar:

```
<xsl:import
  href= uri-reference />

<xsl:include
  href= uri-reference />
```

For example, if you have stylesheets auth.xsl, auth_inc1.xsl, and auth_inc2.xsl, you may combine them in the following manner:

```
<!-- stylesheet auth.xsl -->
<!-- In this example, all stylesheets are assumed to be in the same physical
directory-->
<xsl:stylesheet version="1.0"
  xmlns:xsl="http://www.w3.org/1999/XSL/Transform">
  <xsl:include href="auth_inc1.xsl"/>
  <xsl:include href="auth_inc2.xsl"/>
</xsl:stylesheet>
```

Another way of combining the stylesheets is to use xsl:import in place of xsl:include. If the template rules and definitions in auth.xsl, auth_inc1.xsl, and auth_inc2.xsl have no conflicts, this will give results identical to that achieved by using xsl:include. However, in case of a conflict, using xsl:include will lead to errors since all elements included in auth.xsl from auth_inc1.xsl and auth_inc2.xsl will be treated equally. By contrast when xsl:import is used, the template rules and definitions from the importing stylesheet take precedence over template rules and definitions in the imported stylesheet.

xsl:strip-space and xsl:preserve-space

The elements `xsl:strip-space` and `xsl:preserve-space` instruct the XSLT processor how the white space characters (space, newline, tab) are to be treated. The syntax for both elements is similar:

```
<xsl:strip-space
  elements="element_list"/>
<xsl:preserve-space
  elements="element_list"/>
```

For example, consider a fragment of a source XML file:

```
<p> My phone number is <areacode>612</areacode>
   <localnumber>5551212</localnumber>. </p>
...
```

The following instruction will remove all white-space nodes within `<p>` elements:

```
<xsl:strip-space elements="p"/>
```

The result will look as follows:

```
My phone number is 6125551212.
```

These two elements may also be combined to remove white space from all nodes except for elements for which the space is to be preserved, as for the element `Address` in the following example:

```
<xsl:strip-space elements="*"/>
<xsl:preserve-space elements="Address"/>
```

xsl:output

The `xsl:output` element is used to control the format of the output of the XSLT transformations. The syntax of this element is shown here:

```
<xsl:output
  method = "xml" | "html" | "text" | qname-but-not-ncname
  version = nmtoken
  encoding = string
  omit-xml-declaration = "yes" | "no"
  standalone = "yes" | "no"
  doctype-public = string
```

```
doctype-system = string
cdata-section-elements = qnames
indent = "yes" | "no"
media-type = string />
```

There are multiple attributes that may be set for this element, all of which are optional. Table 4-1 provides a brief description of these attributes. A more detailed discussion about controlling the output can be found in Chapter 11.

xsl:key

The `xsl:key` element can be used to define a named index of nodes from the source XML tree(s). It is used with the `key()` function defined elsewhere in the book. Its syntax is shown here:

```
<xsl:key
  name = qname
  match = pattern
  use = expression />
```

Here, `name` is simply the name of the key. The attribute `match` is used to specify the nodes that are in this key set, whereas `use` specifies the expression within each node that identifies the key.

Let us say that the source file includes names of telephone companies:

```
...
<companyList>
  <company name="ATT" id="111"/>
  <company name="Sprint" id="222"/>
  <company name="Worldcom" id=333"/>
...
</companyList>
```

You can define a key called phonecompany in the XSLT file:

```
<xsl:key name="phoneCompany" match="company" use="@id"/>
```

The code to search for the company with id 333 would then look like this:

```
<xsl:apply-templates select="key('phoneCompany','333')"/>
```

Attribute	Description
Method	The output format may be XML, HTML, WML, text, and so on.
Version	Specifies the XML version of the output.
Encoding	Specifies the character encoding to be used for the output: for example, `iso-8859-1` for ANSI output.
Omit-xml-declaration	If the value of this attribute is "no", the XML declaration (`<?xml...?>`) will be included in the output. If you do not want this, you can set this attribute to a value of "yes".
Standalone	Optional. A value of "yes" indicates that the result should be a stand-alone document; a value of "no" indicates that the result should not be a stand-alone document.
Doctype-public	The standard public identifier to be used in the `<!doctype>` declaration in the output as used in any XML document..
Doctype-system	The standard system identifier to be used in the `<!doctype>` declaration in the output as used in any XML document.
cdata-section-elements	Specifies a list (separated by white space) of elements whose content is to be output in CDATA sections.
Indent	The result tree can be output in an indented fashion to indicate the hierarchical structure by setting this attribute to "yes". If you prefer not to indent, set this attribute to "no".
media-type	Defines the media type, also known as the mime type, of the output. This does not mean that the output content will be altered; that responsibility still remains with the developer. It merely means that you may direct that the output file be treated as if it were of the specified media type.

Table 4-1 *Attributes of the Top-Level Element* `xsl:output`

The element `xsl:key` and the associated function `key()` are discussed in detail in Chapter 10.

xsl:decimal-format

The `xsl:decimal-format` element defines the format of the numbers in a document and is used in conjunction with the `format-number` function. You can specify the thousands separator, the decimal indicator, and other format specifications shown in the following syntax statement:

```
<xsl:decimal-format
  name = qname
  decimal-separator = char
  grouping-separator = char
  infinity = string
  minus-sign = char
  NaN = string
  percent = char
  per-mille = char
  zero-digit = char
  digit = char
  pattern-separator = char />
```

An example of the usage is shown here:

```
<xsl:decimal-format name="custom_format" decimal-separator="."
 grouping-separator=","/>

<xsl:template match="/">
<p> The invoice price of this model of the car is $ </p>
<xsl:value-of
select="format-number(48660.22, '#,###.00', 'custom_format')"/>
</xsl:template>
```

The application of the specified format to the price of the car will produce this output:

```
The invoice price of this model of the car is $ 48,660.22
```

In a European context, you might have have used the period (.) as the group separator and the comma (,) as the decimal separator.

The element `xsl:decimal-format` and the associated function `format-number()` are discussed in detail in Chapter 10.

xsl:namespace-alias

The `xsl:namespace-alias` element is used to map a namespace from the
stylesheet to one in the output. This element is particularly useful when the output
is also a stylesheet, since this is the only way to declare two prefixes with the same
namespace without having the XSLT processor treat both prefixes as the same
namespace. This element may also be useful even when the output is not another
stylesheet, but when you still need a way to resolve colliding namespaces. Thus,
both attributes `stylesheet-prefix` and `result-prefix` in the following
syntax statement are mandatory:

```
<xsl:namespace-alias
  stylesheet-prefix = prefix | "#default"
  result-prefix = prefix | "#default" />
```

xsl:attribute-set

The `xsl:attribute-set` element is used to define a named set of attributes that
may be applied as a whole to the output elements.

Note that this element is different from `xsl:attribtute`, which is used to
create an attribute node and to attach it to an output element.

The syntax for `xsl:attribute-set` is as follows:

```
<xsl:attribute-set
  name = qname
  use-attribute-sets = qnames>
  <!-- Content: xsl:attribute* -->
</xsl:attribute-set>
```

The following simple example of this element's usage creates a named set of
properties, called myStyle:

```
<xsl:attribute-set name="omhStyle">
  <xsl:attribute name="font-family">verdana</xsl:attribute>
  <xsl:attribute name="font-size">20pt</xsl:attribute>
</xsl:attribute-set>
```

This attribute set may be used as follows:

```
...
    <xsl:template match="Address">
      <I>
```

```
      <P xsl:use-attribute-sets="omhStyle">
        <xsl:apply-templates/>
      </P>
    </I>
  </xsl:template>
...
```

xsl:variable and xsl:param

The `xsl:variable` and `xsl:param` elements are used to define named variables and parameters within `xsl:stylesheet` or `xsl:template`. They share a similar syntax and are used similarly:

```
<xsl:variable
  name = qname
  select = expression>
  <!-- Content: template -->
</xsl:variable>
```

The nuance for `xsl:param` is that it can be used either to define a global parameter (as a child node of `xsl:stylesheet`) or to define a local parameter (as a child node of `xsl:template`).

This example defines a variable and later accesses it using the function `xsl:value-of`:

```
<xsl:variable name="consulting" select="'eFORCE'">
...
<xsl:value-of select="item[$consulting]"/>
```

Note that `select` is not a mandatory attribute, and if you did not assign it to a value, the value of the variable would be an empty string.

Variables and parameters are discussed in detail in Chapter 8.

xsl:template

Last but not least is the ubiquitous `xsl:template` element, which is used to define template rules for the output. Each template rule is defined for nodes of a particular type and operates within that context that is defined by the attribute `match` in the following syntax statement:

```
<xsl:template
  match = pattern
  name = qname
```

```
   priority = number
   mode = qname>
   <!-- Content: (xsl:param*, template) -->
</xsl:template>
```

This element is the heart of XSLT programming, since the end goal of XSLT code is to find pattern matches and apply template rules to them. By this time, you have seen numerous examples of its usage, and you will see a lot more in the rest of this book. Chapter 6 will provide a detailed treatment of template rules.

Embedding Stylesheets

It is perfectly legal for an XSLT stylesheet to be embedded within the XML document that it applies to, as shown in the following example:

```
<?xml version="1.0"?>
<?xml-stylesheet type="text/xml" href="#stylesheet"?>
<!DOCTYPE doc [
<!ATTLIST xsl:stylesheet
   id   ID    #REQUIRED>
              ]>
<doc>

<!-- stylesheet specifications begin -->
<xsl:stylesheet id="stylesheet"
                version="1.0"
                xmlns:xsl="http://www.w3.org/1999/XSL/Transform">

    <xsl:template match="/">
      <html>
        <xsl:apply-templates/>
      </html>
    </xsl:template>  <!-- rest of your stylesheet -->

    <xsl:template match="All_authors">
      <xsl:apply-templates/>
    </xsl:template>

    <xsl:template match="Name">
      <B>
        <xsl:value-of select="."/>
```

```
      </B>
    </xsl:template>

    <xsl:template match="Address">
      <P>
        <xsl:value-of select="."/>
      </P>
    </xsl:template>
</xsl:stylesheet>
<!-- stylesheet specifications begin -->

<!-- data specifications begin -->
<All_authors>
  <Author>
  <Name>
    <First_name>Chris</First_name>
    <Last_name>von See</Last_name>
  </Name>
  <Address>
    <Address_line1>111 Mansion Boulevard</Address_line1>
    <Address_line2>Suite 100</Address_line2>
    <City>Chicago</City>
    <State>IL</State>
  </Address>
  </Author>
  <Author>
    <Name>
    <First_name>Nitin</First_name>
    <Last_name>Keskar</Last_name>
    </Name>
  <Address>
    <Address_line1>222 Metropolis Street</Address_line1>
    <Address_line2>P.O. Box 500</Address_line2>
    <City>Minneapolis</City>
    <State>MN</State>
  </Address>
  </Author>
</All_authors>
<!-- data specifications end -->

</doc>
```

This will produce the following output:

```
<html>
   <B> Chris von See </B>
   <P>
      111 Mansion Boulevard
      Suite 100
      Chicago
      IL
   </P>
   <B> Nitin Keskar </B>
   <P>
      222 Metropolis Street
      P.O. Box 500
      Minneapolis
      MN
   </P>
</html>
```

As seen here, the element `xsl:stysheet` is not the outermost element in this stylesheet as it would have been had the transformations been separated from the data.

NOTE

It is mandatory to have a DTD that defines the `xsl:stylesheet` element as having an `id` attribute of type ID. Without this, `href` will not have the reference needed to locate the stylesheet, although it is embedded in the same document!

Although there may be specific instances where you may want to use embedding, we would caution against it as a general practice. We think that the whole point of separating data (XML), presentations (XSL FO), and transformations (XSLT) is lost when you use this functionality as a matter of course.

Summary

In this chapter, we discussed the general structure of an XSLT stylesheet. In its most fundamental form, a stylesheet reads a source XML tree, looks for nodes to which given template rules are to be applied, and outputs the result tree. We discussed the top-level child elements of `xsl:stylesheet`, which is the outermost element when a stylesheet is separated from the source XML file. Using these elements, you should already be able to accomplish a lot, although discussions about writing XSLT programs including familiar programming constructs such as looping and conditional processing are yet to come.

In the next chapter, we will discuss XPath and its significance in XSLT programming. We will also describe the syntax of XPath expressions and their use in developing stylesheets.

CHAPTER

5

Expressions

IN THIS CHAPTER:

XSLT and XPath Expression Overview

Coding XPath Expressions

XPath Functions

Summary

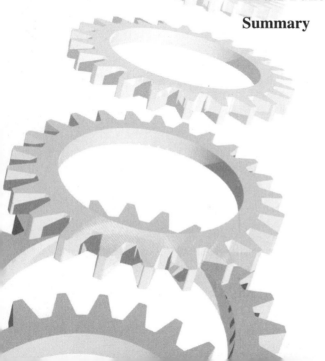

Chapter 2 discussed the hierarchical view that XSLT processors have of XML documents, the terminology used to identify the various parts of the hierarchy, and the relationships that nodes can have to each other: parent-child, sibling, descendant-ancestor, and so on. Now, with this view of the document hierarchy firmly locked in your mind, we will examine how XSLT expressions can be used to identify one or more nodes in the hierarchy, specify conditions to be evaluated when processing nodes, and perform operations on selected nodes in the hierarchy. Understanding the use of expressions in XSLT is key to using XSLT effectively, so this chapter will explore this topic in some depth.

If you've studied the XSLT stylesheets you've seen so far in this book, you've probably noticed that the expression syntax used in XSLT differs substantially from the familiar XML-based command syntax. This expression syntax is described by a separate W3C specification called the XML Path Language, or XPath. The XPath specification grew out of the common needs of two major XML technologies, XSL/XSLT and the XML Pointer Language (XPointer), and it provides both a highly concise syntax for identifying the location of any set of nodes in an XML document and a set of built-in functions that allow users to create powerful conditional expressions and convert among Boolean, numeric, and string data types.

In the course of this chapter, you will learn about XPath and its relationship to XSLT. You will also learn to identify and use XPath expressions to specify the location of elements in an XML document and to perform basic operations on string, numeric, and Boolean values.

XSLT and XPath Expression Overview

In the way of many Internet-related technology specifications, the W3C XPath specification uses highly precise (and somewhat arcane) language to describe XPath's syntax and functionality. While at first glance XPath isn't intuitively obvious, with a little bit of study you'll find that it's actually very easy to use and provides a wealth of features that give you excellent control over XSLT stylesheet processing. In the next few pages, we'll cover general XPath concepts and syntax, and then we'll dive into each class of expression, looking at the common syntax used and what XSLT and XPath do in response to each type.

Location Addressing

We'll start our discussion of XPath expressions by examining the way that XSLT processes XML documents.

When an XML document is processed using an XSLT stylesheet, each template in the stylesheet selects one or more nodes for processing based on the nodes' absolute location in the document hierarchy, their location relative to each other, and their content and attributes. The search starts with the document's root node and proceeds through all of the nodes in a document order (top to bottom, left to right) traversal of the hierarchy. If multiple nodes in the hierarchy match the template's selection criteria (as might be the case if you select all occurrences of a certain element), each matching node is processed by the template in the order in which it is encountered. For example, consider the document hierarchy shown in Figure 5-1.

If we code a template that selects all `book` nodes, the template will process only the document element node, since that is the only `book` node found in the document. However, if we code a template that selects all `chapter` nodes, there are now four nodes to be processed; in this case, the template will process the first and second `chapter` nodes under the first `part` node, and then the first and second `chapter` nodes found under the second `part` node, as shown in Figure 5-2.

The document traversal order can be modified by using the `xsl:apply-templates select="expression" /` and `xsl:call-template` commands to jump to the processing of a particular set of nodes or call a template with a specific name, respectively.

While a template is processing a given node, the node being processed is considered to be the *current node*, and it provides context for all of the operations inside the template. It then becomes possible for XSLT commands within the template to specify the location of other nodes in the document relative to the current node. If the template is processing the first `chapter` node in the example shown in Figure 5-2, it's possible to extract content from that node's parent (the first `part` node) or any other node using relative addressing. The benefit of relative addressing, of course, is that you can specify rules that apply regardless of where the selected node resides in the document hierarchy, as long as the node is used in the same context (same parent and sibling nodes and so on). In this example, the addressing specification

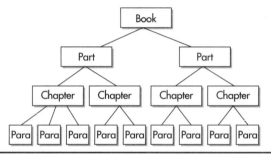

Figure 5-1   *A book document*

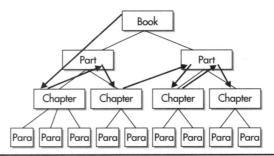

Figure 5-2 *Navigating the book document to locate all* `chapter` *nodes*

used to locate the first `chapter` element's parent (the first `part` node) will still work when the last `chapter` node (whose parent is the second `part` node) is being processed.

For situations where no template in the stylesheet matches a given node, XSLT provides a set of built-in templates that ensure that processing of the document continues uninterrupted. The built-in template that matches the root node, for example, simply calls `xsl:apply-templates` to process its children, and the built-in template that matches all text and attribute nodes copies their values to the stylesheet output.

For XSLT stylesheets to do their work, therefore, XSLT expressions must provide a method for identifying a set of nodes in the document hierarchy that match certain criteria, and must allow both very explicit identification (the fifth `chapter` node under the parent node `book`, for example) and more general identification (all `chapter` nodes). The method must also allow for both absolute addressing (starting with the document root) and relative addressing (starting with the current node). Given the flexibility that XML provides to document designers, creating a tool to handle these location expressions can be quite a challenge. This is where XPath enters the picture.

Fundamentally, everything in XPath revolves around satisfying this need to locate sets of nodes in a document hierarchy. XPath's approach to this problem is to break the identification of a set of nodes into subexpressions, each of which itself identifies a set of nodes that match a given criterion; later subexpressions act on the set of nodes returned by those that came before. Going back to our earlier example, we might specify the location of the first `chapter` node by giving XPath the following instructions:

1. Start with the set of nodes that contains all root nodes (in reality, there is never more than one root node in a document hierarchy, but it's important to remember

that each step in an XPath expression returns a *set* of nodes, not a single node—even if the set only has one node in it).

2. From the children of each node returned from step 1, select the set of element nodes that consists of the first `part` node.

3. From the children of each node returned from step 2, select the set of nodes that consists of the first `chapter` node.

Because of the way the search criteria were specified in the preceding example, the result set from each step contained exactly one node, allowing us to uniquely identify that node within the entire document. This same mechanism can be used to select multiple nodes; in that case, we could approach the problem from two perspectives. In the first instance, we could follow these steps:

1. Start with the set of nodes that contains all root nodes.

2. From the children of each node returned from step 1, select the set of element nodes named `part`.

3. From the children of each node returned from step 2, select the set of element nodes named `chapter`.

Or, more simply:

▶ Select the set of all element nodes named `chapter` that are descendants of the root node.

In support of this capability, XPath provides both a set of intrinsic functions and the ability to generate Boolean, numeric, and string values. Both of these features can be included in a node's location information, making it possible to specify very explicit rules for finding nodes with certain characteristics. As an added benefit, XSLT uses some of these features to provide its conditional processing and value computation functions.

Data Types

Four data types can be used in XPath expressions:

▶ *Node sets* are generated as a result of the evaluation of XPath's node selection process, and they contain all of the nodes in the document hierarchy that match a given expression. Although node sets are not technically a data type, it is possible to perform conversions, comparisons, and other operations on node sets in a way similar to that for the other data types.

▶ *Boolean* values are generated as a result of comparison operations between two objects, whether they are node sets, numeric values, or strings. Boolean values can have only one of two values: true or false.

▶ *Numeric* values are generated primarily by certain XPath functions, such as `position()`, or by conversion of string values. Numeric values are stored as 64-bit floating-point numbers and can include positive and negative zero, positive and negative infinity, and a special "not a number" (NaN) value similar to that found in JavaScript. XPath includes several mathematical functions (+, −, /, *, and mod, among others) that allow simple calculations to be performed.

▶ *String* values are generated by converting nodes in the document hierarchy to their corresponding string values (as when retrieving attribute values, for example) or by the XPath string functions. Strings are composed of zero or more unicode characters and can be of arbitrary length.

Of course, Boolean, numeric, and string values can also be specified as literals.

Data types in XPath aren't quite the same thing as those in traditional programming languages. Programming languages typically provide the ability to define variables of a certain data type and then perform type-specific operations on those variables (addition and subtraction for numbers, substring functions for string values, and so on). XPath does provide a set of type-specific operations, but in most typical cases XPath's transparent type conversion capabilities relieve you of the need to understand the data types and their properties in detail. XPath uses data types primarily to classify values returned from node selection, value retrieval, intrinsic functions, and so on and to allow specification of explicit conversion rules among these values.

XPath converts among data types using the rules shown in Table 5-1.

Although most of the data type conversion operations in XPath behave as one might expect, one topic that deserves special mention is the conversion of root nodes and element nodes to their corresponding string values. In both of these cases, the string value of the node is the concatenation of the string values of all of the node's descendants, in document order, and not the value of the individual node. This has implications for comparison operations and can affect the output of the stylesheet.

	To Number	**To String**	**To Boolean**	**To Node Set**
From Number		Converted to a string representation with a sign, or NaN if not a number. Positive and negative 0 are converted to 0, and positive and negative infinity are converted to +Infinity and –Infinity, respectively.	Converted to true if the number is positive and nonzero; converted to false otherwise.	No conversion possible.
From String	Converted to a floating-point number if the string is a series of digits (optionally preceded by a sign); converted to NaN otherwise.		Strings with nonzero length are converted to true; zero-length strings are converted to false.	No conversion possible.
From Boolean	Converted to 1 if true, to 0 if false.	Converted to true if true, to false if false.		No conversion possible.
From Node Set	Converted to a string value first and then to a number, according to the rules for strings.	Converted to the string value of the first node in the node set, in document order.	Converted to true if the node set is not empty; converted to false otherwise.	

Table 5-1   *XPath Data Type Conversion Rules*

Intrinsic Functions

XPath provides a wealth of intrinsic functions designed to make selection of nodes from a document hierarchy and manipulation of data both easier. These functions are categorized according to the major data type they operate on—node sets, Booleans, numbers, and strings—and include functions to convert from one data type to another, perform basic mathematical and counting operations, perform substring operations, and so on. Many of the functions accept arguments, and XPath is intelligent enough to accept any value that can be converted to the required data type.

You'll make extensive use of these functions in location path predicates and in XSLT conditional processing, both of which are explained on the next few pages. A complete list of the available functions, along with brief descriptions of each, can be found at the end of this chapter; for a complete list, refer to the XPath specification.

Coding XPath Expressions

In this section, we'll explore general XPath expression syntax and then discuss in detail the methods in which XPath can be used to meet the three major XSLT requirements. Some of the more advanced concepts, such as the use of XSLT variables in XPath expressions, are covered later in this book.

In general, XPath expressions are used in three ways:

▶ To identify one or more nodes for processing, as with `xsl:template` and `xsl:apply-templates`.

▶ In conjunction with looping and conditional constructs such as `xsl:for-each`, `xsl:if`, `xsl:choose`, and `xsl:when` to specify conditions that must be evaluated to determine a path for stylesheet processing.

▶ To generate text that is to be included in the stylesheet's output, using commands such as `xsl:value-of`.

Function calls and the three data types can be used together with location addressing to meet each of these needs. In this section, we'll explain the XPath syntax used in these situations.

Using Location Path Addressing

There are two syntaxes for XPath location addressing: an unabbreviated syntax and an abbreviated syntax. Because the unabbreviated syntax more clearly expresses the meaning of a location path, we'll use it here to describe the concepts behind an expression. Most stylesheet developers, however, will want to use the abbreviated syntax, so following our discussion of location paths we'll also explain how to translate what you've learned about the unabbreviated syntax into the abbreviated version.

A *location path* is the set of instructions that must be followed to identify a set of nodes to be processed. Location paths are composed of one or more *location steps*;

each location step in the path returns a set of zero or more nodes, and every location step must select at least one node for the location path to find what it's looking for. Location steps that occur later in the path act on the node sets that are returned by earlier steps, providing a progressive narrowing of the results until the desired nodes are found.

A location step has three parts: the axis, the node test, and the predicate. The axis and node test are separated by a double colon (::) and are always required; the predicate, which is optional, immediately follows the node test if specified and is enclosed in opening and closing brackets ([]). Each location step in the location path is separated from the others by a forward slash (/). If the search for a node is to start with the root node (an absolute path), the first location step starts with a forward slash as well.

In the XPath unabbreviated syntax, a generic two-step location path looks like this:

```
axis::node-test[predicate]/axis::node-test[predicate]/...
```

Here are some examples:

Location path	Meaning
`Child::para`	A single-step location path that selects all `para` element children of the current node. In this example, `child` is the axis name, and `para` is the node test.
`/child::para`	A single-step location path that selects all `para` element children of the root node. In this example, `child` is the axis name, and `para` is the node test. Note the slash on the front of the location step; this indicates that the location path is to start from the root node.
`child::para[position()=2]`	A single-step location path that selects the second `para` element child of the current node. In this example, `child` is the axis name, `para` is the node test, and `[position()=2]` is the predicate.
`child::para/child::div`	A two-step location path that first selects all `para` elements that are children of the current node and then selects all `div` elements that are children of the previously selected `para` elements. In both location steps, `child` is the axis name, and `para` and `div` are the node tests.

Location steps can be as generic or as specific as needed to move toward the desired set of nodes.

Axes

Think of an *axis* as being the set of nodes in the document hierarchy that bear a certain specific relationship to the current node. The child axis of the current node, for example, consists of the set of all child nodes of the current node. The attribute axis of the current node contains all of the attribute nodes assigned to the current node (assuming, of course, that the current node is an element node—the only node that can have attributes).

Axes can express relationships among the seven types of nodes: the root node, element nodes, attribute nodes, text nodes, namespace nodes, processing instruction nodes, and comment nodes. The following table shows the possible axes that can be specified, along with the node types they can contain.

Axis	Types of Nodes That Can Be Contained in the Axis
The *child* axis indicates that nodes are to be selected from among the children of the current node.	Element, attribute, text, namespace, processing instruction, and comment nodes
The *descendant* axis indicates that nodes are to be selected from among the nodes lower in the hierarchy than the current node (that is, children, grandchildren, and so on).	Element and text nodes
The *parent* axis indicates that the node to be selected is the parent of the current node.	Element and root nodes
The *ancestor* axis indicates that nodes are to be selected from among the nodes higher in the hierarchy than the current node (that is, parents, grandparents, and so on).	Element and root nodes
The *following-sibling* axis indicates that nodes are to be selected from among the siblings of the current node that come after it in the document hierarchy.	Element and text nodes
The *preceding-sibling* axis indicates that nodes are to be selected from among the siblings of the current node that come before it in the document hierarchy.	Element and text nodes

Axis	Types of Nodes That Can Be Contained in the Axis
The *following* axis indicates that nodes are to be selected from among the nodes that follow the current node in document order, excluding the direct descendants of the current node.	Element, text, processing instruction, and comment nodes
The *preceding* axis indicates that nodes are to be selected from among the nodes that precede the current node in document order, excluding the direct ancestors of the current node.	Element, text, processing instruction, and comment nodes
The *attribute* axis indicates that nodes are to be selected from among the attributes of the current node (remember: in XML, attributes are considered to be nodes!).	Attribute nodes
The *namespace* axis indicates that nodes are to be selected from among the namespace nodes of the current node. This axis will be empty unless the current node is an element node.	Namespace nodes
The *self* axis indicates that the node to be selected is the current node.	Root, element, attribute, text, namespace, processing instruction, and comment nodes
The *descendant-or-self* axis indicates that nodes are to be selected from the current node and the nodes lower in the hierarchy.	Element, attribute, text, namespace, processing instruction, and comment nodes
The *ancestor-or-self* axis indicates that nodes are to be selected from the current node and the nodes higher in the hierarchy.	Root, element, attribute, text, namespace, processing instruction, and comment nodes

The descendant, ancestor, preceding, following, and self axes together contain all of the nodes in the document except for attribute and namespace nodes, with no overlaps.

Axes that contain the current node and all nodes after it in document order are considered to be *forward axes*. Axes that contain the current node and all nodes before it in document order are considered to be *reverse axes*. The self axis can be considered either a forward or reverse axis—it doesn't really matter.

To better understand the axis concept, take a look at the following XML document fragment:

```
<Book xmlns:dc="http://purl.org/dc/elements/1.1/" >
   <dc:Title>Web Design: A Beginner's Guide</dc:Title>
   <dc:Creator>Wendy Willard</dc:Creator>
   <numberOfPages>496</numberOfPages>
   <price unit="USD">20.99</price>
</Book>
```

Figure 5-3 shows the axis relationships in this document fragment.
   Here are some of the axis relationships shown in Figure 5-3:

▶   When the current node is Book, selection on the child or descendant axis will return all of the child nodes of Book.

▶   When the current node is dc:Title, dc:Creator, numberOfPages, or price, selection on the parent or ancestor axis will return the Book node.

▶   Because of the namespace definition on the Book element, every element child of Book has the dc: namespace in scope. If you select on the namespace axis for any of these nodes, therefore, you will see a namespace node representing the dc: namespace.

▶   The price element has an attribute called unit, so if you select on the attribute axis for this element, you will see an attribute node called unit. Selection on the attribute axis for any other element will return an empty node set.

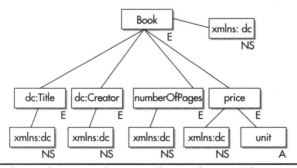

Figure 5-3   *Node relationships in a document hierarchy (E = Element nodes; NS = Namespace nodes; A = Attribute nodes)*

Node Tests

A *node test* is the portion of a location step that identifies the name or type of the nodes that are to be included in the result set for that location step. Node tests can be specific, identifying the elements to be selected by name, or generic, selecting nodes by type.

In the first form, the node test contains the name of the node type (attribute name for the attribute axis, namespace name for the namespace axis, and element names for all other axes) that is to be selected for that location step. This form of the node test can be used to select any node type except text, processing instructions, and comments.

To see the operation of this form of node test, we'll use the location step `child:
:para`. In this example, the node test specifies `para`, and the location step returns all `para` nodes that are children of the current node (because of the `child` axis specification). Likewise, in the two-step location path `child::foo/ child:
:bar`, `foo` is the node test for the first location step (which will find all children of the current node that are called `foo`), and `bar` is the node test for the second location step (which will examine the `bar` element children of each node returned from the previous location step). An `xsl:template` element using this location path might look like this:

```
<xsl:template match="child::foo/child::bar" >
   The content of the "bar" element is <xsl:value-of select="." />
</xsl:template>
```

Names specified in this form of node test can be namespace qualified. If, for example, you're looking for nodes with a `dc:` namespace prefix and an element name of `Creator`, you might code a template that looks like the following (note, however, that the `dc:` namespace prefix is resolved in the stylesheet as well as in the XML document):

```
<xsl:stylesheet version="1.0"
                xmlns:xsl=http://www.w3.org/1999/XSL/Transform
                xmlns:dc="http://purl.org/dc/elements/1.1/" >
  <xsl:template match="dc:Creator" >
     The author named <xsl:value-of select="." /> wrote
        <xsl:value-of select="parent::node()/attribute::title" />
  </xsl:template>
</xsl:stylesheet>
```

This example also illustrates the use of the two-step location path `parent:
:node()/attribute::title` to select the `title` attribute on the parent
of the selected `dc:Creator` node.

You can use the node test `*` as a wildcard to indicate that any node along the
requested axis is to be selected. For example, the location step `child::*` will
select all children of the current node, and the location step `ancestor::*` will
select all ancestors of the current node. It's also possible to use `/` to select the root
node of the document, but be careful: the root node of the document hierarchy is *not*
the same as the document element of an XML document (that is, the element that
has all other elements of the document as its children). The document element is
actually considered to be a child of the root node.

The second, more generic form of node test uses some of XPath's intrinsic functions.
In this form, the functions `node()`, `text()`, `processing-instruction()`,
and `comment()` are used to indicate that the location step is to select all nodes,
text nodes, processing instructions, or comments, respectively. The location step
`/descendant::text()`, for example, will select all text nodes in the document,
starting with the root node.

Predicates

Predicates are filters that can be used to further qualify the set of nodes returned by
the axis and node test. Predicates can be used to examine each node returned by the
axis and node test, evaluating it against a set of criteria to determine whether it
should be included in the result of the location step. Predicates return a Boolean
value; if the predicate evaluates to true for a node, then the node is included in the
location step's result set; if it evaluates to false, then the node is not included.

Let's say we want to specify the location of the second `part` node in the book
document shown in Figure 5-2. One location path that would return this node might
look like this:

```
/child::book/child::part[position()=2]
```

The first location step (`/child::book`) returns all `book` element nodes that
are children of the root node (of which there is only one). The second location step
first uses the axis and node test to select all `part` element nodes that are children of
the `book` element node and then filters this set to return only the second instance.

Predicates can leverage some of the more powerful features of XPath to work
their magic. Not only can you specify literals in predicates, as in the prior example,
but you can also specify predicates that include expressions containing XPath
function calls. If we want to retrieve the last `part` element node from our book, we
could use a location path such as

```
/child::book/child::part[position()=last()]
```

which leverages both the `position()` function to retrieve the position of the node in the node set returned by the axis and node test, and the `last()` function to retrieve the position of the last node in the node set returned by the axis and node test. By comparing the return values of these two functions, we can determine whether the `part` element node being examined by the filter is the last one, and then include only that one node. The key point in using predicates is that they must return a Boolean value (or something that can be converted to a Boolean value) that can be used to determine whether or not to retain the node being examined.

We can also specify `and`/`or` relationships in predicates. There are two ways to specify an `and` relationship: by separating sections of the predicate with `and` or by specifying two predicates. If we want to select the last `chapter` node if and only if it also has an `id` attribute whose value is this-one, we could specify the predicate as

```
child::chapter[position()=last() and attribute::id="this-one"]
```

or as

```
child::chapter[position()=last()][attribute::id="this-one"]
```

To specify an `or` relationship, we would include the `or` phrase in the predicate. If we want to indicate that *either* the last chapter child of the current node *or* the chapter children of the current node whose `id` attribute is equal to this-one should be selected, the previous example could be modified to read as follows:

```
child::chapter[position()=last() or attribute::id="this-one"]
```

To allow negation to be specified, XPath provides the `not()` function. This function can be used in a predicate to express the opposite of whatever phase is provided: for example, a predicate of `[not(position()=last())]` selects all but the last node.

Location Path Abbreviated Syntax

Now that you have a good handle on the unabbreviated syntax, let's take a look at what's different in the abbreviated syntax.

The major difference between the unabbreviated syntax you've seen so far in this book and the abbreviated syntax is that the `child` axis specification can be totally eliminated. For example, where the unabbreviated syntax requires a location step such as `child::chapter` to indicate that the `chapter` children of the current node are to be selected, the abbreviated syntax allows you to specify simply `chapter`.

Since the `child` axis is by far the most widely used, this change in itself saves a lot of typing.

Here are other differences you'll see in the abbreviated syntax:

▶ Location steps specifying attributes can be specified by adding the prefix @ to the attribute name, converting unabbreviated location steps such as `attribute:id` to `@id`.

▶ The descendant-or-self axis can now be specified by adding the prefix // to the node test. A location path specified as `descendant-or-self::node ()/child::part` in the unabbreviated syntax becomes `//part` in the abbreviated syntax.

▶ The . location step can be used in place of `self::node()`, and the location step `..` can be used in place of `parent::node()`. Thus, you can specify `.//para` to select the descendants of the current node, and `../@id` to select the attribute `id` of the parent of the current node.

▶ Where you might have used an unabbreviated predicate such as `[position()=5]` to select the fifth node in a set, in the abbreviated syntax you can simply specify the number itself, like this: `[5]`.

There are still situations in which you'll need to use the unabbreviated syntax. The abbreviated syntax does not include a way to specify less-common axes such as following or preceding, for example, and some XSLT processors require you to use `self::node()` and `parent::node()` in some situations where `./` and `../` would normally be appropriate.

To help you understand the abbreviated syntax and its differences from the unabbreviated syntax, as well as to help reinforce the location path concept, the following list provides a wide range of examples that show exactly how to perform a wide range of node set selections.

Unabbreviated: /
Abbreviated: /
Meaning: Selects the document root.

Unabbreviated: `child::para`
Abbreviated: `para`
Meaning: Selects all `para` element nodes that are children of the current node.

Unabbreviated: `/child::para`
Abbreviated: /`para`
Meaning: Selects all `para` element nodes that are children of the root node (note the difference from the previous example).

Unabbreviated: `descendant::para`
Abbreviated: `.//para`
Meaning: Selects all `para` element nodes that are descendants of the current node.

Unabbreviated: `/descendant::para`
Abbreviated: `//para`
Meaning: Selects all `para` element nodes that are descendants of the root node (note the different from the previous example).

Unabbreviated: `attribute::id`
Abbreviated: `@id`
Meaning: Selects all `id` attributes of the current node.

Unabbreviated: `attribute::*`
Abbreviated: `@*`
Meaning: Selects all attributes of the current node.

Unabbreviated: `child::chapter[position()=5]`
Abbreviated: `chapter[5]`
Meaning: Selects the fifth `chapter` element node that is a child of the current node.

Unabbreviated: `child::chapter[attribute::id="this-one"]`
Abbreviated: `chapter[@id="this-one"]`
Meaning: Selects all `chapter` element nodes that are children of the current node and have an `id` value of this-one.

Unabbreviated: `child::chapter[not(attribute::include="y")]`
Abbreviated: `chapter[not(@include="y")]`
Meaning: Selects all `chapter` element nodes that do not have an attribute value of y.

Unabbreviated: `/descendant::text()`
Abbreviated: `//text()`
Meaning: Selects all `text` nodes that are descendants of the root node (that is, all text nodes in the document).

Unabbreviated:
`child::part[attribute::num="1"][attribute::draft="y"]`
Abbreviated: `part[@num="1"][@draft="y"]`
Meaning: Selects all `part` nodes that are children of the current node if they have a `num` attribute with a value of 1 and a `draft` attribute with a value of y.

Unabbreviated: `parent::node()[attribute::include="y"]`
Abbreviated: `..[@include="y"]`
Meaning: Selects the parent of the current node if the parent has an `include` attribute with a value of y.

Unabbreviated: `/descendant::chapter[attribute::id and attribute::include]`
Abbreviated: `//chapter[@id and @include]`
Meaning: Selects all `chapter` element nodes with both an `id` attribute and an `include` attribute (regardless of the value).

Location Path Examples

Before leaving the subject of location paths, let's look at a concrete example. The following XML document implements a basic book catalog. Each book entry contains some basic information about the book, such as its author, subject, physical dimensions, and price. The catalog uses elements from the Dublin Core Metadata Element Set (http://www.dublincore.org) to provide much of the information; elements that come from the Dublin Core are distinguished by the dc: namespace prefix.

```xml
<?xml version="1.0" encoding="UTF-8" ?>
<BookCatalog name="Book Catalog - XSLT Example"
           xmlns:dc="http://purl.org/dc/elements/1.1/" >
   <Book>
      <dc:Identifier system="ISBN">0072133902</dc:Identifier>
      <dc:Title>Web Design: A Beginner's Guide</dc:Title>
      <dc:Creator>Wendy Willard</dc:Creator>
      <dc:Subject>Web design</dc:Subject>
      <dc:Description>Explains basic Web page design and development
      </dc:Description>
      <dc:Publisher>Osborne McGraw-Hill</dc:Publisher>
      <dc:Date>June, 2001</dc:Date>
      <dc:Language>en-US</dc:Language>
      <dc:Format>Paperback print</dc:Format>
      <dimensions unit="inches">
         <thickness>1.24</thickness>
         <height>9.18</height>
         <width>7.42</width>
      </dimensions>
      <numberOfPages>496</numberOfPages>
      <price unit="USD">20.99</price>
      <readerRating unit="stars">5</readerRating>
   </Book>
   <Book>
      <dc:Identifier system="ISBN">0072130261</dc:Identifier>
      <dc:Title>HTML: A Beginner's Guide</dc:Title>
      <dc:Creator>Wendy Willard</dc:Creator>
      <dc:Subject>HTML</dc:Subject>
      <dc:Description>Explains basic HTML tags and usage</dc:Description>
      <dc:Publisher>Osborne McGraw-Hill</dc:Publisher>
      <dc:Date>November 15, 2001</dc:Date>
      <dc:Language>en-US</dc:Language>
      <dc:Format>Paperback print</dc:Format>
```

```
    <dimensions unit="inches">
        <thickness>1.34</thickness>
        <height>9.03</height>
        <width>7.34</width>
    </dimensions>
    <numberOfPages>569</numberOfPages>
    <price unit="USD">20.99</price>
    <readerRating unit="stars">5</readerRating>
</Book>
<Book>
    <dc:Identifier system="ISBN">0072126302</dc:Identifier>
    <dc:Title>Perl Developer's Guide</dc:Title>
    <dc:Creator>Ed Peschko</dc:Creator>
    <dc:Subject>Perl</dc:Subject>
    <dc:Description>Reference guide for Perl
programming</dc:Description>
    <dc:Publisher>McGraw-Hill Professional
Publishing</dc:Publisher>
    <dc:Date>June 8, 2000</dc:Date>
    <dc:Language>en-US</dc:Language>
    <dc:Format>Paperback print</dc:Format>
    <dimensions unit="inches">
        <thickness>2.11</thickness>
        <height>9.18</height>
        <width>7.54</width>
    </dimensions>
    <numberOfPages>912</numberOfPages>
    <price unit="USD">41.99</price>
    <readerRating unit="stars">4</readerRating>
</Book>
<Book>
    <dc:Identifier system="ISBN">0079136982</dc:Identifier>
    <dc:Title>Perl 5 Developer's Guide</dc:Title>
    <dc:Creator>Ed Peschko</dc:Creator>
    <dc:Subject>Perl</dc:Subject>
    <dc:Description>Reference guide for Perl 5 programming
    </dc:Description>
    <dc:Publisher>McGraw-Hill Professional
Publishing</dc:Publisher>
    <dc:Date>June 12, 1998</dc:Date>
    <dc:Language>en-US</dc:Language>
    <dc:Format>Paperback print</dc:Format>
    <dimensions unit="inches">
```

```
            <thickness>2.19</thickness>
            <height>9.20</height>
            <width>7.39</width>
        </dimensions>
        <numberOfPages>1232</numberOfPages>
        <price unit="USD">54.99</price>
        <readerRating unit="stars">4</readerRating>
    </Book>
    <Book>
        <dc:Identifier system="ISBN">0072129514</dc:Identifier>
        <dc:Title>HTML: The Complete Reference, Third
Edition</dc:Title>
        <dc:Creator>Thomas A. Powell</dc:Creator>
        <dc:Subject>HTML</dc:Subject>
        <dc:Description>Complete reference for HTML</dc:Description>
        <dc:Publisher>McGraw-Hill Professional
Publishing</dc:Publisher>
        <dc:Date>December 14, 2000</dc:Date>
        <dc:Language>en-US</dc:Language>
        <dc:Format>Paperback print</dc:Format>
        <dimensions unit="inches">
            <thickness>2.42</thickness>
            <height>9.08</height>
            <width>7.34</width>
        </dimensions>
        <numberOfPages>1208</numberOfPages>
        <price unit="USD">27.99</price>
        <readerRating unit="stars">4.5</readerRating>
    </Book>
</BookCatalog>
```

If we wanted to render this book catalog in HTML, one possible solution (and the most illustrative for the purposes of this book) is to code an XSLT stylesheet that renders each element as HTML individually and leverages the features of XSLT to connect the pieces together. Here's an example stylesheet, with some comments that should help you understand what's going on and why.

```
<!--
    This is the start of our stylesheet.  Note that we included both the
    xsl" namespace (which is required in all stylesheets) and the "dc"
    namespace (which is used to resolve references to the Dublin Core element
    set found in the source XML document.
-->
```

```
<xsl:stylesheet version="1.0"
            xmlns:xsl=http://www.w3.org/1999/XSL/Transform
            xmlns:dc="http://purl.org/dc/elements/1.1/" >

<!--
    We'll match on the root element to generate the basic HTML framework, as
    well as the title of our page.  Note that the title of our catalog comes
    from the "BookCatalog" element's "name" attribute, which is referenced in
    the <xsl:value-of> command using a relative location path.  Notice that
    we specify the <body> element, then an <xsl:apply-templates /> command,
    and then the closing </body> element - this inserts all of the content
    generated by other templates between the opening and closing "body" tags.
-->
    <xsl:template match="/" >
        <html>
        <head><title>Book catalog name: <xsl:value-of
                    select="BookCatalog/@name" />
        </title></head>
        <body>
        <xsl:apply-templates />
        </body>
        </html>
    </xsl:template>


<!--
    Now we'll generate the headings for our catalog, which display the name
    of the catalog and the number of books in the catlog.  The name of the
    catalog is extracted from the "name" attribute.  We've used the XPath
    count() function to find out how many "Book" elements are in this
    document and then opened a table to put the book descriptions into.
-->
    <xsl:template match="BookCatalog" >
        <h1>Book catalog name: <xsl:value-of select="@name" /></h1>
        <h2>There are <xsl:value-of select="count(Book)" /> books in this
            catalog</h2>
        <table>
        <xsl:apply-templates />
        </table>
    </xsl:template>

<!--
    In this template, we process all of the "Book" elements in the document
    by generating table rows with a yellow background containing the title of
    the book.  Specifying each <xsl:apply templates select="elementname" />
    separately allows us to control the order in which things get displayed;
    we could just as easily have removed the "select" attributes and let the
    subelements get displayed in the order in which they appear in the
```

```
source document (but to do so, we would have to assume that everything is
in the same order for every book entry in the catalog, which may not be a
safe assumption).

Notice that the Dublin Core elements are referenced using the namespace
prefix.  You must be sure that the URI this prefix resolves to in your
stylesheet matches that used in the source document, or your templates
won't find the element.
-->
   <xsl:template match="Book" >
      <tr bgcolor="yellow">
      <td><b><xsl:value-of select="dc:Title" /></b></td>
      </tr>
      <tr><td><p>
      <xsl:apply-templates select="dc:Identifier" />
      <xsl:apply-templates select="dc:Subject" />
      <xsl:apply-templates select="dc:Creator" />
      <xsl:apply-templates select="dc:Publisher" />
      <xsl:apply-templates select="dimensions" />
      <xsl:apply-templates select="numberOfPages" />
      <xsl:apply-templates select="readerRating" />
      </p></td></tr>
      <tr><td>
      </td></tr>
   </xsl:template>


<!--
   We'll select the "system" attribute (which tells us what kind of
   identifier this is) and the value of the identifier itself and place
   them into the "Identifier" line in the HTML.
-->
   <xsl:template match="dc:Identifier" >
      Identifier (<xsl:value-of select="@system" />): <xsl:value-of
               select="." /><br/>
   </xsl:template>


<!--
   The value of the "dc:Subject" element goes into the "Subject" line in the
   HTML.
-->
   <xsl:template match="dc:Subject" >
      Subject: <xsl:value-of select="." /><br/>
   </xsl:template>


<!--
   The value of the "dc:Creator" element goes into the "Author" line in the
   HTML.
```

```
-->
    <xsl:template match="dc:Creator" >
       Author: <xsl:value-of select="." /><br/>
    </xsl:template>

<!--
    The value of the "dc:Publisher" element goes into the "Publisher" line in
    the HTML.  Note that we're also referencing the "dc:Date" element to
    provide the book's release date; because "dc:Date" and "dc:Publisher" are
    at the same level in the hierarchy, we get this information by
    referencing the parent of this element and then navigating to the
    dc:Date element from there.
-->
    <xsl:template match="dc:Publisher" >
       Publisher: <xsl:value-of select="." /> (Released <xsl:value-of
                select="../dc:Date" />)<br/>
    </xsl:template>

<!--
    The value of the "dimensions" element goes into the "Dimensions" line in
    the HTML.  The unit of measurement (which comes from the "unit" attribute
    of the "dimensions" element) is shown, along with the values from the
    "height", "width", and "thickness" subelements.  These are placed into
    the "h x w x d" format using <xsl:value-of> with relative addressing.
-->
    <xsl:template match="dimensions" >
       Dimensions (in <xsl:value-of select="@unit" />):
                <xsl:value-of select="height" /> x
                <xsl:value-of select="width" /> x
                <xsl:value-of select="thickness" /><br/>
    </xsl:template>

<!--
    The value of the "numberOfPages" element goes into the "Number of pages"
    line in the HTML.
-->
    <xsl:template match="numberOfPages" >
       Number of pages: <xsl:value-of select="." /><br/>
    </xsl:template>

<!--
    The reader rating value is placed into the HTML.  Note that we're using
    <xsl:if> to see if the rating value (which is converted to a number using
    the XPath number() function) is greater than 4, and, if it is, we add some
    CSS information to make the rating value red.
-->
    <xsl:template match="readerRating" >
```

```
        This book was rated <span><xsl:if test="number(.) > 4">
            <xsl:attribute name="style">color: red; font-weight: bold
            </xsl:attribute></xsl:if><xsl:value-of select="." /><xsl:text>
            </xsl:text><xsl:value-of select="@unit" /></span><br/>
    </xsl:template>

<!-- -->
</xsl:stylesheet>
```

Running this spreadsheet against the XML file provided yields the result shown in Figure 5-4.

XPath and Conditional Expressions

We'll talk a lot about conditional processing in Chapter 8, but right now we'll touch on the use of XPath expressions in XSLT conditional logic. Conditional expressions

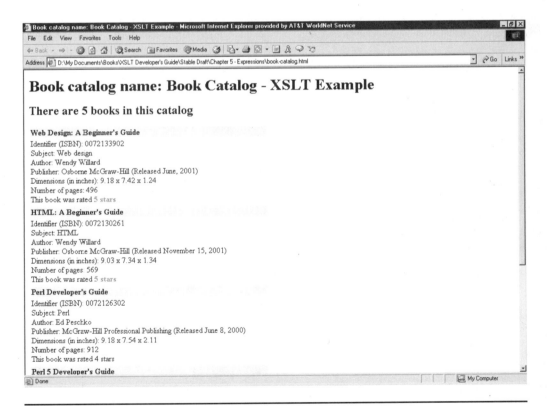

Figure 5-4   *The output of our BookCatalog stylesheet*

in XSLT are just like those in any other programming language in that the expression you provide must somehow resolve to a Boolean value: true or false. Because XPath provides good support for the Boolean data type and for conversion from node sets, numbers, and strings to Boolean values, the stylesheet designer has a fair amount of latitude when expressing conditional logic.

We've seen some examples of conditional expressions in this book already. Templates containing expressions such as the following are quite common in XSLT:

```
<xsl:template match="part">
   <xsl:if test="position()=1">
      <!-- generate a header -->
   </xsl:if>
   <xsl:if test="position()=last()">
      <!-- generate a trailer -->
   </xsl:if>
</xsl:template>
```

Code such as this, which performs special processing for the first and last nodes of the node set selected by the xsl:template statement, allows you to generate lists with headers and footers and add unique styles to certain portions of the output document.

It's also common to compare the value of a node or one of its attributes to a string value, as in the following:

```
<xsl:template match="part" >
   <xsl:if test="@num='1'">
      This is part 1!!!
   </xsl:if>
</xsl:template>
```

This example generates an output message if the part element node selected by the xsl:template statement has a num attribute with the value 1.

Thanks to XPath's data type conversion features, any location path can be converted to a conditional expression. You can, for example, take action depending on whether an element node with a certain attribute value exists:

```
<xsl:template match="BookCatalog" >
   <xsl:if test="Book[@id='121-232004']" >
      There's a book with the right ID!!!
   </xsl:if>
</xsl:template>
```

In this example, the `xsl:template` statement selects all element nodes named `BookCatalog`, and the `xsl:if` statement then tests to see if there are any `Book` element node children with an `id` attribute of 121-232004. The node set returned, which will be empty if there are no qualifying children, is then automatically converted to a Boolean value (true if the node set is nonempty, and false if it is empty), and processing continues depending on the result of that evaluation.

All of XPath's intrinsic functions can be used to perform conditional processing. The following example uses the `count()` function to determine whether the `BookCatalog` element has any children and then includes the number of children in the output message:

```
<xsl:template match="BookCatalog" >
   <xsl:if test="count(./*)" >
      There are <xsl:value-of select="count(./*)" /> books in this
catalog.
   </xsl:if>
</xsl:template>
```

If there are two child elements of the `BookCatalog` element node, then the output of this example would look like this:

```
There are 2 books in this catalog.
```

Generating String Values

Most output from an XSLT stylesheet is composed of a combination of literal strings and string values generating form nodes selected by a template. Using the `xsl:value-of` statement, you can specify a location path to select text from any node in the document hierarchy and include it in the output of your stylesheet.

The most basic example is this:

```
<xsl:value-of select="." />
```

This example generates the string value of the current node and inserts it at the point where the `xsl:value-of` statement occurs.

A template that combines literal and generated text might look like this:

```
<xsl:template match="dc:Title" >
   Book title: <xsl:value-of select="." />
</xsl:template>
```

This template extracts the value of the selected dc:Title element node, prefixes it with the literal Book title:, and places it in the stylesheet output.

The use of the xsl:value-of statement and other ways to generate stylesheet output will be covered in more detail in Chapter 7.

XPath Functions

This section contains a list of the XPath intrinsic functions, along with a brief description of each. For comprehensive descriptions of these functions, refer to the XPath specification at http://www.w3.org/TR/1999/REC-xpath-19991116.

Node Set Functions

The XPath functions below operate on node sets. The most valuable are the last(), position(), and count() functions, which can be used in predicates to find specific nodes or to return the number of nodes in the list.

last()   Returns the index of the last node in the node set, relative to 1.

position()   Returns the position of the current node within the node set, relative to 1.

count()   Returns the total number of nodes in the node set.

id(*object*)   Returns a node set containing the node with the unique ID specified in *object*.

local-name(*node-set*)   Returns a string containing the local part of the name of the node that is first in the node set provided as an argument to the function.

namespace-uri(*node-set*)   Returns a string containing the namespace URI of the node that is first in the node set provided as an argument to the function.

name(*node-set*)   Returns a string containing the expanded name of the node that is first in the node set provided as an argument to the function.

String Functions

These XPath string functions can come in handy when manipulating the data in your input document or when combining input document data with literals specified in the stylesheet itself.

string(*object*)   Converts the specified object to its string representation.

concat(*string1, string2, ...*)   Returns the concatenation of the arguments specified.

starts-with(*string1, string2*)   Returns true if the first argument string starts with the second argument string.

contains(*string1, string2*)   Returns true if the first argument string contains the second argument string.

substring-before(*string1, string2*)   Returns a string containing the substring of the first argument string that occurs before the first occurrence of the second argument string.

substring-after(*string1, string2*)   Returns a string containing the substring of the first argument string that occurs after the first occurrence of the second argument string.

substring(*string1, pos, len*)   Returns a string containing the substring of the first argument string that starts at the position specified in the second argument (relative to 1) and extends for the length specified in the third argument. The third argument is optional; if it is not specified, the resulting substring extends to the end of the source.

string-length(*string*)   Returns the number of characters in the string specified as an argument to the function.

normalize-space(*string*)   Returns the string specified as an argument to the function with all leading and trailing whitespace removed and replaced with a single space.

translate(*string, string, string*)   Returns the string specified as an argument to the function with all occurrences of the second argument string replaced by the third argument string.

Boolean Functions

The Boolean functions, and particularly the not () function, are valuable in conditional expressions and in predicates.

boolean(*object*)   Converts the object provided to the function as an argument into a Boolean value.

not(*boolean*)   Returns true if the argument is false, and false if the argument is true.

true()   Returns true.

false()   Returns false.

lang(*string*)   Returns true if the language of the current node is the same as or a sublanguage of the language specified as an argument to the function.

Number Functions

The number functions are valuable for performing data type conversions as part of your stylesheet's output.

number(*object*)   Returns the object specified in the function argument, converted to a number.

sum(*node-set*)   Converts each node in the node set specified as an argument into a number and then computes and returns the sum.

floor(*number*)   Returns the largest possible integer that is less than the number specified as an argument to the function.

ceiling(*number*)   Returns the smallest possible integer that is not less than the number specified as an argument to the function.

round(*number*)   Returns the nearest integer value to the number specified as an argument to the function.

Summary

XSLT's XPath expression mechanism provides very strong functionality for expressing the location of a single node or set of nodes in an XML document. It's possible to specify very explicit expressions that can select nodes based on their content, attributes, and location relative to each other, and (thanks to XPath's intrinsic functions) it's possible to perform some fairly complex operations on the data once you find it. When you master this topic, you will have harnessed XSLT's power, and you'll be ready to start using this powerful technology almost immediately.

CHAPTER 6

Template Rules

IN THIS CHAPTER:

X SLT is primarily used to transform a *source* XML tree into a *result* XML tree, which may by then be output in a variety of presentation formats as we will see later in the book. Template rules are the heart of an XSLT stylesheet since the desired transformation from the source to the result XML tree is specified by defining one or more *template rules* for nodes on the source tree that you want to process. An XSLT processor traverses the source tree recursively, starting at the root node, and processes each node according to the template rules defined in the stylesheet. We start this chapter with a brief overview of the XSLT processing model. Later, we discuss the built-in template rules, and how custom rules can be defined to override the built-in rules. We also discuss the use of modes and named templates in XSLT programming.

XSLT Processing Model

When an XSLT processor performs the requisite transformations, it follows three steps:

▶ **Matches patterns**   It searches through the patterns specified in the template rules and identifies all template rules in which the pattern matches the current node.

▶ **Instantiates a template**   Once all template rules for the current node have been identified, the processor chooses the *best* template rule and instantiates its template to create a part of the result tree. To choose the best rule from among several possible candidates, XSLT has a conflict resolution mechanism, described in "Applying Conflict Resolution Template Rules" later in this chapter.

▶ **Selects additional nodes**   The template for the given node may optionally contain instructions to select and process additional nodes from the source tree.

The XSLT processor follows these steps for all nodes, starting at the root node, and proceeds recursively. If it does not find any template rule for a given node, it uses the built-in rules, as described later in "Using Built-in Template Rules."

Defining and Applying Template Rules

For an XSLT stylesheet to transform a source tree into a result tree, you first create templates using `<xsl:template>` tags and then apply the templates to specific nodes using the `<xsl:apply-templates>` tag.

The pervasive `xsl:template` element in an XSLT stylesheet is a top-level element: that is, it is a child element of `xsl:stylesheet` (or its synonym, `xsl:transform`). This element is used to define template rules and follows the syntax shown here:

```
xsl:template
  match = pattern
  name = qname
  priority = number
  mode = qname>
  <!-- Content: xsl:param*, template) -->
</xsl:template>
```

All templates, other than named templates that are discussed in "Using Named Templates," must have a `match` attribute. This attribute specifies a pattern to look for in a node. For example, the pattern / stands for a root node, . stands for the current node, `Author` stands for all `Author` nodes in the source tree, `//Author` stands for only the `Author` nodes that are child nodes of the root node, and so forth. According to the 1.0 specification, the `pattern` value may not be a VariableReference. For a detailed treatment of patterns, refer to Chapter 5.

To apply a template to the current node or its descendants, you use the following syntax:

```
<!-- Category: instruction -->
<xsl:apply-templates
  select = node-set-expression
  mode = qname>
  <!-- Content: (xsl:sort | xsl:with-param)* -->
</xsl:apply-templates>
```

The `select` attribute is optional, and the *node-set-expression* value specified for it is basically an XPath expression that typically applies to the descendants of the current node. For example, the following template rule applies to the node `Name` and puts the values of the child nodes `First_name` and `Last_name` between the HTML tags `<B></B>` and `<I></I>`, respectively:

```
...
    <xsl:template match="Name">
      <B>
        <xsl:apply-templates select="First_name"/>
```

```
      </B>
      <I>
        <xsl:apply-templates select="Last_name"/>
      </I>
    </xsl:template>
...
```

Notice that we just used more than one `xsl:apply-template` element in this template rule, which is perfectly valid. If we want to interchange the order of the `First_name` and `Last_name` elements and place them together between `<B></B>` tags, we can do that simply by using the following code:

```
...
    <xsl:template match="Name">
      <B>
        <xsl:apply-templates select="Last_name"/>
        <xsl:apply-templates select="First_name"/>
      </B>
    </xsl:template>
...
```

In the following example, a `select` attribute is not specified for `xsl:apply-templates`:

```
...
    <xsl:template match="Name">
      <B>
        <xsl:apply-templates/>
      </3>
    </xsl:template>
...
```

In this case, the XSLT processor will start at the `Name` node and process the source tree recursively until it reaches the leaf nodes. This is the default behavior when the `select` attribute is not used. So in this case, the processor will evaluate the value of the `Name` node and place it between the `<B></B>` tags. This is because we have not specified any additional templates for either of the child nodes. For this reason, the following example using the `xsl:value-of` element will work in an identical manner:

```
...
    <xsl:template match="Name">
```

```
    <B>
      <xsl:value-of select="."/>
    </B>
  </xsl:template>
...
```

The earlier examples of xsl:apply-template processed only the descendants of the current node. The following code sample shows how other related *branches* of the source tree may be accessed using ancestor-descendent relationships. In this case the current node is the Name node, and the Address node that is accessed lies on a different branch.

```
<xsl:template match="Name">
   The author
     <B> <xsl:apply-templates select="First_name"/></B>
   lives at
     <I><xsl:apply-templates select="ancestor::Author/Address"/></I>.
</xsl:template>
```

In this case, the processor will use the context of the current node, First_name, locate its ancestor, Author, and apply the template rule for the child element, Address, of this author. For the sample source tree in Chapter 2, the preceding code will result in the following HTML fragment:

```
The author
<B>Chris</B>
lives at
<I>
111 Mansion Boulevard
Suite 100
Chicago
IL
31313
</I>.

The author
<B>Nitin</B>
lives at
<I>
222 Metropolis Street
P.O. Box 500
Minneapolis
MN
55455
</I>.
```

A word of caution: check your XSLT code for the possibility of infinite loops, since the W3C specification does not expressly ask the processor implementers to check for these. For example, an infinite loop may occur if you use `xsl:apply-templates` with the current node as the *node-set-expression* value for the `select` attribute, as shown here:

```
<xsl:template match="Name">
   The author
     <B> <xsl:apply-templates select="."/></B>
   lives at
     <I><xsl:apply-templates select="ancestor::Author/Address"/></I>.
</xsl:template>
```

On the surface, it might appear that this code is simply trying to output the complete name of the author along with the address. But remember that `xsl:apply-templates` works recursively. So when the XSLT processor encounters the reference to the current node—that is, `Name`, used for the `select` attribute—it goes back to template matching, which results in nonterminating output, as shown here:

```
   The author
   <B>
      The author
      <B>
         The author
         <B>
...
```

Specific implementations may check for this kind of trap, but the XSLT 1.0 specification does not require them to do so. Such a loophole could possibly be exploited for a denial-of-service attack.

Applying Conflict Resolution Template Rules

In the discussion of the XSLT processing model, we saw that once all template rules for a node have been identified, the *best* template rule is acted upon, and its template is instantiated. But what does *best* mean in this context, and how does the processor make such an evaluation?

In a nutshell, this choice is driven by the rules about import precedence and the `priority` value that is optionally specified for each template rule. As we saw in

Chapter 4, in general, the template rules in the importing stylesheet take precedence over those in the imported stylesheet. Once the import tree is formed, each template rule inherits its import precedence from the `xsl:stylesheet` element that contained it. Accordingly, the XLST processor will short-list the matching template rules to the ones with highest import precedence. Thereafter, the processor will use the `priority` values of the template rules as the next step in deciding the *best* rule. For this, it will first look for the assigned `priority` value (any positive or negative number) for the template rule. In the absence of an explicitly stated priority, the processor computes the default value for that template rule based on the pattern specified by the `match` attribute. In general, the more specific the pattern, the higher the priority (up to +0.5). Conversely, the less specific the pattern, the lower is the priority (down to –0.5). For example, `*` is less specific than `Name`, which, in turn, is less specific than `Author/Name` (because you may have a `Name` node that is a descendant of a `Book_title` node or of an `Author` node). If the template rule's `pattern` attribute specified more than one kind of node, the processor will assign priorities as if there are a set of template rules: one for each alternative. An example of such a template rule is shown here:

```
<xsl:template match="Last_name | First_name">
```

If all else fails—that is, if the XSLT processor ends up with multiple template rules that have identical import precedence as well as `priority` values—the processor may choose to report an error, or it may choose the last template rule that occurs in the stylesheet. To avoid this, you should write your stylesheets in such a way that the XSLT processor will be able to make an unambiguous choice. Since this is easier said than done, particularly for very complex stylesheets, it is best to test your mission- critical code with multiple XSLT processors to ensure that you get identical results.

Overriding Template Rules

We saw earlier that the template rules from the importing stylesheet take precedence over those from the imported stylesheet. In certain instances, you may want to get around the normal precedence rules and apply a template from the imported stylesheet that was overruled. You can do this by using the element `xsl:apply-imports`, the syntax of which follows:

```
<!-- Category: instruction -->
<xsl:apply-imports />
```

Consider this example, which displays the name of an author in boldface using the
`Author.xsl` stylesheet:

```
...
<-- Body of Author.xsl stylesheet to be imported in the next example -->
    <xsl:template match="Name">
      <B>
        <xsl:value-of select="First_name"/>
      </B>
      <I>
        <xsl:value-of select="Last_name"/>
      </I>
    </xsl:template>
...
```

You may want to reuse this stylesheet by importing it into another stylesheet
called `Display.xsl`:

```
...
<-- Larger stylesheet Display.xsl that imports Author.xsl, and
uses xsl:apply-imports -->
<xsl:import href="AuthorName.xsl"/>
    <xsl:template match="Author/Name">
        <xsl:apply-imports/>
    </xsl:template>
...
```

Application of `Display.xsl` to the source tree will result in the following:

```
...
<B> Chris </B>
<I> von See </I>
<B> Nitin </B>
<I> Keskar </I>
...
```

NOTE

The template rules in `Display.xsl` *would normally take precedence over those in the
imported stylesheet,* `AuthorName.xsl`, *but we instructed the processor to override the
default template rule and use the one in the imported stylesheet instead.*

The value of overriding template rules can be seen more clearly by noticing what would happen in the absence of `xsl:apply-imports`. Consider the following code:

```
...
<-- Larger stylesheet Display.xsl that imports Author.xsl,
but does not use
xsl:apply-imports -->
<xsl:import href="AuthorName.xsl"/>
    <xsl:template match="Author/Name">
        <xsl:apply-templates/>
    </xsl:template>
...
```

In this case, the built-in template rule will be invoked for the node `Author/Name`, which simply outputs the value of the node without specifying any special formatting for the child nodes `First_name` and `Last_name`, as shown here:

```
...
Chris
von See
Nitin
Keskar
...
```

Using Modes

We saw that mode is an optional attribute for the elements `xsl:template` and `xsl:apply-templates`. This attribute may be used to process the corresponding element multiple times, each time producing a different result. For example, you may want to display the name of the author in different colors (red or blue) depending on certain conditions. In this case, you would define two modes for the `Author` node as follows:

```
...
<xsl:template match="Author" mode="blue">
<DIV style="color:blue">
<xsl:value-of select="."/>
</DIV>
```

```
</xsl:template>


<xsl:template match="Author" mode="red">
<DIV style="color:red">
<xsl:value-of select="."/>
</DIV>
</xsl:template>
...
```

The following example shows how you can use the modes defined in the preceding code:

```
...
<!-- Condition for the red-mode met -->
<xsl:template match="//Author">
<xsl:apply-templates select="." mode="red"/>
</xsl:template>
...
```

The resulting output looks as follows:

```
...
      <DIV style="color:red">
         Chris
         von See
      </DIV>

      <DIV style="color:red">
         Nitin
         Keskar
      </DIV>
...
```

Note that for xsl:template, you can specify the mode attribute only when the match attribute is specified as well. When you use this attribute in xsl:apply-templates, it will be applied to only those template rules for which the mode attribute has the same value. By the same token, if you were applying a template without a mode attribute, that attribute would apply only to those template rules that do not have a mode specified for them.

Using Built-in Template Rules

In the code examples discussed so far, you may have noticed that sometimes we specify specific template rules for certain nodes, and sometimes we do not. Regardless, the XSLT processor is still able to sort through the source tree and apply the transformations to all nodes. The W3C specification defines several built-in rules, which we discuss in this section. In some instances you can use them to your advantage and keep the code compact; that's why you should be familiar with them. More often, however, you will need to override the built-in rules with template rules required to solve the problem at hand.

Recursive Processing of Nodes and Elements

Let us consider an extreme example where we do not specify any template rules in our stylesheet:

```
<xsl:stylesheet version="1.0"
    xmlns:xsl="http://www.w3.org/1999/XSL/Transform'>
<!-- No template rule specified -->
</xsl:stylesheet>
```

When applied to the source XML file `auth.xml` that we used in Chapter 4, this code will still produce the following output:

```
<?xml version="1.0" encoding="utf-8"?>
    Chris
    von See
    111 Mansion Boulevard
    Suite 100
    Chicago
    IL
    31313

    Nitin
    Keskar
    222 Metropolis Street
    P.O. Box 500
    Minneapolis
    MN
    55455
```

This is because there is a built-in template rule for recursive processing of all nodes as well as the root node. By writing your own template rules, you are, in fact, overriding this built-in rule. Explicitly stated, this template rule is as follows:

```
<xsl:template match="*|/">
  <xsl:apply-templates/>
</xsl:template>
```

To apply this template rule, the XSLT processor will begin at the root node and continue processing its descendants until it encounters an overriding template for a node. When it finds such a template for a node, it processes that node and *its* descendants until the leaf nodes are reached.

Processing Template Modes

The built-in rule for processing mode enables recursive processing to continue in the same mode as that in the current context, unless a pattern match is found for an explicitly stated template rule in the stylesheet that instructs otherwise. Explicit statement of this rule is shown below:

```
<xsl:template match="*|/" mode="xyz">
  <xsl:apply-templates mode="xyz"/>
</xsl:template>
```

Processing Text and Attribute Nodes

If you have plain text in your XML source tree, a built-in rule passes this text through to the output. Consider the following data file excerpt:

```
<Author>
  <Name>
  <First_name>Nitin </First_name>
  <Last_name>Keskar</Last_name>
    Just plain text ...
  </Name>
...
  </Author>
```

In this case, the XSLT processor will strip the XML tags and output the nodes along with the untagged plain-text content:

```
Nitin
Keskar
  Just plain text ...
```

The same treatment is given to attribute nodes as well. That is, the following statement of this built-in rule will copy the attribute nodes, along with the text nodes, to the output tree:

```
<xsl:template match="text()|@*">
  <xsl:apply-templates select="."/>
</xsl:template>
```

Processing Instructions, Comments, and Namespace Nodes

The built-in template rule for comments and instruction nodes is:

```
<xsl:template match="comment()|processing-instruction()"/>
```

The statement of the built-in rule for namespace nodes is:

```
<xsl:template match="namespace()"/>
```

These built-in rules for instructions, comments, and namespace nodes instruct the XSLT processor simply to ignore them. In fact, you cannot override the built-in rule with an explicit template rule for a namespace node because such a node is specified by a URI, and hence no pattern can match a namespace node.

Using Named Templates

In the syntax of the xsl:template element, you probably noticed the name attribute, which can optionally be used to name a template. A named template can be then invoked using the xsl:call-template element, which uses the following syntax:

```
<!-- Category: instruction -->
<xsl:call-template
  name = qname>
  <!-- Content: xsl:with-param* -->
</xsl:call-template>
```

Sometimes you will have multiple templates specified for a node and you want to use a particular one in a particular instance. This is where the named templates will come in handy. Such a situation may occur, for example, when the output has to have different style attributes (such as font color, size, or type) in different places. Consider the following example that illustrates how names may be specified for templates:

```
...
<xsl:template match="Name" name="red-template-for-Author-Name">
<DIV style="color:red">
<xsl:value-of select="."/>
</DIV>
</xsl:template>

<xsl:template match="Name" name="blue-template-for-Author-Name">
<DIV style="color:blue">
<xsl:value-of select="."/>
</DIV>
</xsl:template>
...
```

To use one of these named templates, you would write code similar to the following:

```
...
<xsl:template match="Name">
<xsl:call-template name="red-template-for-Author-Name"/>
</xsl:template>
...
```

This will result in the expected output, as shown here:

```
...
  <DIV style="color:red">
    Chris
    von See
  </DIV>
...
    <DIV style="color:red">
    Nitin
```

```
Keskar
</DIV>
```
. . .

Note the following points about named templates:

▶ Although we have specified the `mode` attribute for the named template in the preceding examples, we do not have to.

▶ The `name` attribute is mandatory for an `xsl:call-template` element. Naming a template does not affect the use of `xsl:apply-templates` elements that invoke that template.

▶ The stylesheet must include a named template with the same `name` attribute as used in `xsl:call-template`.

▶ Templates must have unique names. Otherwise, the processor will end up with two templates that have the same name and precedence and so report an error, even if you explicitly specified priorities that are different.

Summary

This chapter discussed the important topic of template rules. In the absence of explicitly stated template rules, the XSLT processor will use built-in rules. This is a useful facility since you do not have to write rules for every single element and node. However, you will frequently custom-code template rules to meet the requirements for the result tree. Template rules follow certain precedence rules that you must be aware of and be able to override when necessary, particularly when you develop multiple complex stylesheets that are linked to each other through `xsl:include` and `xsl:import` elements. For code readability and maintainability, you can name templates and call them from elsewhere. We also discussed how the `mode` attribute of `xsl:template` and `xsl:apply-templates` may be used to process the corresponding element multiple times, each time with a different result.

The following list shows all child elements allowed for `xsl:template`. This chapter discussed only `xsl:apply-imports`, `xsl:apply-templates`, `xsl:call-template`, and `xsl:value-of`. The treatment of the rest of the templates is deferred until later in this book.

- ▶ xsl:apply-imports
- ▶ xsl:apply-templates
- ▶ xsl:attribute
- ▶ xsl:call-template
- ▶ xsl:choose
- ▶ xsl:comment
- ▶ xsl:copy
- ▶ xsl:copy-of
- ▶ xsl:document
- ▶ xsl:element
- ▶ xsl:fallback
- ▶ xsl:for-each
- ▶ xsl:if
- ▶ xsl:message
- ▶ xsl:number
- ▶ xsl:processing-instruction
- ▶ xsl:text
- ▶ xsl:value-of
- ▶ xsl:variable

Creating the XSLT Result Tree

U p to this point, we've focused on the structure of XSLT stylesheets, the definition and behavior of templates, the XPath language as a tool for identifying nodes to be processed, coding conditional and repetition expressions, and selecting node content. While this is all very interesting stuff, when it comes right down to it, the whole point of an XSLT stylesheet is to generate output—HTML, XML, text, or something equally useful. The first step toward that goal is to use the information from the input XML document to generate nodes in the result tree, which is the focus of this chapter. The first part of this chapter deals with the details of generating nodes using XSLT's `xsl:element`, `xsl:attribute`, and related elements, and the second part deals with the conditional processing elements, `xsl:if` and `xsl:choose`, which give you more control over how things are generated.

In many cases, much of what comes out of the XSLT transformation process is a combination of data that is hard-coded in the stylesheet itself, and data extracted from nodes in the input document—you've seen this done in many of the examples in this book. In some applications, such as when stylesheets are used to generate other stylesheets, almost all of the output must be dynamically generated based on data from multiple sources. While we'll revisit the mechanisms used to generate output using hard-coded data, most of this chapter will focus on this dynamic generation process and how it can be used to create various types of XML nodes. In the remainder of this chapter, we'll extend the discussion with an explanation of variables and parameters as a tool to inject other data into the node creation process; Chapter 8 will explain how to get the new result tree into HTML, XML, or text format.

You have probably come across looping and conditional processing while working with other programming languages. Such processing lets you perform repetitive actions in a controlled loop, or deal with multiple alternatives based on whether certain conditions are met. XSLT also gives you the power to develop such logic in dealing with XML source trees. The current chapter focuses on XSLT elements such as `xsl:for-each`, `xsl:if`, and `xsl:choose`.

What Comes Out of an XSLT Stylesheet?

Back in Chapter 2, we talked about the document hierarchy: a collection of nodes arranged in a tree and related to each other through parent, child, sibling, and ancestor relationships. When we process an XML document using XSLT, we use templates to select nodes from this hierarchy based on some combination of their position or relationship relative to other nodes in the tree or their attributes and content. The XSLT stylesheet processor works its way through the input document hierarchy, calling templates as it goes, until all nodes in the input have been processed.

XSLT is a language meant to transform one XML document into another XML document (even if that output XML document is composed of nothing but text). The only way a stylesheet can generate output (aside from error messages) is by creating another document hierarchy containing whatever the templates in that stylesheet want written—elements and attributes, text, processing instructions, and so on. This output XML document is called the *result tree*.

The result tree is seen as a document hierarchy by the XSLT processor, just like the input document. It's composed of a root node, which is generated automatically by XSLT, and some number of nodes that are produced by the stylesheet using a combination of literals, content, and attributes from the input document, and even parameters passed into the stylesheet processor. The stylesheet must insert a single node directly underneath the root node; this element (which is the html element for HTML documents, the document node for XML documents, or an arbitrary node for text documents) forms the foundation for the rest of the tree.

In the sample HTML result tree shown in Figure 7-1, you can see the html node inserted under the root node, forming the foundation of the result tree. Notice the location of the xsl:apply-templates element in the template shown at the left; because this appears between the <html> and </html> tags, any nodes created by templates executed as a result become children of the html node (the head and body nodes in the figure, for example). If the xsl:apply-templates element had appeared before or after the opening and closing <html> tags, the nodes generated by templates executed by xsl:apply-templates would have been siblings, not children, of the <html> tag (which, of course, would be invalid HTML!). This is a key point to remember when working with XSLT: the parent-child and sibling relationships among elements are determined by the placement of the XSLT elements that create nodes (or cause nodes to be created) in the result tree.

Templates aren't restricted to the creation of a single element. If desired, a template can create multiple elements itself, and can even call xsl:apply-templates multiple times (with different select attributes, for example) to create additional child element types. In this way, the result tree is built into a well-formed document that can then be written as HTML, XML, or text.

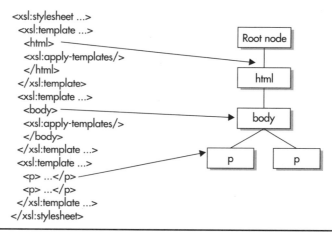

Figure 7-1 *A sample HTML result tree, showing the* `html` *node and its children*

Creating the Result Tree

To kick off our discussion of the techniques for creating result tree elements, let's go back and review one of our examples from Chapter 5. In that chapter, we used a book catalog example that included a series of book entries, such as the one shown here:

```
<Book>
    <dc:Identifier system="ISBN">0072129514</dc:Identifier>
    <dc:Title>HTML: The Complete Reference, Third Edition</dc:Title>
    <dc:Creator>Thomas A. Powell</dc:Creator>
    <dc:Subject>HTML</dc:Subject>
    <dc:Description>Complete reference for HTML</dc:Description>
    <dc:Publisher>McGraw-Hill Professional Publishing</dc:Publisher>
    <dc:Date>December 14, 2000</dc:Date>
    <dc:Language>en-US</dc:Language>
    <dc:Format>Paperback print</dc:Format>
    <dimensions unit="inches">
        <thickness>2.42</thickness>
        <height>9.08</height>
        <width>7.34</width>
    </dimensions>
    <numberOfPages>1208</numberOfPages>
    <price unit="USD">27.99</price>
    <readerRating unit="stars">4.5</readerRating>
</Book>
```

The stylesheet we used to process this document had several templates, each of which processed a given element type in the document. For example, the template used to process the `dc:Subject` element looked like this:

```
<xsl:template match="dc:Subject" >
   Subject: <xsl:value-of select="." />
</xsl:template>
```

This template is a very basic example of the first method of generating stylesheet output: combining hard-coded text from the stylesheet with content from the input XML document. In this case, we're combining the literal `"Subject:"` with the value of the current node (that is, the `dc:Subject` element) to create a text node in the result tree containing the following text:

```
Subject: HTML
```

More often than not, you'll use some form of this ability to combine static and dynamic content to produce nodes in the result tree and, therefore, output from your XSLT stylesheet. Of course, we could just as easily have left out the content of the `dc:Subject` element entirely, if, for example, our point was only to detect the presence of a certain element and notify the user:

```
<xsl:template match="dc:Subject" >
   Subject element detected!<br/>
</xsl:template>
```

Or we could have left out the literal output and displayed only the element content, as we might if we want to produce an output document containing only the text content of the input document:

```
<xsl:template match="dc:Subject" >
   <xsl:value-of select="." />
</xsl:template>
```

Extracting Content from Elements and Attributes

XSLT provides an element called `xsl:value-of` to allow templates to retrieve element content or attribute values from nodes in the document hierarchy. The syntax for this element is

```
<xsl:value-of
  select = "XPath-expression "
  disable-output-escaping = "yes" | "no" />
```

The `xsl:value-of` element uses an XPath expression to designate the node from which content is to be extracted, and it returns the string value of the selected node. Perhaps the simplest example is the statement `xsl:value-of select= "." /`, which extracts the content of the current node (recall that "." is XPath's abbreviated syntax designating the current node). Extracting the value of an attribute of the current node is equally straightforward:

```
<xsl:template match="readerRating" >
    This book uses <xsl:value-of select="@unit" /> as the rating unit.
</xsl:template>
```

This example retrieves the value of the `unit` attribute (again, using XPath's abbreviated syntax), combines it with literal text, and writes a new text node containing

```
This book uses stars as the rating unit.
```

There are many situations where it's necessary to retrieve information from an element that is not the template's current node. Using XPath, we can identify the relative or absolute relationship the desired node has to the current node and write an expression to retrieve its content using `xsl:value-of`. The following code uses the book catalog example to illustrate retrieval of content from children of the current node using the `dimensions` element and its children:

```
<xsl:template match="dimensions" >
    Dimensions (in <xsl:value-of select="@unit" />):
            <xsl:value-of select="height" /> x
            <xsl:value-of select="width" /> x
            <xsl:value-of select="thickness" />
</xsl:template>
```

By selecting the `dimensions` element and then referencing each of its children using `xsl:value-of` and the appropriate XPath expressions, we can generate a text node containing

```
Dimensions (in inches): 9.08 x 7.34 x 2.42
```

Parents of the current node can be referenced in a similar fashion. If we want to combine the value of the dc:Publisher and dc:Date elements in a single text node, we could use the following template:

```
<xsl:template match="dc:Publisher" >
   Publisher: <xsl:value-of select="." /> (Released <xsl:value-of
           select="../dc:Date" />)<br/>
</xsl:template>
```

To retrieve the value of the dc:Date element, the xsl:value-of element's XPath expression first references the parent of the current node (using the location step "..") and then retrieves the dc:Date child of that parent.

By default, XSLT automatically escapes all characters (such as < and >) which, if left alone, would prevent the stylesheet's output from being well-formed XML. Take a look at this XML document:

```
<?xml version="1.0" encoding="UTF-8" ?>
<Book>
   <Title>Good HTML, Bad HTML</Title>
   <Description>Explains the difference between good &lt;html&gt; &amp; bad
 &lt;html&gt;</Description>
</Book>
```

Note that the description element contains escaped characters (< for <, > for >, and & for &), which allow these characters to be included in the element's content while still maintaining the document's well-formedness. Now let's process this document using the stylesheet shown here:

```
<xsl:stylesheet version="1.0"
                xmlns:xsl="http://www.w3.org/1999/XSL/Transform" >
   <xsl:output method="html" />
   <xsl:template match="Title" >
      The title of this book is <xsl:value-of select="." />
   </xsl:template>
   <xsl:template match="Description" >
      The description of this book is <xsl:value-of select="." />
   </xsl:template>
</xsl:stylesheet>
```

By default, the stylesheet processor ensures that all characters that need to be escaped to create a valid HTML document are handled. If we used this stylesheet as is, the output would be as follows:

```
The title of this book is Good HTML, Bad HTML
The description of this book is Explains the difference between good
&lt;html&gt; &amp; bad &lt;html&gt;
```

By disabling output escaping when we extract the content of the `description` element, we can prevent the XSLT processor from escaping these characters. This ability may be valuable, for example, if the XSLT processor's output is to be reprocessed by another program later. The following stylesheet shows output escaping disabled for the `description` element:

```
<xsl:stylesheet version="1.0"
                xmlns:xsl="http://www.w3.org/1999/XSL/Transform" >
   <xsl:template match="Title" >
      The title of this book is <xsl:value-of select="." />
   </xsl:template>
   <xsl:template match="Description" >
      The description of this book is <xsl:value-of select="."
disable-output-escaping="yes" />

   </xsl:template>
</xsl:stylesheet>
```

This stylesheet leaves the <, >, and & characters unescaped, resulting in the following output:

```
The title of this book is Good HTML, Bad HTML
The description of this book is Explains the difference between good <html>
 & bad <html>
```

Output escaping works with both HTML and XML output. Because text output does not have to be escaped, the `disable-output-escaping` attribute of `xsl:value-of` is ignored when the output is set to text mode using `xsl:output method="text"`.

Dynamically Generating Elements and Attributes

Let's say that we want to use the content of an input XML document to generate an output XML document, determining output element names, attribute names, and so on by retrieving this information from the input. A simple approach to doing this

might be to build an XML document that contains information about the elements
and attributes that comprise the desired output:

```
<?xml version="1.0" ?>
<dynDoc name="BookCatalog">
    <dynElem name="Book">
        <dynElem name="dc:Identifier">
            <dynAttr name="system" value="ISBN" />
            <dynElemValue>0072133902</dynElemValue>
        </dynElem>
        <dynElem name="dc:Title">
            <dynElemValue>Web Design: A Beginner's Guide</dynElemValue>
        </dynElem>
        <dynElem name="dc:Description">
            <dynElemValue>Explains basic Web page design and development
            </dynElemValue>
        </dynElem>
    </dynElem>
</dynDoc>
```

When designing the stylesheet to perform this transformation, you might attempt
the obvious first choice—to simply wrap `xsl:value-of` elements that extract the
names and values in escaped < and > characters to construct elements and attributes.

```
<xsl:template match="dynElem" >
    &lt;<xsl:value-of select="@name" />&gt;
    <xsl:value-of select="dynElemValue" />
    &lt;/<xsl:value-of select="@name" />&gt;
</xsl:template>
```

Unfortunately, this doesn't work because the XSLT processor keeps the escaped
< and > characters, resulting in a malformed XML output document. What's needed
is a way to tell the XSLT processor that you want to generate XML and to place the
names and values of elements and attributes where they need to go. To address
problems like this that require dynamic generation of output based on an input XML
document, XSLT provides three elements—`xsl:element`, `xsl:attribute`,
and `xsl:attribute-set`—and a new construct, the *attribute value template*.

Attribute Value Templates

Normally, templates include data from the input document by using `xsl:value-of`
elements to extract the relevant content and insert it into the stylesheet's output.
When content from the input document is to be inserted into an attribute that is itself

dynamically generated, however, the `xsl:value-of` element can't be used, because doing so would violate the well-formedness of the stylesheet, as you can see in the following example:

```
<body bgcolor="<xsl:value-of select="@bgcolor" />>
```

In this case, another mechanism is needed, and XSLT has just the solution: attribute value templates.

With the exception of their syntax, attribute value templates function almost exactly the same way as `xsl:value-of`. An attribute value template is an XPath expression surrounded by curly braces—{ and }—and it's used with `xsl:element`, `xsl:attribute`, and several other XSLT elements. The entire attribute value template (including the curly braces) is replaced with the value generated by evaluating the XPath expression contained within the template.

For example, if we want to retrieve the name attribute from an input element and include it as the element name in an `xsl:element` element, we can code the following:

```
<xsl:element name="{@name}">
... content goes here
</xsl:element>
```

We'll look at more examples of attribute value templates as we explore the XSLT elements in which they are used.

Using xsl:element to Dynamically Generate Elements

The `xsl:element` element provides an easy way to tell the XSLT processor that you want to include a dynamically generated XML element in your output document and to provide the information needed to build that element. The syntax for `xsl:element` is as follows:

```
<xsl:element
   name = " name "
   namespace = " uri "
   use-attribute-sets = "name1 name2 ... name-n">
</xsl:element>
```

Only the `name` attribute, which provides the name of the element to be generated, is required. Additional XSLT elements or literal content that generates children of the generated node can be provided inside the opening and closing xsl:element tags; typically, stylesheet developers use xsl:apply-templates to drive other templates to generate these children.

Here's an example of a basic use of xsl:element to generate output, using the XML document shown earlier in this section:

```
<xsl:stylesheet version="1.0"
                xmlns:xsl="http://www.w3.org/1999/XSL/Transform"
                xmlns:dc=http://purl.org/dc/elements/1.1/ >
<xsl:template match="dynDoc" >
   <xsl:element name="{@name}" >
      <xsl:apply-templates select="dynElem" />
   </xsl:element>
</xsl:template>
<xsl:template match="dynElem" >
   <xsl:element name="{@name}" >
      <xsl:if test="dynElemValue" >
         <xsl:value-of select="dynElemValue" />
      </xsl:if>
      <xsl:apply-templates select="dynElem" />
   </xsl:element>
</xsl:template>
</xsl:stylesheet>
```

In the first template of this stylesheet, which matches on the input dynDoc element, the name attribute of xsl:element extracts the name attribute of the current node using an attribute value template, using this string to create the name of the new element. The xsl:apply-templates select="dynElem" / element inside this xsl:element element forces the XSLT processor to execute the second template, which creates children of this first element (we know that children are created instead of siblings because the xsl:apply-templates element appears inside xsl:element, not outside).

The second template, which matches on dynElem elements, also uses xsl:element to generate elements with the content specified in the input document. Because not all of the elements contain text content, we use xsl:if in this second template to check for the presence of an dynElemValue element and, if one exists, print its value. By inserting an xsl:apply-template select="dynElem" / element inside the xsl:element, we can recursively process any number of levels of dynElem elements in the input document, and any elements created by the stylesheet's second template become children of nodes generated in the previous recursion. The final output of this stylesheet looks like this:

```
<?xml version="1.0" encoding="UTF-8"?>
<BookCatalog xmlns:dc="http://purl.org/dc/elements/1.1/">
   <Book>
      <dc:Identifier>0072133902</dc:Identifier>
      <dc:Title>Web Design: A Beginner's Guide</dc:Title>
      <dc:Description>Explains basic Web page design and development
      </dc:Description>
   </Book>
</BookCatalog>
```

While this demonstrates how elements can be generated, there are still some pieces missing—the attributes! Next, we'll demonstrate how the xsl:attribute element can be used in cooperation with xsl:element to generate attributes in our output document.

Using xsl:attribute and xsl:attribute-set to Dynamically Generate Attributes

The xsl:attribute element functions in a very similar way to xsl:element in that it takes values from the input document and dynamically generates attributes on an element. The xsl:attribute element can be used to create dynamic attributes on both elements generated using xsl:element (by inserting xsl:attribute elements between the opening and closing tags of the xsl:element) and on hard-coded elements (by specifying the xsl:attribute elements inside the hard-coded element's opening and closing tags).

The syntax for xsl:attribute is as follows:

```
<xsl:attribute
   name = " name "
   namespace = " uri" >
</xsl:attribute>
```

The name of the generated attribute is taken from the name attribute of xsl:attributes, and the value of the attribute come from the xsl:attribute element's content. As with xsl:element, only the name attribute is required.

Let's modify our earlier stylesheet to add support for attributes:

```
<xsl:stylesheet version="1.0"
                xmlns:xsl="http://www.w3.org/1999/XSL/Transform"
                xmlns:dc=http://purl.org/dc/elements/1.1/ >
<xsl:template match="dynDoc" >
   <xsl:element name="{@name}" >
      <xsl:apply-templates select="dynElem" />
   </xsl:element>
</xsl:template>
<xsl:template match="dynElem" >
   <xsl:element name="{@name}" >
      <xsl:apply-templates select="dynAttr"/>
      <xsl:if test="dynElemValue" >
         <xsl:value-of select="dynElemValue" />
      </xsl:if>
      <xsl:apply-templates select="dynElem" />
   </xsl:element>
</xsl:template>
<xsl:template match="dynAttr" >
   <xsl:attribute name="{@name}">
      <xsl:value-of select="@value" />
   </xsl:attribute>
</xsl:template>
</xsl:stylesheet>
```

There are two major changes to this stylesheet, which are highlighted in bold. First, we've added a third template that matches on dynAttr elements in the input document and uses xsl:attribute to generate attributes. This template uses an attribute value template to create the name attribute and extracts the value attribute from the content of the current dynAttr node to create the value for the new attribute. Second, it uses xsl:apply-templates select="dynAttr" / inside the template that matches on input dynElem nodes; this causes the new template to be called when elements are generated, and it adds the new attributes to that element. We know the new attributes will get added to the element generated in this template because the xsl:apply-templates select="dynAttr" / element appears inside, not outside, the xsl:element element (having it appear outside would generate an invalid result tree, and most likely an XSLT processor error as well).

```
<?xml version="1.0" encoding="UTF-8"?>
<BookCatalog xmlns:dc="http://purl.org/dc/elements/1.1/">
   <Book>
      <dc:Identifier system="ISBN">0072133902</dc:Identifier>
      <dc:Title>Web Design: A Beginner's Guide</dc:Title>
      <dc:Description>Explains basic Web page design and development
      </dc:Description>
   </Book>
</BookCatalog>
```

You'll notice that the system="ISBN" attribute has been added to the dc:Identifier element in response to the dynAttr element in the input XML document. This same technique can be used to add other attributes, such as namespace attributes or xml:lang attributes.

XSLT also provides a way to combine xsl:attribute elements into a set, which can then be included on any number of generated elements. The element that performs this function is called xsl:attribute-set, and its syntax is shown here:

```
<xsl:attribute-set
  name = "name "
  use-attribute-sets = "name1 name2 ... name-n">
</xsl:attribute-set>
```

Only the name attribute, which gives the name by which this attribute set can be referenced, is required. The attributes that comprise the attribute set are specified by inserting xsl:attribute elements inside the attribute set; these attributes will be created using the current node in effect when the attribute set is invoked. Attribute sets can also invoke other attribute sets by specifying their names in a space-separated list using the use-attribute-sets attribute.

Here's an example of an attribute set that includes a set of attributes whose characteristics are specified as literal values:

```
<xsl:attribute-set name="as1"
   <xsl:attribute name="attr1">Attribute 1</xsl:attribute>
   <xsl:attribute name="attr2">Attribute 2</xsl:attribute>
</xsl:attribute>
```

You can also use attribute value templates and elements such as xsl:value-of and xsl:text to generate attributes in an attribute set. In our earlier example, we used a template that matched on dynAttr elements in the input XML document, combined with xsl:attribute elements that generated the appropriate attributes on the enclosing element; we can accomplish the same goal using attribute sets:

```
<xsl:stylesheet version="1.0"
                xmlns:xsl="http://www.w3.org/1999/XSL/Transform"
                xmlns:dc=http://purl.org/dc/elements/1.1/ >
<xsl:template match="dynDoc" >
   <xsl:element name="{@name}" >
      <xsl:apply-templates select="dynElem" />
   </xsl:element>
</xsl:template>
<xsl:template match="dynElem" >
   <xsl:element name="{@name}"
                   use-attribute-sets="as1" >
      <xsl:if test="dynElemValue" >
         <xsl:value-of select="dynElemValue" />
      </xsl:if>
      <xsl:apply-templates select="dynElem" />
   </xsl:element>
</xsl:template>
<xsl:attribute-set name="as1" >
   <xsl:attribute name="{dynAttr/@name}">
      <xsl:value-of select="dynAttr/@value" />
   </xsl:attribute>
</xsl:attribute-set>
</xsl:stylesheet>
```

The xsl:element elements invoke attribute sets using their use-attribute-sets attribute, which provides a space-separated list of attribute set names that are to be invoked for that element. Each attribute set named in the list is invoked, in turn, to generate its attributes onto that element using the current node's content. In the previous example, the attribute set as1 contains an xsl:attribute element that reads the dynAttr/name and dynAttr/value attribute values to generate its output.

Attribute sets can also be applied to elements defined as literals in the stylesheet simply by specifying the use-attribute-sets attribute in the literal element:

```
<Book name="Benji" use-attribute-sets="as1">
```

Creating Text, Processing Instructions, and Comments

Hopefully you've seen up to this point that XSLT uses a fairly consistent approach to dynamically generating content: provide a framework using literal text, `xsl:element`, or `xsl:attribute`, and then fill in the blanks using content extracted from the input document using `xsl:value-of` or attribute value templates. There are three additional elements that follow this same pattern: `xsl:text`, `xsl:processing-instruction`, and `xsl:comment`, which generate text, XML processing instructions, and XML comments, respectively. Just as when you create text, processing instructions (PIs), or comments by hand, the content generated by these elements is subject to the rules described in the XML specification; processing instructions, for example, cannot use the reserved string XML as their target, and comments must appear only outside of elements.

Using xsl:text to Create Text Nodes

XSLT provides the `xsl:text` element to allow stylesheets to generate text to be included in the output document. When you include literal strings in your stylesheet that are to be written to the output document, XSLT internally converts those strings to `xsl:text` elements.

The syntax of `xsl:text` elements is as follows:

```
<xsl:text
   disable-output-escaping = "yes" | "no" >
</xsl:text>
```

Content to be generated as a text node is included between the `xsl:text` and `/xsl:text` elements. For example, if we modify the template from the earlier example to generate additional element content using `xsl:text`, we might end up with the following:

```
<xsl:template match="dynElem" >
   <xsl:element name="{@name}" >
      <xsl:apply-templates select="dynAttr"/>
      <xsl:if test="dynElemValue" >
         <xsl:value-of select="dynElemValue" />
      </xsl:if>
      <xsl:text> This content generated using &lt;xsl:text&gt;</xsl:text>
      <xsl:apply-templates select="dynElem" />
   </xsl:element>
</xsl:template>
```

Each element generated using this template would have the string enclosed by `xsl:text` included as part of its output.

As you might expect, dynamic text can also be built by combining `xsl:text` with `xsl:value-of`. For example, if we want to include the name of the element in the text generated by the earlier example, we could include an `xsl:value-of` element in the appropriate place inside the `xsl:text` element:

```
<xsl:text>This content for the <xsl:value-of select="@name" /> element was
  generated using &lt;xsl:text&gt;</xsl:text>
```

This, for the `dc:Title` element, would generate the following text:

```
<xsl:text>This content for the dc:Title element was generated using
  &lt;xsl:text&gt;</xsl:text>
```

Creating Processing Instructions Using xsl:processing-instruction

The `xsl:processing-instruction` element follows much the same path as `xsl:text`, except that it has an additional attribute that allows templates to specify the target of the PI:

```
<xsl:processing-instruction
  name = "target-name" >
</xsl:processing-instruction>
```

The target of the PI is specified using the `name` attribute, and the actual content of the PI is specified as content of the `xsl:processing-instruction` element. If, for example, you want to specify a processing instruction in the document generation example that told programs reading the output document that it had been generated by XSLT, you can do so with the `xsl:processing-instruction` element shown here:

```
<xsl:processing-instruction name="target">
documentGenerator=&quot;xslt&quot;
</xsl:processing-instruction>
```

This would generate the following PI:

```
<?target documentGenerator="xslt" ?>
```

One tip to keep in mind when generating processing instructions: because XML reserves the `?>` string to denote the end of a processing instruction's content, it is an error to either embed these characters in `xsl:processing-instruction` content or to cause them to be embedded by dynamically generating the string using `xsl:value-of` or `xsl:text`. XSLT processors are supposed to complain about this, but some will silently insert a space between the offending question mark and slash.

Creating Comments Using xsl:comment

XML comments can be generated in much the same fashion as processing instructions and text by using the `xsl:comment` element. Content to be included in the comment, whether it be from `xsl:text`, `xsl:value-of`, or literal text, is included inside the `xsl:comment` element. Here are some examples:

```
<xsl:comment>This is a comment</xsl:comment>
<xsl:comment><xsl:value-of select="." /></xsl:comment>
```

Handling Namespaces

Although misunderstood early in the life of XML, namespaces have become an integral part of many XML applications, with tangible benefits from the reuse of standard XML vocabularies. XSLT makes the use of namespaces in generated documents practically painless with very straightforward rules for determining what namespaces are in scope for a given set of generated output.

Recall from the XML namespace specification that namespaces are declared by including `xmlns` attributes specifying a namespace prefix and the Uniform Resource Identifier (URI) of the namespace. The names of attributes specifying namespace URIs are built by adding the namespace prefix to the `xmlns` string; for example, you've seen the namespace specification for XSLT specified on the `xsl:stylesheet` element in examples throughout this book:

```
<xsl:stylesheet version="1.0"
                xmlns:xsl="http://www.w3.org/1999/XSL/Transform">
```

The `xmlns:xsl` attribute name indicates that this is a namespace attribute that uses the `xsl` prefix to identify elements from that namespace, and whose URI is http://www.w3.org/1999/XSL/Transform. In many of the same prior examples, you've also seen a namespace attribute identifying the Dublin Core namespace, showing how multiple namespace declarations can be provided on the same element:

```
<xsl:stylesheet version="1.0"
                xmlns:xsl="http://www.w3.org/1999/XSL/Transform"
                xmlns:dc="http://purl.org/dc/elements/1.1/">
```

The xmlns:dc attribute identifies the namespace prefix (dc) and the namespace URI (http://purl.org/dc/elements/1.1/) for the Dublin Core namespace.

The scope of a declared namespace is identified in the XML Namespaces specification as including the element on which the xmlns attribute declaring the namespace is specified, plus any child elements. By specifying the XSLT namespace identifier on the xsl:stylesheet element, we've effectively indicated that the xsl prefix is valid for the entire XSLT stylesheet.

Generating elements with namespace declarations is very straightforward. There are two techniques that can be used: declaring the namespace on the xsl:template element, and declaring it on the xsl:element element. Both techniques require the namespace prefix to be specified as part of the dynamically generated element's name; XSLT automatically makes the connection between this prefix and the namespace. Using the first technique keeps you from having to specify the namespace on every xsl:element element in the template; using the second technique allows you to extract the namespace URI from the input document using an attribute value template.

If we want to declare the namespace on the xsl:template element, we can code something similar to the following:

```
<xsl:template match="document" xmlns:doof="http://www.doof.com/ns">
   <xsl:element name="doof:{@name}" >
      This element was dynamically generated!
   </xsl:element>
</xsl:template>
```

Alternatively, if we want to declare the namespace directly on the dynamically generated element, we can code something like this:

```
<xsl:template match="document" >
   <xsl:element name="doof:{@name}" namespace="http://www.doof.com/ns" >
      This element was dynamically generated!
   </xsl:element>
</xsl:template>
```

In either case, the resulting output has both the generated element name (prefixed with the doof namespace prefix) and the namespace declaration itself:

```
<?xml version="1.0" encoding="UTF-8"?>
<doof:BookCatalog xmlns:doof="http://www.doof.com/ns">
      This element was dynamically generated!
</doof:BookCatalog>
```

Any children of this element that bear the doof namespace prefix will automatically be in scope.

Sometimes it's necessary to use the XSLT namespace itself in the output of the stylesheet (as when an XSLT stylesheet is being used to generate another XSLT stylesheet). Because XSLT relies on the XSLT namespace URI to identify its own elements, it's not possible to use this URI on the output; to address this problem, XSLT provides the `xsl:namespace-alias` element:

```
<xsl:namespace-alias stylesheet-prefix = prefix | "#default"
  result-prefix = prefix | "#default" />
```

The `stylesheet-prefix` and `result-prefix` attributes specify namespace prefixes that are in scope when the `xsl:namespace-alias` element is encountered. The actual URIs for these prefixes are specified earlier in the stylesheet and must be in scope when the `xsl:namespace` element is encountered. XSLT uses the information in this element to substitute the namespace URI for the prefix specified in `result-prefix` for the namespace URI of the prefix specified in `stylesheet-prefix` in the output document. The final result is that all elements with the prefix specified in `stylesheet-prefix` now point to the namespace URI of the prefix specified in `result-prefix`.

Here's a very basic example that illustrates the use of `xsl:namespace-alias`. Let's say that we're using an XSLT stylesheet to generate another XSLT stylesheet. Our first stylesheet might look like this:

```
<xsl:stylesheet version="1.0"
                xmlns:xsl="http://www.w3.org/1999/XSL/Transform"
                xmlns:doof="http://www.doof.com/ns/" >
<xsl:namespace-alias stylesheet-prefix="doof" result-prefix="xsl" />
<xsl:template match="/" >
   <doof:stylesheet>
      <doof:apply-templates />
   </doof:stylesheet>
</xsl:template>
</xsl:stylesheet>
```

Our stylesheet has one template that, upon encountering the input document's root element, generates a simple XSLT stylesheet. Note that the output stylesheet has the `doof` prefix (instead of the usual `xsl`), and that the `doof` prefix is resolved to its namespace URI by the `xmlns:doof` attribute on the `xsl:stylesheet` element. The `xsl:namespace-alias` element maps this namespace to the namespace URI for the `xsl` prefix, so that when the output is written, the `doof` namespace prefix is mapped to the XSLT namespace URI:

```
<?xml version="1.0" encoding="UTF-8"?>
<doof:stylesheet xmlns:doof="http://www.w3.org/1999/XSL/Transform">
<doof:apply-templates/>
</doof:stylesheet>
```

Note that the doof namespace prefix is now mapped to the XSLT namespace URI. Because it's the namespace URI, not the namespace prefix, which uniquely identifies the namespace as belonging to XSLT, this stylesheet can be successfully executed by an XSLT processor.

The xsl:namespace-alias element also provides a special value, #default, that can be specified for either the stylesheet-prefix or result-prefix attribute. This value indicates that the default namespace URI should be used as either the source (result-prefix) or target (stylesheet-prefix) of the remapping operation.

Copying Nodes and Subtrees

Sometimes, all you need to do in an XSLT stylesheet is copy nodes from the input XML document to the output document, perhaps with some additional tweaks to each node along the way. XSLT provides a nice feature, xsl:copy, that can make this mundane task much easier. The syntax of this element is as follows:

```
<xsl:copy use-attribute-sets = "name1 name2 … name-n">
</xsl:copy>
```

The xsl:copy feature makes a copy of the current node. If the current node has children or attributes (that is, if it's the root node or an element node), these are *not* included in the copy—it's your responsibility to copy those for yourself. This simplicity is the element's strength, however, because it allows you to copy any kind of node—text, processing instructions, comments, attributes, and elements—without necessarily understanding what type of node it is. The use-attribute-sets attribute of xsl:copy allows you to apply attribute sets during the copy operation, providing a space-separated list of attribute sets to be processed just as with the xsl:element element.

To copy a node with no children or attributes, use xsl:copy with no attributes or content. The following example will insert an exact copy of every text, processing instruction, and comment node in the input document into the output document:

```
<xsl:template match="text() | processing-instruction() | comment()" >
  <xsl:copy />
</xsl:template>
```

In this case, there's no need for XSLT elements inside `xsl:copy` because the nodes being processed don't allow children or attributes.

Making an exact copy of a node and its children and attributes, regardless of what mode type it is, is as simple as defining a template that matches on attributes and nodes and then invokes `xsl:copy`:

```
<xsl:template match="@*|node()">
  <xsl:copy>
    <xsl:apply-templates select="@*|node()"/>
  </xsl:copy>
</xsl:template>
```

The `xsl:apply-templates` element inside the `xsl:copy` element ensures that all children and attributes of the current node get copied; this statement, of course, forces the same template to be called again, recursively processing the entire input document. If you want to add attributes or elements to the copied node, simply put the appropriate literals or XSLT elements (`xsl:attribute`, `xsl:apply-templates`, or `xsl:element`) inside the `xsl:copy` element.

Performing Conditional Processing

XSLT's conditional processing elements fill a substantial gap in the XSLT model by allowing some processing decisions to be made inside of templates, instead of having to call other templates to perform processing on a subset of nodes. Although not as powerful as those found in programming languages such as Java, these elements still allow a fair amount of control over template behavior.

Using xsl:for-each to Control Looping

When you want to perform repetitive actions for a known sequence of nodes of the same type, you use the almost self-explanatory element `xsl:for-each`. The syntax of this element is shown here:

```
<!-- Category: instruction -->
<xsl:for-each
  select = node-set-expression>
  <!-- Content: (xsl:sort*, template) -->
</xsl:for-each>
```

To understand how `xsl:for-each` works, let us go back to an excerpt from the stylesheet `auth.xsl` that we first encountered in Chapter 4:

```
<xsl:template match="Name">
  <b>
    <xsl:value-of select="."/>
  </b>
</xsl:template>


<xsl:template match="Address">
  <i>
    <p>
      <xsl:apply-templates/>
    </p>
  </i>
</xsl:template>
```

In this case, we are implicitly looping over all `Name` nodes and inserting the value of the node between `<B></B>` HTML tags. Similarly, the `Address` value for each of the `Author` nodes is formatted using the respective HTML tags.

Since this code processes the `Author` node in a predictable repetitive fashion, we can rewrite it using `xsl:for-each`. Here is the modified version of `auth.xsl` with the new code highlighted in bold letters:

```
<?xml version="1.0"?>

<!-- stylesheet specifications begin -->
<xsl:stylesheet version="1.0"
    xmlns:xsl="http://www.w3.org/1999/XSL/Transform">

  <xsl:template match="/">
    <html>
      <head>
        <title>Information about OMH authors</title>
      </head>
      <body>
        <xsl:apply-templates select="All_authors"/>
      </body>
    </html>
  </xsl:template>
```

```
<xsl:template match="All_authors">
  <xsl:for-each select="Author">
    <b>
      <xsl:value-of select="./Name"/>
    </b>
    <i>
      <p>
        <xsl:value-of select="./Address"/>
      </P>
    </i>
  </xsl:for-each>
</xsl:template>

</xsl:stylesheet>
<!-- stylesheet specifications end -->
```

When viewed in a web browser, the HTML output resulting from this new code appears as shown in Figure 7-2.

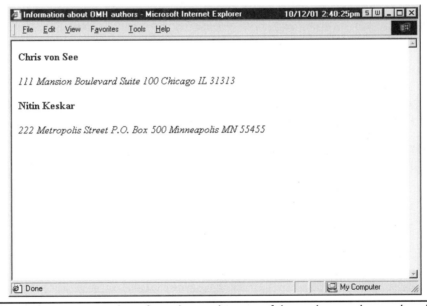

Figure 7-2 *The output resulting from the application of the code sample, rendered in IE5.5*

Using Conditional Logic in XSLT

The simplest form of conditional logic is based on if-then scenarios. In XSLT, this is programmed using the following syntax:

```
<!-- Category: instruction -->
<xsl:if
  test = boolean-expression>
  <!-- Content: template -->
</xsl:if>
```

As you will notice, the form of the `if` instruction is similar to that used in most high-level programming languages. For the `xsl:if` element, `test` is a required attribute that tests whether `boolean-expression` is true or false. Note that in XSLT, any kind of data can be transformed into a Boolean value. This conversion is implicitly performed by the XSLT processor when you use a string, node set, result tree fragment, or number in the expression in coding the `xsl:if` logic.

The content of the `xsl:if` element is a template. This template is instantiated if the result of the Boolean expression evaluation is true, and the output would result according to the instructions contained in this template.

Consider the previous code sample in which we used `xsl:for-each`. Let us say that we want to display a dashed line after the information for each author is output. We can do as follows:

```
<xsl:template match="All_authors">
  <xsl:for-each select="Author">
    <b>
      <xsl:value-of select="./Name"/>
    </b>
    <i>
      <p>
        <xsl:value-of select="./Address"/>
      </p>
    </i>
    <p> -------------------------------- </p>
  </xsl:for-each>
</xsl:template>
```

The HTML output resulting from the application of this code is shown in Figure 7-3. Here we have added a third, fictitious author, John Galt, for the purpose of illustration.

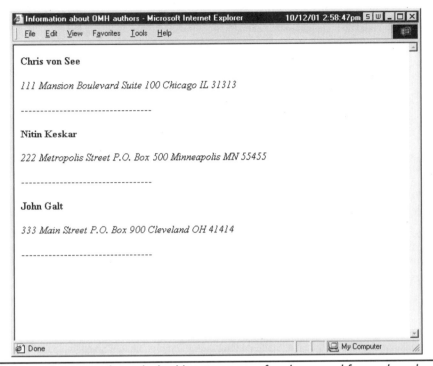

Figure 7-3   *In this example, a dashed line is output after the record for each author is displayed*

Now consider an additional requirement for the output: that of omitting the dashed line after the record for the *last* author is shown. To accomplish this, we can use `xsl:if` as shown in the following code sample:

```
<xsl:if test="not(position()=last())">
  <p> -------------------------------- </p>
</xsl:if>
```

The resulting output is shown in Figure 7-4.

Although the use of `xsl:if` is similar to the use of the `if-then-else` statement found in many programming languages, there is a difference: the XSLT 1.0 specification does not support an `else` or `elseif` clause. Therefore, you can use this element to test for only a single condition at a given time. However, you can use nesting of `xsl:if` elements or multiple clauses in the XPath expression to match on multiple conditions, and the functionality of `else` and `elseif` can be

Figure 7-4   *In this example, the dashed line is output after the record for each author, except for the last one*

achieved using the xsl:choose element described in the next section. An example of the use of nested xsl:if clauses to test for multiple conditions is shown here:

```
<xsl:if test= "@First_name='John'">
  <xsl:if test= "@State='OH'">
    <p style="color: red">
      <xsl:value-of select="."/>
    </p>
  </xsl:if>
</xsl:if>
```

The first xsl:if test determines whether the current element contains a First_name attribute with a value of John, and the second, nested xsl:if test determines whether that same element has a State attribute with a value of OH.

Choosing from Multiple Alternatives

The `xsl:choose` element provides a more generalized, and therefore a more powerful, means of implementing conditional logic. It is reminiscent of the `SWITCH-CASE` statements found in many other programming languages. It uses this syntax:

```
<!-- Category: instruction -->
<xsl:choose>
  <!-- Content: (xsl:when+, xsl:otherwise?) -->
</xsl:choose>
<xsl:when
  test = boolean-expression>
  <!-- Content: template -->
</xsl:when>
<xsl:otherwise>
  <!-- Content: template -->
</xsl:otherwise>
```

To test for the multiple alternatives, a child element, `xsl:when`, is used with each of the alternatives. As in the case of the `xsl:if` element, the content of `xsl:when` and `xsl:otherwise` is also a template. Although `xsl:otherwise` is optional within `xsl:choose`, you will often find it useful to instruct the XSLT processor about the template(s) to be instantiated if all when conditions fail.

When `xsl:choose` is used, the `xsl:when` elements are serially processed, and the content of only the first one that holds true is instantiated, and the rest of the `xsl:when` elements and `xsl:otherwise` element (if present) are ignored. If all when conditions fail, the XSLT processor moves to `xsl:otherwise`, if present, and instantiates its content.

Consider the following example in which we display the output in different colors depending on the version of the XSLT specification that the processor supports:

```
<xsl:template match="Name">
  <b>
    <xsl:choose>

      <xsl:when test="system-property('xsl:version') >= 2.0">
        <p style="color: red">
          <xsl:new-element-in-v2.0/>
        </p>
      </xsl:when>
```

```
      <xsl:when test="system-property('xsl:version') >= 1.1">
        <p style="color: yellow">
          <xsl:new-element-in-v1.1/>
        </p>
      </xsl:when>

      <xsl:otherwise>
        <p style="color: green">
          <xsl:value-of select="."/>
        </p>
      </xsl:otherwise>

    </xsl:choose>
  </b>
</xsl:template>
```

Summary

In this chapter, you learned about XSLT mechanisms that create elements and support controlled looping and conditional processing. You can leverage your prior development experience to draw parallels to the way that these mechanisms are handled in other programming languages. Since XSLT is designed primarily to deal with source XML trees, not every feature that you might expect is supported at the present time. As the language evolves further and the need for more sophisticated processing becomes apparent, more features will likely be added to these mechanisms in future XSLT specifications.

Now that you understand the basic control structures in XSLT, it's time to move on to a discussion of variables and parameter handling, in the next chapter.

Variables and Parameters

IN THIS CHAPTER:

I n this chapter, you will learn about the use of variables and parameters in XSLT. In particular, you will learn about the elements `xsl:variable` and `xsl:param`, each of which may be used to create a name-value pair at one place within a stylesheet and then used elsewhere within it. Although these two elements share a common syntax and appear to have a similar purpose in the XSLT framework, there is, in fact, a difference in the way they work. You will learn about their use through examples. You will also learn about a new data type for variables, the result tree fragment data type. The discussion of global and local variables is deliberately deferred until then. Finally, we will discuss the use of `xsl:param` in stylesheets, and how parameters are passed to templates.

Variables and Parameters Defined

The elements `xsl:variable` and `xsl:param` are used to bind a name to a value. We will refer to them collectively as variables, although the context will clarify which element we are referring to. For each variable, the name-value binding is visible only within a certain context that defines its *scope*, which is discussed later in the chapter. The difference between these two elements is that `xsl:variable` defines a value once, and this value cannot be overridden within the same scope or context, whereas `xsl:parameter` defines merely a default value, which can be overridden by a passed value when the template defining the variable is called with a different value.

Use of variables helps you write better organized and more easily maintainable code, because, once defined, a variable may be referenced elsewhere in the stylesheet, subject to the *scope* constraints on that variable. Thus, the general philosophy underlying the use of variables is similar to that of other programming languages, though the specifics differ. The biggest difference is perhaps that `xsl:variable` is really used to define a constant in XSLT: that is, once a variable is defined, it cannot be overridden within the same scope. By contrast, most programming languages allow you to reassign variable values as many times as you want.

The two elements used to specify variables share a similar syntax as shown here:

```
<xsl:variable
  name = qname
  select = expression>
  <!-- Content: template -->
</xsl:variable>
```

and

```
<xsl:param
  name = qname
  select = expression>
  <!-- Content: template -->
</xsl:param>
```

For both types of variables, `name` is a mandatory attribute. The `select` attribute and the content are optional: in fact, you can either specify the `select` attribute or have content, but not both. Declaration of each variable of either type requires a separate `xsl:variable` or `xsl:parameter` statement. As usual, *expression* is an XPath expression defining the value of the variable.

Consider the following examples of variable definitions. Here is how you can define a variable using the select attribute:

```
<!-- Defining a variable using the select attribute -->
<xsl:variable name="publisher" select="OMH"/>
...
```

Here is how a variable with content may be defined. Of course since the content is specified, we cannot specify the `select` attribute in this instance:

```
...
<xsl:variable name="publisher">
OMH
</xsl:variable>
...
```

The difference in the preceding two definitions will become clear shortly as we discuss the different data types for variables.

A variable may also be defined in terms of another variable, as shown in the following example. Some nuances of such definitions are discussed in "Boolean Variables," later in the chapter.

```
...
<xsl:variable name="omh" select="$omh2"/>
...
<xsl:variable name="omh2" select=" 'Osborne-McGraw Hill' "/>
...
```

The elements `xsl:variable` and `xsl:param` are required to be well formed. When the `select` attribute is used in defining a variable, the element is automatically well formed or self-closing. When the content is specified for either of these elements, the use of an explicit closing element, `</xsl:variable>` or `</xsl:param>`, is mandatory.

Variable Data Types

XSLT supports five data types: the familiar XPath data types number, string, Boolean, node-set, and a new data type called result tree fragment. In order to use the XPath data types, the `select` attribute must be used in defining the variable. Let us look at some examples to see how variables of different types may be defined. Although these examples use the element `xsl:variable`, definitions using xsl:param would look similar.

Number and String Variables

Variables of the number or string data type are defined in a straightforward manner. For most XSLT processors, the following two ways of defining string variables will be synonymous.

```
...
<xsl:variable name="publisher" select="'OMH'"/>
...
<xsl:variable name="publisher" select="OMH"/>
...
```

The first definition uses single quotation marks around the name of the string variable to explicitly indicate that it is a string name, not a node name. A point of confusion may occur if you used the second definition, and your original XML file has a node called OMH. W3C's XSLT specification does not mandate whether or not single quotation marks are to be used; it leaves that choice to the implementor providing the XSLT processor. When in doubt as to what a particular XSLT processor will do in such a situation, you are better off using the first definition because it does not leave anything to chance.

Now consider the following variable definitions:

```
<!-- Defining a variable of the number datatype -->
<xsl:variable name="n_number" select="10"/>
...
```

```
<!-- Defining a variable of the literal string datatype ... -->
<xsl:variable name="n_string" select=" '10' "/>
<!-- ... or a little differently by changing the order of the quotes -->
<xsl:variable name="n_string" select=' "10" '/>
...
```

We deliberately chose an example in which a value—in this case, 10—is assigned to either a number or a string data type of your choice. Note that there is no explicit mention of the type of the variable in XSLT; you must provide enough context to the XSLT processor to make the type unambiguous. Thus, when you use one pair of quotation marks around the value 10, the XSLT processor interprets the variable to be of the number type. When you use the single- and double-quotation marks, as shown in the example, the XSLT processor implicitly assigns the variable to the string data type. When the choice is not clear, the processor will indicate an error, as in the following example:

```
<!-- An erroneous variable definition -->
<xsl:variable name="n_number" select="10_value"/>
...
```

Boolean Variables

Consider the following example, which shows how a Boolean variable may be defined:

```
<!-- Defining a variable with a Boolean datatype: it tests
whether the variables $omh and $omh2 have the same value. In this
case it will happen to get assigned to a "true" value. -->
<xsl:variable name="title_text">
  Information about <xsl:value-of select="$omh"/> authors
</xsl:variable>
...
<xsl:variable name="omh" select="$omh2"/>
...
<xsl:variable name="omh2" select=" 'Osborne-McGraw Hill' "/>
...
<xsl:variable name="myBoolean" select=" $omh = $omh2 "/>
...
```

This example also illustrates the following points:

► Variables may be defined in terms of other variables. Here the definition of title_text is based on that of omh, which, in turn, is based on that of omh2. In defining the variable omh in terms of another variable, omh2, we have used the optional select attribute. This ensures that omh is assigned the same data type as omh2.

▶ As long as all variables are defined within the same context, the order in which they are defined does not matter. For example, title_text is defined in terms of omh, which is defined *after* title_text. This is a powerful feature of XSLT, and it distinguishes XSLT from most other programming languages that you may be familiar with. This feature is a clear manifestation of a key design principle behind XSLT: the final result of the transformations should not depend on the sequence of steps outlined in the stylesheet. For the same reason, the order in which templates are defined does not affect the result tree.

Node-Set Variables

Consider the following example in which a node-set variable, AuthorNameNodeSet, is defined. When the variable is used, the descendant Last_name of the node Name is accessed using the familiar / operator.

```
<xsl:for-each select="Author">
  <xsl:variable name="AuthorNameNodeSet" select="./Name"/>
...
  <P> This author's last name is
    <B>
      <xsl:value-of select="$AuthorNameNodeSet/Last_name"/>
    </B>
  </P>
...
</xsl:for-each>
```

The New Result Tree Fragment Data Type

When content is specified for xsl:variable, the value of the variable is a result tree fragment. This is a new data type in XSLT and is available in addition to other familiar data types discussed previously. When a template is instantiated within the specification of a variable, the result tree fragment consists of a single root node and its descendants that were produced during the process of instantiation. The operations that are valid on a result tree fragment are a subset of that permitted on a node set: in particular, the use of the operators /, //, and [..] is not permitted on a result tree fragment.

If we want to extract a certain portion of a result tree and use it in defining a variable, we can do so using the element xsl:copy-of, as shown here:

```
<xsl:variable name="Author_names">
  <xsl:template match="Author">
    <xsl:copy-of select="Name"/>
    <xsl:apply-templates/>
  </xsl:template>
</xsl:variable>
```

In this case, the data type of the variable Author_names is a result tree fragment. Had we used xsl:value-of in defining the variable, the result would have been implicitly converted to a string data type.

Consider the following simple example, which helps further clarify the definition of a result tree fragment:

```
<xsl:variable name="n">10</xsl:variable>
```

In this case, the variable n is not of the number type since we did not use an expression to define it, so we cannot use it to select a node that is at the tenth position. However, if we use the select attribute, the desired result is obtained by specifying the following:

```
<xsl:variable name="n" select="10"/>
...
<xsl:value-of select="item[$n]"/>
```

Setting Default Values

Consider the following source XML tree in which we have assigned an AuthID attribute for the node Author:

```
<?xml version="1.0"?>

<!-- data specifications begin-->
<All_authors>
  <Author AuthID="77">
  <Name>
    <First_name>Samuel</First_name>
    <Last_name>Clemens</Last_name>
```

```
  </Name>
...
  </Author>
</All_authors>
<!-- data specifications end -->
```

Let us say we want to create a variable `Author_ID` that uses the value of the `AuthID` attribute, if available. If not, we want to set an easily identifiable default value for `Author_ID` that can be used in later processing. If we know that all valid `AuthID` values are positive integers, perhaps we should set the default value of `Author_ID` to a negative number, as shown in the folloing example:

```
<xsl:variable name="Author_ID">
  <xsl:choose>
    <xsl:when test="@AuthID">
      <xsl:value-of select="@AuthID">
    </xsl:when>
    <xsl:otherwise>
      -1
    </xsl:otherwise>
  </xsl:choose>
</xsl:variable>
```

Note that we have specified content in defining this variable `Author_ID`. Therefore it will be of the type result tree fragment.

In procedural programming languages such logic could also be implemented using the following pseudo-code, in which we first set the default value, and then override it if `AuthID` is a positive number:

```
Author_ID=-1
If (AuthID >0 ) Author_ID=AuthID
```

As we have seen before, the value of a variable defined using `xsl:variable` cannot be changed once it is set. Therefore, there is no analog of the preceding logic in XSLT programming. However, `xsl:parameter` works differently in that you set a default value first, which is overridden when you call a template containing a value. We will see this in more detail in "Use of `xsl:param`," later in the chapter.

Global and Local Variables

Variables may be defined at either the top level or within a template. Where the variable is defined determines the context, or scope, within which the name-value binding is applicable. For example, if you define the same variable at multiple places within a stylesheet, only the innermost definition will apply when you reference the variable. In other words, if you were to define the same variable at the top level and, again, within a template, the second definition will apply if you used the variable within that template. XSLT allows only one definition of a variable within any given context. Hence, if you attempt to redefine a variable while a previous definition applies within the immediate context, you will trigger an error.

Variables defined at the top level are accessible anywhere within the stylesheet and are considered *global* variables. By contrast, variables defined within a template have a limited scope within that template and are called *local* variables.

If a stylesheet has more than one definition of a top-level, or global, variable with the same name and import precedence, the XSLT processor will report an error since there is no way to resolve the definitions unambiguously. If a top-level variable is redefined within a template, that is, locally, the local definition will override the global definition within the template. In this case, we say that the local binding *shadows* the global binding.

It is legal to have multiple definitions of local variables, as long as no more than one definition occurs within any given template. In this case, the definition closest to the point of use will override all other definitions. For a variable defined inside a template, the binding is visible to all descendants of that template.

Within a given template, a local variable, defined using either `xsl:variable` or `xsl:param`, is not permitted to shadow another variable with the same name. Thus, the following will lead to a syntax error:

```
<xsl:template match="All_authors">
  <xsl:variable name="omh">
    Osborne-McGraw Hill Corporation __local_definition_1
  </xsl:variable>

  <xsl:param name="omh">
    Osborne-McGraw Hill Corporation __local_definition_1
  </xsl:param>
```

```
<P>
   The following authors are working together with
   <xsl:value-of select="$omh"/> on this project:
</P>
...
</xsl:template>
```

Use of xsl:variable at the Global and Local Levels

If you plan to use the string "Osborne-McGraw Hill" at multiple places within a stylesheet, you can define it as follows:

```
<!-- stylesheet specifications begin -->
<xsl:stylesheet version="1.0"
     xmlns:xsl="http://www.w3.org/1999/XSL/Transform">

<xsl:variable name="omh">
  Osborne-McGraw Hill
</xsl:variable>

    <xsl:template match="/">
...
```

In this case, `xsl:variable` is used as a top-level element. Thus defined, the variable becomes a global variable. To refer to the variable `omh` within a template, you would prefix it with the symbol $, as shown here:

```
...
    <xsl:template match="All_authors">
      <P>
        The following authors are working together with
        <xsl:value-of select="$omh"/> on this project:
      </P>
      <xsl:for-each select="Author">
<!-- rest of the template content to follow -->
...
      </xsl:for-each>
    </xsl:template>
...
```

Although the variable omh is already defined at the top level, it is legal to redefine it within a template, as shown next:

```
...
    <xsl:template match="All_authors">
      <xsl:variable name="omh">
        Osborne-McGraw Hill Corporation
      </xsl:variable>
      <P>
        The following authors are working together with
        <xsl:value-of select="$omh"/> on this project:
...
```

The second definition is for a local variable with the same name as the global variable, and it overrides the previous one within the scope of the template All_authors, although this does not mean that the value of the variable has been overwritten for good. Thus, if the variable were to be referred to again at the top level, the original definition will apply. The following example, showing the complete stylesheet, clarifies this point further:

```
<?xml version="1.0"?>
<!-- stylesheet specifications begin -->
<xsl:stylesheet version="1.0"
    xmlns:xsl="http://www.w3.org/1999/XSL/Transform">
<xsl:variable name="omh">
  Osborne-McGraw Hill
</xsl:variable>
    <xsl:template match="/">
      <html>
        <head>
          <title>Information about OMH authors </title>
        </head>
        <body>
          <xsl:apply-templates select="All_authors"/>
          <P>
            End of the information about the
            <xsl:value-of select="$omh"/> authors
          </P>
```

```
      </body>
     </html>
   </xsl:template>

   <xsl:template match="All_authors">
     <xsl:variable name="omh">
       Osborne-McGraw Hill Corporation
     </xsl:variable>
     <P>
       The following authors are working together with
       <xsl:value-of select="$omh"/> on this project:
     </P>
     <xsl:for-each select="Author">
<!-- rest of the template content to follow -->
       <B>
         <xsl:value-of select="./Name"/>
       </B>
       <I>
         <P>
           <xsl:value-of select="./Address"/>
         </P>
       </I>
       <xsl:if test="not(position()=last())">
         <P> -------------------------------- </P>
       </xsl:if>
     </xsl:for-each>
   </xsl:template>
</xsl:stylesheet>
<!-- stylesheet specifications end -->
```

Figure 8-1 shows the output from this example.

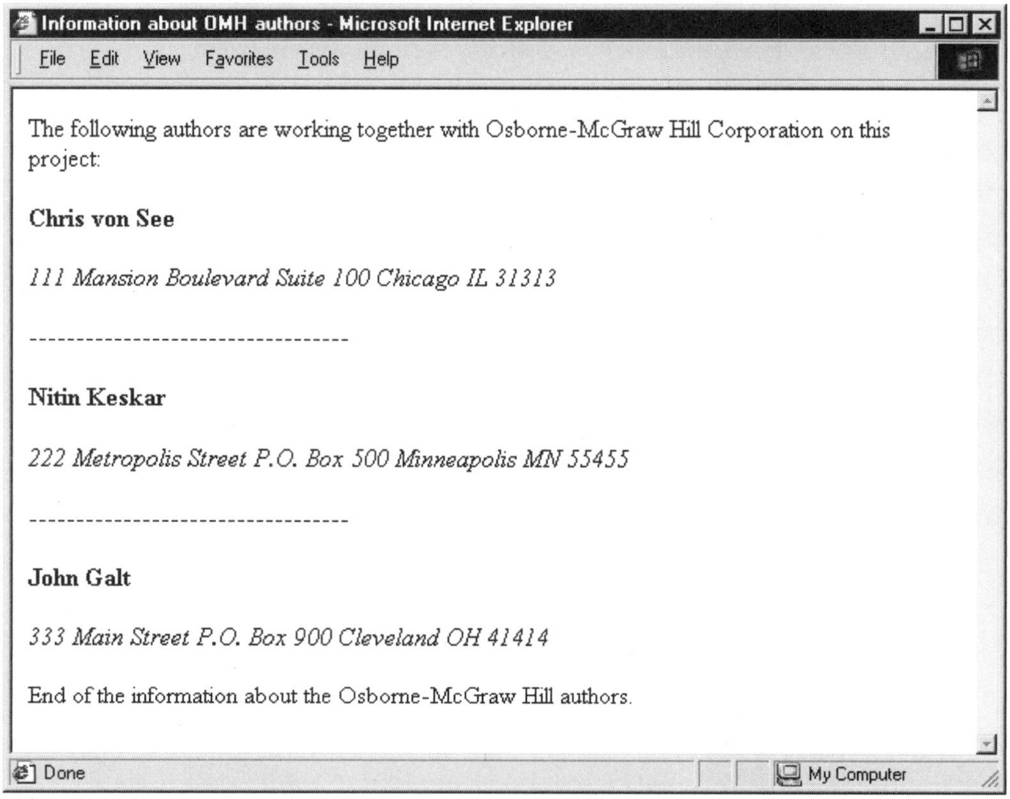

Figure 8-1   *The output* `auth.htm` *resulting from the application of* `auth.xsl` *to* `auth.xml`, *rendered in IE 5.5*

A variable can refer to another variable, or even to XSLT instructions, as shown in the following example:

```
<?xml version="1.0"?>

<!-- stylesheet specifications begin -->
```

```
<xsl:stylesheet version="1.0"
    xmlns:xsl="http://www.w3.org/1999/XSL/Transform">

<xsl:variable name="omh">
  Osborne-McGraw Hill
</xsl:variable>

<xsl:variable name="title_text">
  Information about <xsl:value-of select="$omh"/> authors
</xsl:variable>

    <xsl:template match="/">
      <html>
        <head>
          <title>
            <xsl:value-of select="$title_text"/>
          </title>
...
```

A variable can refer to another variable, provided that the referenced variable has also been declared in the stylesheet. In the following example, notice that $omh refers to $omh2, which is defined later in the stylesheet. This is valid since the XSLT processor is able to resolve all variable references unambiguously.

```
...
<xsl:variable name="omh">
  <xsl:value-of select="$omh2"/>
</xsl:variable>

<xsl:variable name="omh2">
  Osborne-McGraw Hill
</xsl:variable>

<xsl:variable name="title_text">
  Information about <xsl:value-of select="$omh"/> authors
</xsl:variable>
...
```

However, XSLT does not allow circular references, either direct or indirect. Thus, the following definition will cause the XSLT processor to report an error:

```
<xsl:variable name="title_text">
  Information about <xsl:value-of select="$title_text"/> authors
</xsl:variable>
```

The following example will also lead to an error, since $omh and $title_text refer to each other:

```
...
<xsl:variable name="omh">
  Osborne-McGraw Hill <xsl:value-of select="$title_text"/>
</xsl:variable>
...
<xsl:variable name="title_text">
  Information about <xsl:value-of select="$omh"/> authors
</xsl:variable>
...
```

Use of xsl:param

So far, we have explored examples of the use of the element xsl:variable. Although xsl:param shares a similar syntax, it is used to specify the default value of a parameter for the *module* (either a stylesheet or a template), which will be replaced when a calling template passes in another value for the parameter.

Chapter 6 discussed the use of named templates and how they can be called from other templates. The following example was presented there:

```
...
<xsl:template match="Name" mode="red" name="red-template-for-Author-Name">
<DIV style="color:red">
<xsl:value-of select="."/>
</DIV>
</xsl:template>
```

```
<xsl:template match="Name" mode="blue" name="blue-template-for-Author-Name">
<DIV style="color:blue">
<xsl:value-of select="."/>
</DIV>
</xsl:template>
...
```

Depending on the color that you want for the author name, you would write the following type of code to invoke one of these templates:

```
...
<xsl:template match="Name">
<xsl:call-template name="red-template-for-Author-Name"/>
</xsl:template>
...
```

Now let us explore the use of xsl:param by examining the following example. In this case, the code creates a named template in which the variable color becomes a parameter:

```
...
<xsl:template match="Name" mode="chosenColor"
name="color-template-for-Author-Name">
  <xsl:param name="chosen_color">
    black
  </xsl:param>
  <DIV style="color:{$chosen_color}">
    <xsl:value-of select="."/>
  </DIV>
</xsl:template>
...
```

This example sets the default value black for the parameter chosen_color. However, we could invoke this template with any desired value of chosen_color, by using xsl:call-template, discussed in Chapter 6. The difference is that here we will do so using the element xsl:with-param, which has this syntax:

```
<xsl:with-param
  name = qname
  select = expression>
```

```
  <!-- Content: template -->
</xsl:with-param>
```

The following example shows how the named template that we just defined can be invoked using the `xsl:with-param` element:

```
<xsl:template match="Name">
  <xsl:call-template name="color-template-for-Author-Name">
    <xsl:with-param name="chosen_color">
      red
    </xsl:with-param>
  </xsl:call-template>
</xsl:template>
```

Instead of using `xsl:call-template`, we could use `xsl:apply-templates` to get exactly the same effect:

```
<xsl:template match="Name">
  <xsl:apply-templates select="." mode="chosenColor">
    <xsl:with-param name="chosen_color">
      red
    </xsl:with-param>
    <xsl:with-param name="does_not_exist">
      fictitious
    </xsl:with-param>
  </xsl:apply-templates>
</xsl:template>
```

To illustrate another point, this example adds a twist to the previous example. In this case, the example sets another parameter, `does_not_exist`, to the value `fictitious`. Of course, the called template does not use this parameter. However, the XSLT processor simply ignores such a parameter and does not generate an error.

Another important point is that you can define a template with as many parameters as you like. In some places, you may want to invoke the template using some of the parameters, and in another case you may want to specify all of the parameters. Remember that the original template has default values for all parameters, so the XSLT processor will process your request regardless of whether you specify none, some, or all of the parameters.

Summary

This chapter discussed variables and parameters and the similarity between them and the differences in their uses. It gave several examples of the familiar XPath data types—number, string, Boolean, and node-set. It also discussed how a result tree fragment can be treated as a data type to create a binding with a variable or a parameter. Finally it discussed scope of variables, and how global and local variables work in XSLT.

The discussion so far has emphasized the basics of XSLT programming. The next chapter brings together several of the concepts we have explored and expands the focus to XSLT power programming.

Creating Stylesheet Output

IN THIS CHAPTER:

Numbering Output

Introducing xsl:output

Generating Informative or Exception
Output with xsl:message

Summary

I f you've worked through the entire book up to this point, you've mastered the most useful and powerful tools that XSLT can provide, and in the examples you've seen how output—usually XML—is generated. Now it's time to learn the finer points of output generation. In this chapter, you will learn how to use `xsl:output` to create more complex XML, HTML, or text that incorporates complex numbering schemes and allows you to change the character encoding, specify your own DTD in the output, and manipulate the way in which the output is written. In particular, you will learn how to number sections of output automatically, using various numbering styles and multiple levels, and how to use `xsl:message` to generate messages during stylesheet processing.

Numbering Output

Numbering is one of those mundane little tasks that always seem to pop up in web- and text-based projects. Although simple numbering (such as the incremental numbering provided by HTML's `<ol>` and `<li>` tags) can be accomplished quite readily, more complex tasks such as outline numbering and range-limited numbering can be difficult to accomplish automatically (and can be almost impossible to maintain manually). XSLT's answer to the numbering problem is `xsl:number`, a handy tool that provides the ability to generate formatted numbers automatically from a literal value, from the contents of the input document, or from a count of specific node types. The real power of `xsl:number` lies in the fact that you can generate numbers of almost any type and almost any format and put them anywhere you need them. As with many other XSLT elements, most of `xsl:number`'s flexibility comes from its ability to accept XPath expressions—in this case, XPath is used both to express counting criteria and to indicate the point from which counting is to begin.

The syntax for `xsl:number` is as follows:

```
<xsl:number
  level = "single" | "multiple" | "any"
  count = pattern
  from = pattern
  value = number-expression
  format = { string }
  lang = { nmtoken }
  letter-value = { "alphabetic" | "traditional" }
  grouping-separator = { char }
  grouping-size = { number } />
```

The attributes of xsl:number you'll use most are the level, count, from, value, and format attributes. In the examples that follow, we'll explore these in detail; explanations of the remaining attributes can be found at the end of this section.

To illustrate the capabilities of xsl:number, we're going to use an XML file called MyList.xml that contains a series of nested ListItem elements. Each ListItem element has an ItemName element that names the item. The source code for MyList.xml is as follows:

```
<?xml version="1.0" ?>
<MyList>
<ListItem>
    <ItemName>Item 1</ItemName>
</ListItem>
<ListItem>
    <ItemName>Item 2</ItemName>
    <ListItem>
        <ItemName>Item 2-1</ItemName>
    </ListItem>
    <ListItem>
        <ItemName>Item 2-2</ItemName>
    </ListItem>
</ListItem>
<ListItem>
    <ItemName>Item 3</ItemName>
    <ListItem>
        <ItemName>Item 3-1</ItemName>
        <ListItem>
            <ItemName>Item 3-1-1</ItemName>
        </ListItem>
    </ListItem>
    <ListItem>
        <ItemName>Item 3-2</ItemName>
        <ListItem>
            <ItemName>Item 3-2-1</ItemName>
        </ListItem>
        <ListItem>
            <ItemName>Item 3-2-2</ItemName>
        </ListItem>
        <ListItem>
            <ItemName>Item 3-2-3</ItemName>
        </ListItem>
```

```
        </ListItem>
    </ListItem>
</MyList>
```

Numbering Items in the Result Tree

We'll start with an example of the simplest way to use xsl:number. Suppose we want to number only the top-level items in a document. The stylesheet that follows and the sample output (see Figure 9-1) show one method for doing this.

```
<xsl:stylesheet version="1.0"
                xmlns:xsl="http://www.w3.org/1999/XSL/Transform" >
<!-- -->
<xsl:template match="/">
    <html>
    <head>
        <title>Example of item sequencing using &lt;xsl:number&gt;</title>
    </head>
    <body>
    <xsl:apply-templates />
    </body>
    </html>
</xsl:template>
<!-- -->
<xsl:template match="ListItem" >
    <p>
    <xsl:number /><xsl:text>. </xsl:text><xsl:value-of select="ItemName" />
    </p>
</xsl:template>
<!-- -->
</xsl:stylesheet>
```

By default, xsl:number counts all of the nodes encountered that are at the same level in the hierarchy and are of the same type as the current node. In the previous example, xsl:number counts all of the ListItem nodes at the topmost level in the document hierarchy; it doesn't count the ListItem nodes farther down in the tree because the template doesn't contain an xsl:apply-templates element (which precludes it from processing children of any ListItem element it finds). Note that in this example, xsl:number generates the number at the beginning of each line, but the period and space after the number are generated by the xsl:text element immediately after the xsl:number element.

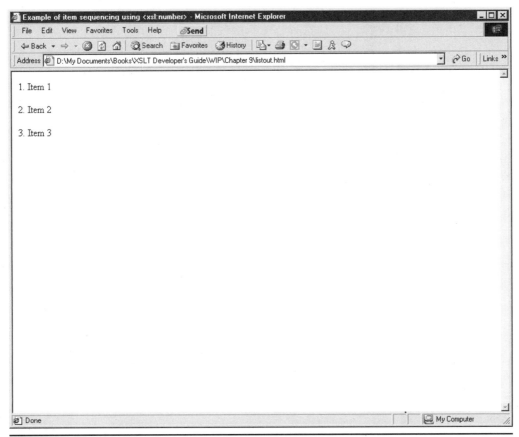

Figure 9-1   *Sequencing of items using `xsl:number`*

You can use the `level` attribute to determine how `xsl:number` groups nodes to count. When `level="single"` is specified or defaulted, nodes at the same level and under the same parent as the current node will be grouped and counted together. Let's modify the template that matches `ListItem` elements on our sample stylesheet to illustrate this point:

```
<xsl:template match="ListItem" >
   <p>
   <xsl:number level="single" /><xsl:text>. </xsl:text><xsl:value-of
             select="ItemName" >
   </p>
   <xsl:apply-templates select="ListItem" />
</xsl:template>
```

There are two changes to note in this template. First, we've added `xsl:apply-templates select="ListItem" /` to allow the template to process all `ListItem` elements (instead of just the first-level elements), and we've specified the `level="single"` attribute on `xsl:number`. Executing this stylesheet generates the result shown in Figure 9-2.

If you look closely at the output, you'll notice that each group of `ListItem` elements that are at the same level and that share a common parent are numbered together. For example, all the `ListItem` elements at the first level of the document hierarchy (and that share the root node as a common parent) are numbered together, all the `ListItem` elements at the second level of the document hierarchy and that share a common parent are numbered together, and so on. As the `ListItem` template executed, it looked at the level of the current node and current parent and

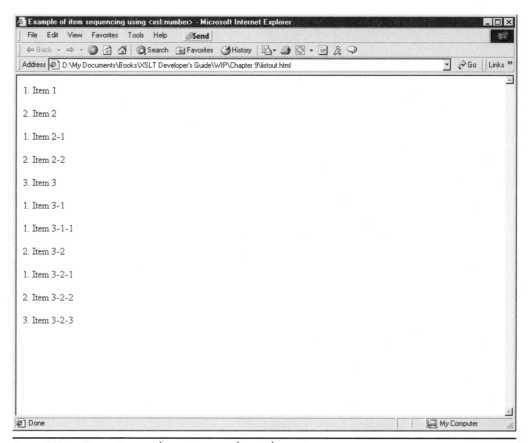

Figure 9-2   *Grouping and counting nodes with* `xsl:number level="single" /`

determined how many other nodes of the same type there were at that level and under the same parent and then sequenced them accordingly.

Now let's change the template to specify `level="multiple"` and see what happens. The updated template is shown here; its output appears in Figure 9-3.

```
<xsl:template match="ListItem" >
    <p>
    <xsl:number level="multiple" /><xsl:text>. </xsl:text><xsl:value-of
                select="ItemName" />
    </p>
    <xsl:apply-templates select="ListItem" />
</xsl:template>
```

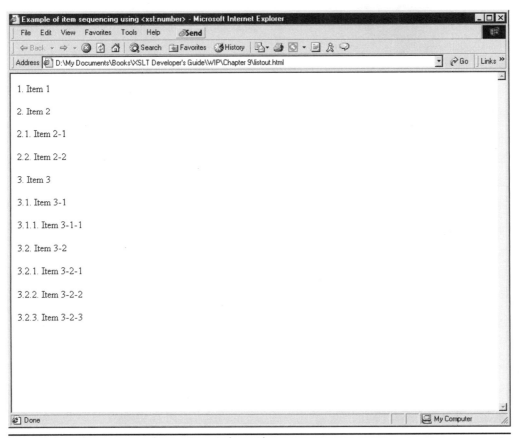

Figure 9-3   Grouping and counting nodes with `xsl:number level="multiple" /`

Now we end up with more of an outline format. In this case, xsl:number has numbered nodes to indicate their relative order in the hierarchy, with nodes at the top of the hierarchy numbered with single-level numbers, and children (or grandchildren) of those nodes numbered with multilevel numbers. The benefit of using level="multiple" is that it uniquely numbers each node selected by the template while still preserving the relative order in the hierarchy.

Like level="multiple", the level="any" attribute uniquely numbers each element selected. Instead of using a numbering scheme that indicates relative position in the hierarchy, however, level="any" numbers all nodes using a single ascending sequence, as shown in the results in Figure 9-4.

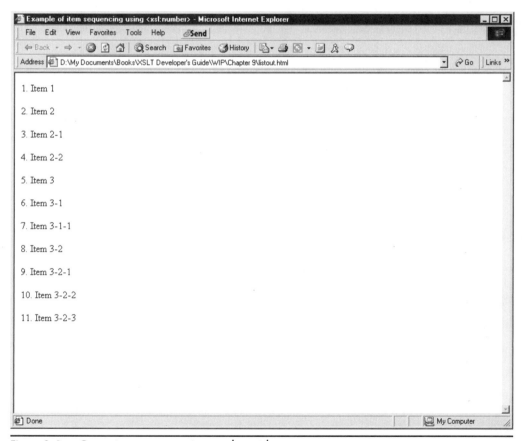

Figure 9-4   *Grouping ans counting nodes with* xsl:number level="any" /

```
<xsl:template match="ListItem" >
   <p>
   <xsl:number level="any" /><xsl:text>. </xsl:text><xsl:value-of
            select="ItemName" />
   </p>
   <xsl:apply-templates select="ListItem" />
</xsl:template>
```

Now the ListItem nodes are numbered without regard to their position in
the hierarchy.

In the preceding examples, we counted nodes of the same type as those selected
by the template in which xsl:number appears. But what if we want to count
something else? We can do that easily using the count attribute, which allows us
to specify an XPath expression that selects the nodes to be counted. To see this,
we'll examine an XML document that simulates the outline of a book, with parts,
units, chapters, and sections nested as shown here:

```
<?xml version="1.0" ?>
<Outline>
<Part title="Part 1">
   <Unit title="Unit 1">
      <Chapter title="Chapter 1">
         <Section title="Section 1">Chapter 1, Section 1</Section>
         <Section title="Section 2">Chapter 1, Section 2</Section>
         <Section title="Section 3">Chapter 1, Section 3</Section>
      </Chapter>
      <Chapter title="Chapter 2">
         <Section title="Section 1">Chapter 2, Section 1</Section>
         <Section title="Section 2">Chapter 2, Section 2</Section>
         <Section title="Section 3">Chapter 2, Section 3</Section>
      </Chapter>
   </Unit>
</Part>
</Outline>
```

Now suppose that we want to number each section to show the part, unit, and
chapter it belongs to, as well as its relative number within each chapter. Using
the count attribute, we can tell xsl:number which node types to count to get
this result:

```
<xsl:template match="Section" >
   <p>
```

```
<xsl:number level="multiple"
            count="Part|Unit|Chapter|Section" />
<xsl:text>. </xsl:text><xsl:value-of select="." />
</p>
</xsl:template>
```

In this template, we've selected each Section element and instructed xsl:number to generate a number based on the count of Part, Unit, Chapter, and Section nodes it finds. The level="multiple" attribute tells xsl:number to search all levels of the document hierarchy prior to the current node and to generate the multilevel numbering scheme we want.

As you can see in the output shown in Figure 9-5, the resulting numbers contain four nodes: one for the part number, one for the unit number, one for the chapter number, and one for the section number. If we had specified level="single" (or allowed it to default), each set of Section elements under a given Chapter parent would have been numbered separately (that is, Chapter 1's sections would have been numbered 1 through 3, and Chapter 2's sections would also have been numbered 1 through 3).

Even more control over the generated number is provided by the xsl:number from attribute, which indicates where in the document hierarchy counting is to start. Like the count attribute, the from attribute specifies an XPath expression; the count includes only those nodes in the node set returned by the count attribute's XPath expression that fall after the point in the document hierarchy specified by the from attribute's XPath expression.

In the previous example, we can indicate that counting is to start with the Unit element rather than the Part element by modifying the xsl:number element in our stylesheet template to use a from attribute:

```
<xsl:template match="Section" >
   <p>
   <xsl:number level="multiple" count="Part|Unit|Chapter|Section"
               from="Part" />
   <xsl:text>. </xsl:text>
   <xsl:value-of select="." />
   </p>
</xsl:template>
```

By specifying from="Part", we've indicated to XSLT that the nodes to be counted (as specified in the count attribute) should fall after—but *not* include—the Part elements in the document hierarchy. In this particular case, we could have

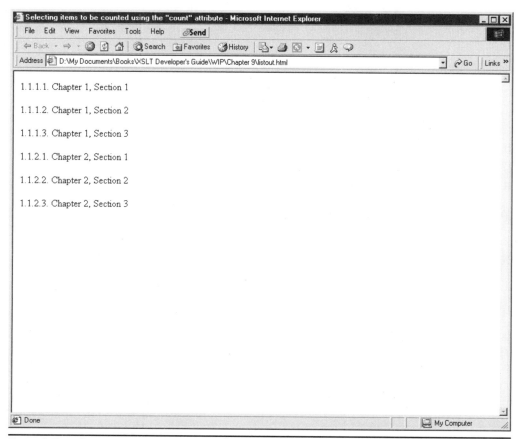

Figure 9-5   *Generating sequence number using the* `xsl:number` `element` `count`
attribute

achieved the same result by removing the `Part` element from the `count` XPath
expression, but that's not always an option. If our document had included elements
specified in the `count` expression both before and after the point at which we
wanted to start counting, for example, the only way to achieve the desired result
would be to use `from`.

Often, you'll want either to use numbers that are provided in the input document
or to hard-code numbers to be formatted by `xsl:number`. The `value` attribute
allows you to explicitly specify (or extract from the input document) the value you
want `xsl:number` to generate. As with the `count` and `from` attributes, `value`
accepts an XPath expression, which is used to retrieve the value to be displayed; this
is similar to the approach used by `xsl:value-of`.

If we want to format hard-coded numbers using roman numerals (I for the number 1, II for the number 2, and so on), we can use the approach illustrated next:

```
<xsl:template match="/">
The string &quot;<xsl:number value="2001" format="I" />&quot; is
 &quot;2001&quot; expressed as a roman numeral.
</xsl:template>
```

In this example, the hard-coded number 2001 is formatted by xsl:number using the roman numeral format (more on the format attribute in the next section). The resulting string gives the correct roman numeral:

```
The string "MMI" is "2001" expressed as a roman numeral.
```

Number Formatting

The xsl:number element provides comprehensive number formatting capabilities that allow you to format values not only as numbers, but as Latin and non-Latin alphabetic characters, roman numerals, mixed numeric and alphabetic values, and multilevel (outline) values. As powerful as they are, these capabilities are extremely easy and intuitive to use.

Number formatting is accomplished by providing xsl:number with a template of the format you want. To get a feel for how these formatting capabilities work, take a look at this stylesheet:

```
<xsl:stylesheet version="1.0"
                xmlns:xsl="http://www.w3.org/1999/XSL/Transform" >
<!-- -->
<xsl:template match="/">
   <html>
   <head><title>Demonstrating number formatting using the
 &quot;format&quot; attribute</title></head>
   <body>
   <xsl:apply-templates />
   </body>
   </html>
</xsl:template>
<!-- -->
<xsl:template match="Part" >
   <p>
   <xsl:number level="multiple" format="A. " />
```

```
        <xsl:value-of select="@title" />
        </p>
        <xsl:apply-templates />
</xsl:template>
<!-- -->
<xsl:template match="Unit" >
        <p>
        <xsl:number level="multiple" format="1. " />
        <xsl:value-of select="@title" />
        </p>
        <xsl:apply-templates />
</xsl:template>
<!-- -->
<xsl:template match="Chapter" >
        <p>
        <xsl:number level="multiple" format="I. " />
        <xsl:value-of select="@title" />
        </p>
        <xsl:apply-templates />
</xsl:template>
<!-- -->
<xsl:template match="Section" >
        <p>
        <xsl:number level="multiple" format="#1. " />
        <xsl:value-of select="." />
        </p>
</xsl:template>
<!-- -->
</xsl:stylesheet>
```

This stylesheet illustrates four of the options for formatting numbers. In the template that selects Part elements, each title is prefixed with a letter value; the first part will be prefixed with A., the second with B., and so on. The template that selects Unit elements prefixes each title with a numeric value, giving the first unit a 1., the second a 2., and so on. The Chapter element titles are given roman numeral prefixes, and the Section elements are given a numeric prefix that starts with a # character. Processing the sample book outline document using this stylesheet generates the output shown in Figure 9-6.

Table 9-1 provides examples of the various format template options for xsl:number.

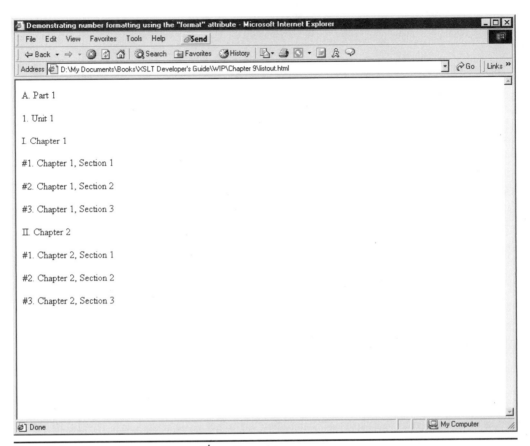

Figure 9-6   *Formatting options with* `xsl:number`

The `lang`, `letter-value`, `grouping-separator`, and `grouping-size` attributes of `xsl:number` refine the use of number format templates. The `lang` attribute allows you to specify the language to be used when formatting numbers as alphabetic values. The `letter-value` attribute allows you to specify the numbering system to be used for languages that support more than one system.

The `grouping-separator` and `grouping-size` attributes work together to allow separation of decimal sequences into groups. For example, if you've specified a format that can generate numbers in the thousands, you may want to split the numbers into multiple three-digit groups (for example, 1,000); by specifying `grouping-separator=","` and `grouping-size="3"`, you can accomplish this quite easily.

If the Format Template Is ...	Your Numbers Will Be Formatted as ...
A	A sequence of ascending capital letters (A, B, C, ..., Z, AA, BB, and so on).
a	A sequence of ascending lowercase letters (a, b, c, ..., z, aa, bb, and so on).
1	A sequence of ascending numeric values (1, 2, 3, ...).
I	A sequence of ascending capital roman numeral values (I, II, III, IV, ...).
I	A sequence of ascending lowercase roman numeral values (i, ii, iii, iv, ...).
Any of the entries in this table, prefixed with a nonalphanumeric character	A sequence as described in this table, with each number or letter in the sequence preceded by the specified nonalphanumeric character. For example, a format of #1 will generate a sequence of #1, #2, #3, and so on.

Table 9-1   *Format Template Options for* `xsl:number`

Introducing xsl:output

Interestingly, the XSLT specification does not require that an XSLT processor be capable of doing anything more than transforming an input document hierarchy into a result tree. While this is fine if you're planning to call XSLT programmatically to transform documents for internal processing, it's bad news indeed if you're trying to actually use the transformed document externally (as HTML to send to a browser, for example). Fortunately, the specification does strongly recommend that conformant processors provide some mechanism for externalizing the result tree, and it even provides a special element to allow users control over what gets generated. This special element is called `xsl:output`, and it provides several parameters that facilitate generation of XML, HTML, and text from the contents of the result tree.

When specified, `xsl:output` must be a top-level element (that is, it should appear prior to any templates in the stylesheet). The default output method when `xsl:output` is not specified depends on the content of the result tree. Essentially, if the root node of the result tree has an element child whose (unqualified) element name is `html`, and if all text nodes that are children of the root node contain only whitespace, then the default method is HTML; otherwise, the default output method is XML. The fact that a given output method was specified or defaulted to doesn't mean, however, that your stylesheet doesn't need to generate appropriate elements (`<p>` for HTML, for example); it simply means that the rules that govern the writing of documents of a particular type are set for that particular output method. For example, if your output method is xml, then the XSLT processor can generate an ?xml? element at the top; if your output method is html, then the processor will ensure that empty tags are handled according to the rules for HTML.

The parameters for xsl:output are shown next. Because their use and meaning varies depending on the type of output desired, the parameters relevant to each output method are covered in more detail in the sections that follow.

```
<xsl:output
  method = "xml" | "html" | "text"
  version = nmtoken
  encoding = string
  omit-xml-declaration = "yes" | "no"
  standalone = "yes" | "no"
  doctype-public = string
  doctype-system = string
  cdata-section-elements = qnames
  indent = "yes" | "no"
  media-type = string />
```

The sections that follow discuss how to generate output using each of the three output methods; they also discuss the parameters of xsl:output that are appropriate for each type of output.

Writing XML Output

It's possible to generate two different types of XML output using a conformant XSLT processor: a complete, well-formed, and valid XML document and an XML fragment suitable for use as an external parsed entity. Let's start by taking a look at the process for generating a complete XML document.

As you know, XML documents have certain structural characteristics that distinguish them from XML fragments:

▶ XML documents start with an ?xml? prolog, providing (at least) the XML version in use.

▶ XML documents can have an optional Document Type Definition (DTD), which is composed of an external subset (a pointer to a set of XML structural definitions in another file) or an internal subset (XML structural definitions embedded in the document), or both.

▶ XML documents have a single element, the root element, which contains all
    other elements in the document. This element name is the same as the name in
    the document type declaration.

Because parsed entities are meant to be included in other XML documents, they
do not contain an XML prolog or document type declaration and can contain many
elements at the highest level of the entity without a single enclosing element.

All of the attributes of the `xsl:output` element are useful when creating XML
documents:

▶ The `version` attribute specifies the version of the XML specification that
    applies to this document. The default is `version="1.0"`, which is the
    current base version of the XML standard.

▶ The `encoding` attribute allows the stylesheet designer to specify the character
    encoding of the output document. XSLT processors are required to support at
    least the UTF-8 and UTF-16 encodings; other encoding schemes registered
    with the Internet Assigned Numbers Authority (IANA) may also be specified.
    Depending on which encoding is used, the XSLT processor may either produce
    an error, if an encoding it doesn't support is specified, or silently produce either
    UTF-8 or UTF-16. In practice, if no encoding is specified, XSLT processors
    usually default to UTF-8.

▶ By default, XSLT processors behave as if the `omit-xml-declaration`
    attribute were set to `no`, indicating that the processor should generate an `?xml?`
    prolog. If you're generating an XML parsed entity or have some other reason you
    don't want this prolog, specify `omit-xml-declaration="yes"`.

▶ The `doctype-system` attribute allows the stylesheet designer to include
    a system DTD identifier in the output XML document. This attribute works
    in conjunction with the `doctype-public` attribute to create a public
    DTD identifier.

▶ The `standalone` attribute specifies whether the output XML document
    is stand-alone (that is, whether it has an external DTD subset). The valid
    values for this attribute are `yes` and `no`; the correct specification depends on
    whether you ask the XSLT processor to include a `!DOCTYPE` element using
    the `doctype-system` and `doctype-public` attributes of `xsl:output`.

▶ The `cdata-section-elements` attribute specifies a whitespace-separated
    list of names of elements in the result tree whose text children are to be written

as XML CDATA sections. Elements named in this list will have their content converted into a CDATA section before being written as output.

▶ The `indent` attribute indicates whether the XSLT processor may indent elements in the output by adding whitespace to make the output more readable. The valid values for this attribute are `"yes"` and no. Note that using indention when the document contains elements using a mixed-content model may provide undesirable results, as the whitespace added may be interpreted as part of element content by other programs reading the document.

▶ The `media-type` attribute specifies the MIME type of the data to be written as output by the XSLT processor. Because XML specifies character encoding information using the `encoding` attribute of the `?xml?` prolog, the charset parameter should not be specified. The default is `media-type="text/xml"`.

Using a modified version of the example stylesheet, we can generate a well-formed XML document fairly easily. First, here's the modified stylesheet, showing updates to create the XML root element and restructure the output as an XML document:

```
<xsl:stylesheet version="1.0"
                xmlns:xsl="http://www.w3.org/1999/XSL/Transform" >
<!-- -->
<xsl:output method="xml" />
<!-- -->
<xsl:template match="/">
<myDoc>
<xsl:apply-templates />
</myDoc>
</xsl:template>
<!-- -->
<xsl:template match="Part" >
<myPart>
<partNumber><xsl:number level="multiple" format="A. " /></partNumber>
<partName><xsl:value-of select="@title" /></partName>
<xsl:apply-templates />
</myPart>
</xsl:template>
<!-- -->
<xsl:template match="Unit" >
<myUnit>
<unitNumber><xsl:number level="multiple" format="1. " /></unitNumber>
<unitName><xsl:value-of select="@title" /></unitName>
```

```
<xsl:apply-templates />
</myUnit>
</xsl:template>
<!-- -->
<xsl:template match="Chapter" >
<myChapter>
<chapterNumber><xsl:number level="multiple" format="I. " /></chapterNumber>
<chapterName><xsl:value-of select="@title" /></chapterName>
<xsl:apply-templates />
</myChapter>
</xsl:template>
<!-- -->
<xsl:template match="Section" >
<mySection>
<sectionNumber><xsl:number level="multiple" format="# 1. " ></sectionNumber>
<sectionName><xsl:value-of select="." /></sectionName>
</mySection>
</xsl:template>
<!-- -->
</xsl:stylesheet>
```

Note that we haven't specified any attributes on the `xsl:output` element at the top of the stylesheet. Running this stylesheet against our sample document produces the following output (which I've rearranged slightly to make it more readable):

```
<?xml version="1.0" encoding="UTF-8"?>
<myDoc>
   <myPart>
      <partNumber>A. </partNumber>
      <partName>Part 1</partName>
      <myUnit>
         <unitNumber>1. </unitNumber>
         <unitName>Unit 1</unitName>
         <myChapter>
            <chapterNumber>I. </chapterNumber>
            <chapterName>Chapter 1</chapterName>
            <mySection>
               <sectionNumber># 1. </sectionNumber>
               <sectionName>Chapter 1, Section 1</sectionName>
            </mySection>
            <mySection>
               <sectionNumber># 2. </sectionNumber>
```

```
                    <sectionName>Chapter 1, Section 2</sectionName>
                 </mySection>
                 <mySection>
                    <sectionNumber># 3. </sectionNumber>
                    <sectionName>Chapter 1, Section 3</sectionName>
                 </mySection>
             </myChapter>
             <myChapter>
                 <chapterNumber>II. </chapterNumber>
                 <chapterName>Chapter 2</chapterName>
                 <mySection>
                    <sectionNumber># 1. </sectionNumber>
                    <sectionName>Chapter 2, Section 1</sectionName>
                 </mySection>
                 <mySection>
                    <sectionNumber># 2. </sectionNumber>
                    <sectionName>Chapter 2, Section 2</sectionName>
                 </mySection>
                 <mySection>
                    <sectionNumber># 3. </sectionNumber>
                    <sectionName>Chapter 2, Section 3</sectionName>
                 </mySection>
             </myChapter>
          </myUnit>
       </myPart>
</myDoc>
```

Note that by default, the XSLT processor generated the `?xml?` prolog with
`version="1.0"` and `encoding="UTF-8"` specified, but no `!DOCTYPE`
element pointing to an external DTD subset. If we want to include a `!DOCTYPE`
element, we can use the `doctype-system` and/or `doctype-public` attribute;
for example, to generate a `SYSTEM` identifier, we could specify

```
<xsl:output method="xml" doctype-system="myDoc.dtd" />
```

which would result in the addition of the correct `!DOCTYPE` element to the document:

```
<?xml version="1.0" encoding="UTF-8"?>
<!DOCTYPE myDoc SYSTEM "myDoc.dtd">
<myDoc>
... rest of document ...
</myDoc>
```

Generating a public identifier is a little trickier—you have to specify both the `doctype-system` and `doctype-public` attributes to get the correct result. A correct `xsl:output` element might look like this:

```
<xsl:output method="xml"
            doctype-system="myDoc.dtd"
            doctype-public="-//CVS//MyDoc DTD//EN" />
```

with the output appearing at the front of the document as:

```
<!DOCTYPE myDoc PUBLIC "-//CVS//MyDoc DTD//EN" "myDoc.dtd">
```

To produce an XML parsed entity, you'll need to ensure that there is no `?xml?` prolog (by specifying `omit-xml-declaration="yes"`) and omit any `!DOCTYPE` declarations (by omitting the `doctype-public` and `doctype-system` attributes). All other attributes can be specified as described earlier.

Writing HTML Output

Creating HTML using XSLT isn't all that different from creating XML. By and large, an XSLT processor will adhere to the HTML rules with respect to empty end tags, character escaping, and so on, so if you know HTML well, you'll be able to code stylesheets to do exactly what you want. Keep in mind that your output will be parsed according to HTML rules, not XHTML rules, so you'll still run into many of the HTML idiosyncrasies that are resolved in XHTML.

One difference between XML and HTML generation is in the `xsl:output` element's `version` attribute. The current version of the HTML spec is 4.01; as with XML, this governs how the XSLT processor interprets your HTML, so if you're generating multiple versions of HTML, you'll need to pay attention to this specification. The default is `version="4.0"`, which is suitable for the vast majority of applications.

The HTML output method converts some of the `xsl:output` attribute values to `<META>` tags to include them in the final document. For example, if you specify an `encoding` attribute for `xsl:output`, you should expect to see a corresponding `<META>` tag with a `charset` attribute specifying your preferred encoding. Interestingly, however, not all attributes are treated this way by all processors; the Apache Xalan XSLT processor, for example, ignores `media-type` attributes of `xsl:output` and always specifies a media type of `text/html`.

Note also that the HTML output method will (unfortunately!) not actually parse your HTML and inform you of errors. The XSLT specification indicates that elements not recognized as valid HTML elements are to be written as "non-empty, inline elements"; this means that unless you're careful, you'll end up with elements that are unrecognizable to web browsers and other HTML processing tools in your document.

As you would expect, some of the attributes of `xsl:output` are meaningless when specified with the HTML output method. The `omit-xml-declaration`, `doctype-public`, and `doctype-system` attributes are all invalid with HTML; however, the behavior of XSLT processors varies when these are encountered, so be careful.

Writing Text Output

To generate output using the text output method, an XSLT processor writes every text node in the document as is, without escaping any special characters. None of the `xsl:output` parameters, except `encoding`, apply; if a text node contains content that cannot be shown using the specified encoding, then the XSLT processor generates an error.

Generating Informative or Exception Output with xsl:message

Sometimes it's helpful to get messages from your stylesheet, whether to report an error, to let the person using the stylesheet know what's going on, or to receive messages that aid in debugging. The XSLT specification provides a handy element, `xsl:message`, which not only generates messages but also allows you to optionally terminate your stylesheet's processing if needed.

The syntax for `xsl:message` is as follows:

```
<xsl:message terminate = "yes" | "no">
  <!-- Content: template -->
</xsl:message>
```

Exactly where the messages created using `xsl:message` come out depends on the processor. When running in command-line mode, most processors write the messages to the console window where the command is running, but windowed versions can provide pop-up alerts, scrolling text boxes, or some other appropriate medium.

To write a message, simply insert an `xsl:message` element at the point in your stylesheet where you want the message to be generated, and provide whatever content you need between the `xsl:message` starting and ending tags. This template shows a message being generated whenever a `Section` element is processed:

```
<xsl:template match="Section" >
<mySection>
<xsl:message terminate="no">
   Now processing: <xsl:value-of select="." />
</xsl:message>
<sectionNumber>
   <xsl:number level="multiple" format="# 1. " />
</sectionNumber>
<sectionName><xsl:value-of select="." /></sectionName>
</mySection>
</xsl:template>
```

Summary

The `xsl:number`, `xsl:output`, and `xsl:message` elements are useful tools that allow you to fine-tune the output from your XSLT stylesheet to your particular needs. They can make tedious tasks like numbering elements much easier, and allow a high level of customization of your document's output.

CHAPTER 1

XSL/XSLT Power Programming

IN THIS CHAPTER:

I n this chapter, you will learn about advanced XSLT concepts such as sorting of the nodes in the output, specification of a decimal format for the number, use of the `format-number` function, and use of keys. You will also learn about XSLT extensions, particularly extension elements and extension functions. XSLT provides accessory functions such as `element-available` and `function-available` to determine whether a particular extension (or a supposedly built-in capability) is indeed available in the particular implementation: if it is not, the programmer can use the `xsl:fallback` element to handle the contingency. The concepts of extensions, functions to check for the availability of extensions, and fallback are tied to the discussion of forwards-compatible processing that we undertook in Chapter 4.

Sorting

In the examples in this book so far, the order of the nodes in the result tree was not managed explicitly: it depended solely on the order in the source tree. To customize the order, the element `xsl:sort` can be used, the syntax of which is shown here:

```
<xsl:sort
   select = string-expression
   lang = { nmtoken }
   data-type = { "text" | "number" | qname-but-not-ncname }
   order = { "ascending" | "descending" }
   case-order = { "upper-first" | "lower-first" } />
```

The `xsl:sort` elements always appear as children of the elements of `xsl:apply-templates` or `xsl:for-each`. Let us look at an example of using `xsl:sort` to sort our author list by the last name:

```
. . .
    <xsl:template match="All_authors">
      <P>
        The following authors are working together with
        <xsl:value-of select="$omh"/> on this project:
      </P>
      <xsl:for-each select="Author">
```

```
            <xsl:sort select=".//Last_name"/>
            <xsl:variable name="AuthorNameNodeSet" select="./Name"/>
            <B>
              <xsl:value-of select="./Name"/>
            </B>
            <I>
              <P>
                <xsl:value-of select="./Address"/>
              </P>
            </I>
          </xsl:for-each>
        </xsl:template>
...
```

When this stylesheet is applied to `auth.xml` we get the following HTML output:

```
<html>
   <head>
      <meta http-equiv="Content-Type" content="text/html; charset=utf-8">
      <title>
         Information about Osborne-McGraw Hill authors
      </title>
   </head>
   <body>
      <P>
```

The following authors are working together with Osborne-McGraw Hill on this project:

```
      </P><B>
         John
         Galt
         </B><I>
         <P>
            333 Main Street
            P.O. Box 900
            Cleveland
            OH
            41414
```

```
        </P></I><B>
        Nitin
        Keskar
        </B><I>
        <P>
            222 Metropolis Street
            P.O. Box 500
            Minneapolis
            MN
            55455
        </P></I><B>
        Chris
        von See
        </B><I>
        <P>
            111 Mansion Boulevard
            Suite 100
            Chicago
            IL
            31313
        </P></I><P>
        End of the information about the Osborne-McGraw Hill authors.
    </P>
  </body>
</html>
```

In the preceding output, notice that the author records are output one after the other without any well-defined delimiters. Thus the rendering of this output using a browser (shown in Figure 10-1) shows no breaks between the author records.

For the short list of authors that we have used as an example, perhaps sorting using one key is sufficient. But for longer lists, you may want to sort using multiple keys. To accomplish this, you would simply use multiple xsl:sort elements one after the other. In that case, the XSLT processor will first sort using the key that appears in the first xsl:sort element, followed by the key that appears in the

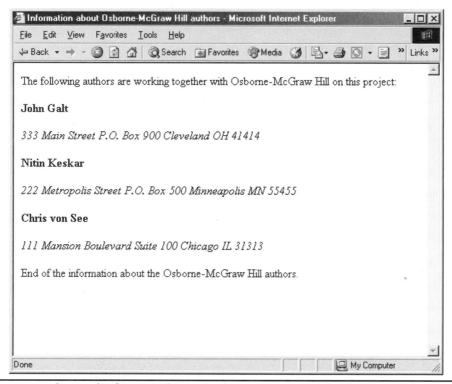

Figure 10-1   *The result of sorting the output by* Last_name *first, followed by sorting by* First_name

second xsl:sort element, and so on. Consider the following example in which we sort by the author's Last_name first and then sort by the First_name:

```
...
    <xsl:template match="All_authors">
      <P>
        The following authors are working together with
        <xsl:value-of select="$omh"/> on this project:
      </P>

      <xsl:for-each select="Author">
```

```
      <xsl:sort select=".//Last_name"/>
      <xsl:sort select=".//First_name"/>

      <xsl:variable name="AuthorNameNodeSet" select="./Name"/>
      <B>
        <xsl:value-of select="./Name"/>
      </B>
      <I>
        <P>
          <xsl:value-of select="./Address"/>
        </P>
      </I>

      <xsl:if test="not(position()=last())">
        <P> -------------------------------- </P>
      </xsl:if>

    </xsl:for-each>
  </xsl:template>
...
```

You will notice that in addition to sorting the data using multiple keys, we have also added some logic to insert a dashed line after each author record, *unless* it happens to be the last record. The resulting output is shown in Figure 10-2.

Of course, the order in which the xsl:sort elements specify the key matters. Thus, if you made a simple interchange of the xsl:sort elements shown in the previous example, the output will be first sorted by First_name and then by the Last_name:

```
<xsl:for-each select="Author">
        <xsl:sort select=".//First_name"/>
        <xsl:sort select=".//Last_name"/>
...
</xsl:for-each>
```

The resulting output is shown in Figure 10-3.

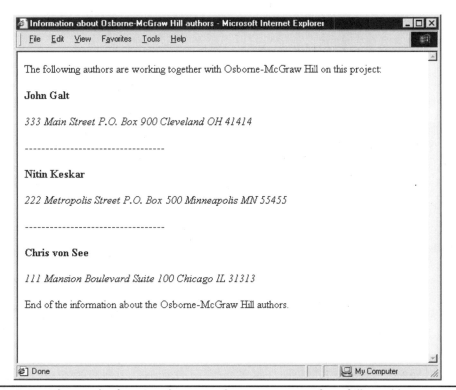

Figure 10-2   *The result of sorting the output by* `Last_name` *first, followed by sorting by* `First_name`

In the preceding examples , the *string-expression* value used for the `select` attribute specified descendant nodes of `Author`. You can also sort on attributes of the `Author` nodes. For instance, consider the following structure for the source tree in which we have added the attributes `age` and `region` for the `Author` nodes:

```
<Author age="88" region="Midwest">
  <Name>
  <First_name>...</First_name>
  <Last_name>...</Last_name>
  </Name>
<Address>
```

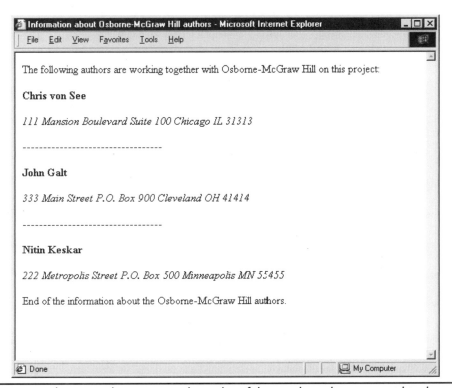

Figure 10-3   *The output by reversing the order of the sort keys that was used in the previous example: sort on the* `First_name` *followed by another sort on the* `Last_name`

To sort the author listing by *descending* order of age, you could use code such as the following. Note that by default, data is sorted in ascending order.

```
<xsl:sort select="@age" order="descending"/>
```

Also note that in this example, we are sorting on a key of the number type. The earlier code samples were for keys of the string, or text, data type, which is the default data type. To sort this data correctly, you must specify the number data type explicitly in the `xsl:sort` element. This is shown in the following code sample:

```
<xsl:sort select="@age" order="descending" data-type="number"/>
```

If you had data with key values starting with lowercase as well as uppercase letters, you could specify `case-order` as follows:

```
<xsl:sort select=".//Last_name" case-order="lower-first" lang="en"/>
```

The default `case-order` value depends on the `lang` (language) attribute, which we explicitly stated in the previous example with a value of `en`.

The current XSLT specification does leave some room for sorting to be implemented a bit differently across different processors, and also to support certain languages while not supporting certain others. Future versions of the specifications may tighten the control further by providing additional attributes to be specified.

Extensions

An extension function or extension element is one that is defined outside the W3C specification. Such extensions may either be user defined or provided by a specific XSLT processor vendor as an additional capability. The current XSLT specification does not mention how such extensions may be defined, but it does provide support for using them within an XSLT stylesheet. It also provides support for determining whether an extension of interest to the programmer is implemented by the current XSLT processor and for specifying fallback instructions for the course of action if the extension is not available.

Extension Elements

Extension elements are user-defined or vendor-defined additional elements that can occur within a template body. To use such elements, you have to use the extension namespace declaration within the `xsl:stylesheet` element. The following example shows how you can define a hypothetical custom namespace called `myExtension`:

```
<xsl:stylesheet version="1.0"
    xmlns:xsl="http://www.w3.org/1999/XSL/Transform"
    xmlns:myExtension="http://www.myWebSite.com/2001/XSLT/Extension">
```

A namespace may also be defined as an extension namespace by using the `extension-element-prefixes` attribute of the `xsl:stylesheet` element, or the `xsl:extension-elements-prefixes` attribute of an extension element itself. In either case, you can specify multiple namespace prefixes separated by whitespaces.

Thus defined, you can use extension elements from the extension namespace, as shown in the following example, which uses the custom-defined element my-own-element:

```
...
   <xsl:template match="All_authors">
       <xsl:for-each select="Author">
         <B> <xsl:value-of select="./Name"/> </B>
         <myExtension:my-own-element select="."/>
       </xsl:for-each>
   <xsl:template match="All_authors">
...
```

Note that the definition of extension elements, and any restrictions thereon, apply only to elements occurring within a template body, and not to top-level elements. The XSLT specification gives the user and the vendor the freedom to define their own top-level elements, provided they use a non-null namespace URI, and as long as they do not alter the behavior of standard top-level elements.

For the XSLT processor, or for the programmer, to determine whether a particular element, built-in, or extension is accessible, the Boolean function element-available is provided by XSLT:

```
element-available(string_for_function_name)
```

The following usage will return a true result since xsl:variable is a legitimate XSLT element:

```
<xsl:value-of select="element-available('xsl:variable')"/>
```

Of course, the following usage will output a false value since the current specification does not support the element xsl:new-element-in-v1.1:

```
<xsl:value-of select="element-available('xsl:new-element-in-v1.1')"/>
```

Extension Functions

Extension functions are functions written by a user or provided by a software vendor outside the XSLT specification. In the code examples seen so far, you probably noticed that we do not use the xsl: prefix while using the built-in XSLT/XPath functions. Thus, if an XSLT processor encounters a function in which a colon appears, it treats that function as an extension function. as shown in the following code sample:

```
<xsl:value-of select="myExtension:myFunction(48660.22, '#,###.00')"/>
```

For the programmer to make an assessment about the availability of a particular function, the built-in Boolean function `function-available` is provided by XSLT:

```
function-available(string_for_function_name)
```

Thus, if a function is available, as shown in the following example, the result will be `true`:

```
<xsl:value-of select="function-available('format-number')"/>
```

If the namespace `myExtension` is accessible, the following call will return a `true` result; if the namespace is not accessible, the result will be `false`:

```
<xsl:value-of select="function-available('myExtension:myFunction')"/>
```

If the result of the `function-available` call is `false`, the processor is not required to indicate an error if the extension function does not get called during the processing of the stylesheet. If, however, it does get called and the processor cannot access it, it must signal an error.

Fallback

Chapter 4 discussed the forwards-compatible mode in XSLT that is enabled when the value of the `version` attribute of the stylesheet element is higher than the version implemented by the processor (currently 1.0), as in the following example:

```
<xsl:stylesheet version="1.1"
    xmlns:xsl="http://www.w3.org/1999/XSL/Transform">

<!-- stylesheet template processing begins -->
    <xsl:template match="/">
      <xsl:new-element-in-v1.1 select=".">
      <html>
        <head>
          <title>Information about OMH authors</title>
        </head>
        ...
      <html>
```

```
...
        </xsl:new-element-in-v1.1>
...
```

In this case, the XSLT processor does not know how to deal with `xsl:new-element-in-v1.1` and must signal an error. To handle such cases gracefully, XSLT provides the `xsl:fallback` element, which is activated only if the instruction element surrounding it cannot be processed by the current XSLT implementation. The `xsl:fallback` element always occurs within a template body and follows the syntax shown here:

```
<!-- Category: instruction -->
<xsl:fallback>
  <!-- Content: template -->
</xsl:fallback>
```

Let us look at the following example, which uses `xsl:new-element-in-v1.1`, which, hypothetically, will provide a standard way of formatting the descendants of the current node. It also provides fallback instructions in case the XSLT processor does not know how to handle this new element. Except for the elements `xsl:new-element-in-v1.1` and `xsl:fallback`, this is the same code used in one of the examples in Chapter 8.

```
<?xml version="1.0"?>
<!-- stylesheet specifications begin -->
<xsl:stylesheet version="1.1"
    xmlns:xsl="http://www.w3.org/1999/XSL/Transform">
<xsl:variable name="omh" select=" 'Osborne-McGraw Hill' "/>
...
    <xsl:template match="All_authors">
      <P>
        The following authors are working together with
        <xsl:value-of select="$omh"/> on this project:
      </P>

      <xsl:new-element-in-v1.1 select=".">
        <xsl:fallback>
          <xsl:for-each select="Author">
            <xsl:variable name="AuthorNameNodeSet" select="./Name"/>
            <B>
              <xsl:value-of select="./Name"/>
            </B>
```

```
        <I>
          <P>
            <xsl:value-of select="./Address"/>
          </P>
        </I>

        <P> ... </P>
        <P> This author's last name is
          <B>
            <xsl:value-of select="$AuthorNameNodeSet/Last_name"/>
          </B>
        </P>
        <xsl:if test="not(position()=last())">
          <P> -------------------------------- </P>
        </xsl:if>
      </xsl:for-each>

    </xsl:fallback>
</xsl:new-element-in-v1.1>
    </xsl:template>
...
```

Let us revisit an example from Chapter 4 in which we controlled the use of xsl:new-element-in-v1.1 explicitly, using the "when ... otherwise" construct:

```
<?xml version="1.0"?>
<!-- stylesheet specifications begin -->
<xsl:stylesheet version="1.1"
    xmlns:xsl="http://www.w3.org/1999/XSL/Transform">
<xsl:variable name="omh" select=" 'Osborne-McGraw Hill' "/>
...
    <xsl:template match="Name">
      <B>
        <xsl:choose>

          <xsl:when test="system-property('xsl:version') >= 1.1">
            <xsl:new-element-in-v1.1 select=".">
              <!-- Content of the element xsl:new-element-in-v1.1-->
              ...
            </xsl:new-element-in-v1.1>
          </xsl:when>
```

```
            <xsl:otherwise>
              <xsl:value-of select="."/>
            </xsl:otherwise>

          </xsl:choose>
        </B>
      </xsl:template>
...
```

The Boolean functions `element-available` and `function-available` can also be used along with the elements `xsl:choose` and `xsl:if` to exercise such explicit control when a particular element (for example, `xsl:new-element-in-v1.1`) or function is not available. These Boolean functions are discussed later in the book. For the moment, let us see how we can rewrite the previous example much more concisely using `xsl:fallback`:

```
<?xml version="1.0"?>
<!-- stylesheet specifications begin -->
<xsl:stylesheet version="1.1"
     xmlns:xsl="http://www.w3.org/1999/XSL/Transform">
<xsl:variable name="omh" select=" 'Osborne-McGraw Hill' "/>
...
    <xsl:template match="Name">
      <B>
            <xsl:new-element-in-v1.1 select=".">
              <!-- Content of the element xsl:new-element-in-v1.1-->
              ...
              <xsl:fallback>
                <xsl:value-of select="."/>
              <xsl:fallback>
            </xsl:new-element-in-v1.1>
      </B>
    </xsl:template>
...
```

Keys

XSLT provides a powerful concept to effectively process source trees that have an implicit structure within them. Such implicit structures may arise from the interrelationships that the diverse nodes have with each other: for example, an XML tree extracted from an RDBMS schema might have such a structure. So XSLT keys can be used to define and process a named index of nodes from the source XML tree. This concept uses two interrelated constructs: the element `xsl:key` and the function `key()`. (Although we have mentioned RDBMS in the example, there is no connection whatsoever between the database keys and XSLT keys!)

XSLT Element xsl:key

The top-level element `xsl:key` follows the syntax shown here:

```
<xsl:key
  name = qname
  match = pattern
  use = expression />
```

All attributes are mandatory in defining the key: `name` is simply the identifier of the key, `match` specifies the pattern of interest that should appear in the nodes that are to be processed, and `use` corresponds to a pointer to the values of the key. Thus, key is a name-value-node triple that you define at the top-level of the stylesheet. The restriction on `pattern` and `expression` is that they should evaluate as literals: that is, they cannot have a variable reference within them. This is to avoid circular definitions within the stylesheet.

In the source document, you may specify the value of a named key in an attribute, in a child element, or in the content of the element. In the example discussed in Chapter 4, we defined the key values using the attribute `id`:

```
...
<companyList>
  <company name="ATT" id="111"/>
  <company name="Sprint" id="222"/>
  <company name="Worldcom" id=333"/>
...
</companyList>
```

Alternatively, we could have specified the values in a child element. ID, as shown in the following example. Note the change of case when specifying ID. This is to set it apart from the built-in `id` attributes of many XSLT elements.

```
...
<companyList>
  <company name="ATT">
```

```
    <ID>111</ID>
  </company>
  <company name="Sprint">
    <ID>222</ID>
  </company>
  <company name="Worldcom">
    <ID>333</ID>
  </company>
...
</companyList>
```

Since the key values can be found in different places, an XPath expression is used in the key definition to pinpoint the location of values for that particular key. For example, in the first case where the id attribute for the company was used, the key is defined as follows:

```
<xsl:key name="phoneCompany" match="company" use="@id"/>
```

In the second case where the key values were stored using the child element ID, the key definition will have to be altered as follows:

```
<xsl:key name="phoneCompany" match="company" use="./ID"/>
```

The power of keys lies behind the flexibility that XSLT attributes to their definition and use. For instance, the value of a key can be any arbitrary string, not just a name. Moreover, within a given source document, you can use the same key name for multiple keys on multiple nodes. Across the nodes, the key values may even be the same, because we can use multiple xsl:key elements in the stylesheet to distinguish among the different keys. Additionally, we can have multiple keys for the same node, as long as they have different values. Last, more than one xsl:key element may match a given node, and in the event that multiple matches occur, all of them will be invoked and used, even if they do not have the same import precedence.

XSLT Function key()

The key() function returns a node set as a result. It follows the syntax shown here:

```
key(key_name_string, object)
```

In its simplest form, the object of the search is a string or any data type other than a node set, as in the following example:

```
<xsl:apply-templates select="key('phoneCompany','333')"/>
```

In such a case, the `object` argument is implicitly converted to a string, and the `key()` function returns a node set for which the object's string value matches that for the node.

When the key values are stored on child elements within a source file, you can use a node set as the `object` argument of the `key()` function, as in the following example:

```
<xsl:apply-templates select="key('phoneCompany','./ID')"/>
```

Let us look at a few more examples that use the source tree shown here. We have modified the original `auth.xml` element a little by adding an `AuthID` attribute on the `Author` nodes:

```
<?xml version="1.0"?>
 <!-- data specifications begin -->
<All_authors>
  <Author AuthID="77">
  <Name>
    <First_name>Chris</First_name>
    <Last_name>von See</Last_name>
  </Name>
  <Address>
    <Address_line1>111 Mansion Boulevard</Address_line1>
    <Address_line2>Suite 100</Address_line2>
    <City>Chicago</City>
    <State>IL</State>
    <ZIP>31313</ZIP>
  </Address>
  </Author>
  <Author AuthID="88">
    <Name>
    <First_name>Nitin</First_name>
    <Last_name>Keskar</Last_name>
    </Name>
  <Address>
    <Address_line1>222 Metropolis Street</Address_line1>
    <Address_line2>P.O. Box 500</Address_line2>
    <City>Minneapolis</City>
    <State>MN</State>
    <ZIP>55455</ZIP>
```

```
    </Address>
    </Author>
    <Author AuthID="55">
      <Name>
      <First_name>John</First_name>
      <Last_name>Galt</Last_name>
      </Name>
    <Address>
      <Address_line1>333 Main Street</Address_line1>
      <Address_line2>P.O. Box 900</Address_line2>
      <City>Cleveland</City>
      <State>OH</State>
      <ZIP>41414</ZIP>
    </Address>
    </Author>
</All_authors>
<!-- data specifications end -->
```

To find an author by the `First_name` descendant node, we would use code similar to that shown here:

```
...
<xsl:key name="myAuthorName" match="Author" use="./Name"/>
...
  <xsl:value-of select="key('myAuthorName','Nitin')"/>
...
```

To find an author by the `AuthID` attribute, the code would look like the following:

```
...
<xsl:key name="myAuthorAuthID" match="Author" use="@AuthID"/>
...
<xsl:value-of select="key('myAuthorAuthID','55')"/>
...
```

Number Formatting

To format numbers in the output, you can use the element `xsl:decimal-format` in conjunction with the `format-number` function. The `xsl:decimal-format` element specifies a number format, which controls the interpretation of the pattern used by the `format-number` function anywhere in the stylesheet. This top-level element was introduced in Chapter 4; now we will take a more detailed look at it. Its syntax is shown here:

```
xsl:decimal-format
  name = qname
  decimal-separator = char
  grouping-separator = char
  infinity = string
  minus-sign = char
  NaN = string
  percent = char
  per-mille = char
  zero-digit = char
  digit = char
  pattern-separator = char />
```

All attributes of `xsl:decimal-format` are optional and are described in Table 10-1.

You can specify multiple named decimal formats at the top-level of the stylesheet, as long as all names are unique. The XSLT processor will indicate an error if it encounters more than one named format with the same name, even if the formats have different import precedence values, unless all declarations have exactly the same values for all attributes. If the optional `name` attribute is not specified, the declaration is considered the default decimal format for that stylesheet, and there can be no more than one default declaration.

The function `format-number` uses the specifications given in the declaration of `xsl:decimal-format` and can be used in an XPath expression, for example, along with a `select` attribute of `xsl:value-of`. Its syntax is shown here:

```
format-number(number,format_pattern_string,format_name_string)
```

The function converts the `number` argument to a string using the pattern specified by the argument `format_pattern_string` and the named decimal format specified by the argument `format_name_string`. If the optional third argument `format_name_string` is not specified, the default format is used.

Attributes other than the `name` attribute of the `xsl:decimal-format` element *correspond* to the methods on Java 1.1's `DecimalFormatSymbols` class. Similarly, the `format_pattern_string` argument of the `number-format` function *follows* the syntax specifications of Java 1.1's

Attribute	Value	Description
Name	name	Optional. Name of decimal format.
Decimal-separator	char	Optional. A character to separate the integer and the fraction part of a number. Default is ".".
Grouping-separator	char	Optional. A character to separate groups of digits. Default is ",".
Infinity	string	Optional. A string to represent infinity. Default is "infinity".
Minus-sign	char	Optional. A character to represent negative numbers. Default is "-".
NaN	string	Optional. A string to represent Not a Number. Default is "NaN".
Percent	char	Optional. A character to represent a percentage sign. Default is "%".
Per-mille	char	Optional. A character to represent a per-mille sign. Default is "‰".
zero-digit	char	Optional. A character to indicate a place where a leading zero digit is required. Default is "0".
Digit	char	Optional. A character to indicate a place where a digit is required. Default is "#".
Pattern-separator	char	Optional. A character to separate format strings. Default is ";".

Table 10-1 *Attributes of the Top-Level Element* `xls:decimal-format`

`java.text.DecimalFormat` class—that is, the output must be formatted *as if* by the `DecimalFormat` class, although the XSLT specification does not mandate that the processor be written in Java or even use the JDK 1.1 implementation.

Additional Functions

This section discusses miscellaneous useful functions provided by XSLT.

current()

The `current()` function does not have any argument, and it returns a node set containing a single node, which is the current node. The simplest usage of this function is shown here:

```
<xsl:value-of select="current()"/>
```

The result of such usage will be identical to that of the following code:

```
<xsl:value-of select="."/>
```

In the preceding example, the function is used within an outermost XPath expression. That is, it appears in an expression that itself is not contained within another expression. Hence, in this case the context node—that is, the node returned by the XPath expression—is the current node itself. In the following example, the `current()` function is used within a predicate, and the context node shares the `First_name` value of the current `Author` node. In effect, we want to process nodes corresponding to all authors whose first name is the same as that of the current author under consideration.

```
<xsl:apply-templates
select="//Author[.//First_name=current()//First_name]"/>
```

To process nodes corresponding to all authors who are the same age as the current author (`Age` being an attribute on the `Author` node), the code is modified as follows:

```
<xsl:apply-templates select="//Author[@Age=current()/@Age"/>
```

generate-id()

The `generate-id` function generates unique identifiers for the node in its argument node set. The XSLT specification gives implementation latitude to software vendors as long as the following conditions are met:

▶ The ID must start with a letter and must contain only ASCII alphanumeric characters.

▶ The same ID must be consistently generated for the same node every time the function is invoked for that node *within the current processing lifecycle*. That is, the implementation need not generate the same ID the next time the same source tree is processed.

▶ Different IDs are generated for different nodes.

A simple example of this function's usage is shown here:

```
...
<xsl:for-each select="Author">
        <xsl:variable name="AuthorNameNodeSet" select="./Name"/>
        <b>
          <a href="#{generate-id(.)}">
           <xsl:value-of select="./Name"/>
         </a>
        </b>
...
</xsl:for-each>
```

Note the distinct values of the generated IDs for each of the nodes in the resulting HTML output:

```
        <b><a href="#d1e5">Chris von See</a></b>
...
        <b><a href="#d1e35">Nitin Keskar</a></b>
...
        <b><a href="#d1e65">John Galt</a></b>
```

system-property()

The `system-property` function takes a string as its input and generates a string as the output. It is used to find a certain property of the current implementation, such as the current version that the XSLT processor supports, as shown here:

```
Current XSLT version =
<xsl:value-of select="system-property('xsl:version')"/>
```

As expected, the output is as follows:

```
Current XSLT version = 1
```

If the input string does not evaluate to a known property, an empty string is output, as in the following example:

```
New property in v1.1 =
<xsl:value-of select="system-property('xsl:new-property-in-v1.1')"/>
```

Implementations are required to provide the system properties `xsl:vendor` and `xsl:vendor-url`. We ran the following code using Instant Saxon:

```
. . .
Vendor = <xsl:value-of select="system-property('xsl:vendor')"/>
Vendor URL = <xsl:value-of select="system-property('xsl:vendor-url')"/>
. . .
```

The following output was obtained:

```
. . .
      Vendor = SAXON 6.2.2 from Michael Kay
      Vendor URL = http://users.iclway.co.uk/mhkay/saxon/index.html
. . .
```

Summary

This chapter discussed power programming concepts such as sorting of the nodes in the output using one or more keys, number formatting, and the use of keys. It also described several functions: `element-available`, `function-available`, `format-number()`, `key()`, `current`, `generate-id`, and `system-property`.

Although version 1.0 is the only available XSLT version at present, you have to be prepared to deal with multiple future versions and multiple vendor implementations. In this regard, the discussions of extensibility, availability of extensions within the current implementation, a fallback plan if an extension is not available, and the forwards-compatible mode (from Chapter 4) should be useful. Equipped with all these tools, you are now in a good position to see how XSLT can be used in real-life practical situations.

Practical XSLT Examples

T his chapter is intended to give you some examples of how XSLT is (or can be) used in the real world. We chose examples that represent some of the most prevalent applications of this technology, while at the same time attempting to illustrate the use of the most common XSLT elements. By viewing the code in these examples, you will see how you can construct similar applications yourself.

Real-World XSLT Applications

Given the vast array of current and potential uses for XML and the processing power provided by XSLT, there's no good way to characterize a typical real-world XSLT application. We can, however, talk about broad categories of applications for which XSLT is a viable solution and discuss how this tool can be used to solve tangible problems, often faster and more efficiently than other methods.

What Type of Problem Is XSLT Well Suited For?

With its roots in presentation-oriented XSL, XSLT offers obvious benefits in the transformation of XML documents into various human-readable formats such as HTML, WML, or text. Whereas XSL required the use of complex formatting objects to produce human-readable output, XSLT provides some very straightforward functions for using HTML and other facilities to create various types of output, and it provides stylesheet designers with great flexibility in their efforts to do so. XPath's ability to locate and retrieve information in a highly structured XML document, combined with XSLT's own template-driven facilities for generating presentation elements, makes creating multiple presentation formats from a single data source a fairly simple process.

One of the major driving forces behind the separation of the XSLT transformation language from XSL's formatting object language was XSLT's appeal as a tool for restructuring XML documents: it allows the easy addition of dynamically generated elements and attributes, conversion from one DTD to another, and removal of information that is no longer needed. In addition to being key to generating presentation-oriented output, this capability is a powerful tool for making structured XML data usable by a wide range of processing programs, both inside and outside the enterprise. When combined with conventional tools for extracting information from relational database management systems, XSLT's restructuring capabilities make it easy to produce highly customized and personalized data formats not only for presentation to users, but for content syndication, electronic commerce, and other applications as well.

An interesting variation on this restructuring capability is the ability to use XSLT stylesheets to generate other stylesheets. For example, a stylesheet designer can use variable or parameter input and documents that describe output branding and style characteristics to produce stylesheets capable of converting a single data source into multiple, individually branded HTML pages. Customizations that are not possible directly, such as the ability to change imported or included stylesheets based on parameters or input document content, can be performed easily by using one stylesheet to generate another.

When Should XSLT Not Be Used?

As powerful as XSLT is, it's not a panacea for all data transformation and presentation generation problems. In its current form, XSLT has several limitations that make it unsuitable for some applications:

► Remember that XSLT is not a programming language. Tasks that require complex manipulation of element content or extensive conditional logic, for example, are often better handled by programs written in Perl, PHP, or Java.

► In most organizations, a significant amount of data is stored in relational databases. XSLT does not provide a way to access this data directly from a stylesheet; stylesheet developers must use data extraction tools or write programs to retrieve data to be processed.

► If high-performance creation of customized content is needed, as might be the case for a high-volume Web site, Java or another programming language is almost always the better choice. Fortunately, there are many personalization tools and tag libraries available for Java application servers that query user profile information or site navigation history to produce customized content in real time.

► XSLT, like some other development tools, is a victim of the 80/20 rule: 80 percent of the tasks for which one might use XSLT can be performed easily, while the remaining 20 percent are so difficult as to be almost impossible. For experienced programmers in particular, it can be much faster to develop a solution using a programming language such as Perl than to try and figure out how to complete the same task using XSLT.

The good news is that XSLT can still play a role in solving many of these problems. By adopting a pipeline approach and breaking the solution down into multiple steps, you can use XSLT where its functionality meets the need, and other tools where they are appropriate or necessary.

XSLT Application Examples

With all that in mind, let's take a look at examples of real-life applications created using XSLT. Keep in mind when reviewing these examples that although they represent situations where XSLT is an appropriate solution, their focus is on how to use XSLT (and, in particular, how to code XSLT stylesheets), not necessarily on providing complete solutions to the problems described.

Modifying Data in an XML Document

Sometimes the content in a document must be modified to suit a particular application: perhaps because the application requires that its input data conform to a different DTD, or because the data must be supplied to an external customer who will use it in a different way from that envisioned when the data was originally created. In situations such as these, XSLT can substantially streamline the process of converting the data into its new, more usable format.

Let's say, for example, that we intend to syndicate content we've developed for use by other content providers. Our goal is to provide a document index, based on our own internal XML-based index document, that is customized to the unique requirements of each content provider, and which the content providers can use to retrieve articles of interest to their customer bases. The starting point for this endeavor is the internal article index document shown here.

```
<?xml version="1.0" encoding="UTF-8" ?>
<articleCatalog>
   <article>
      <dc:Identifier system="internal">20011126-00345</dc:Identifier>
      <dc:Title>Java vs C++: Another Perspective</dc:Title>
      <dc:Creator>Frank deFord</dc:Creator>
      <dc:Subject>Programming</dc:Subject>
      <dc:Subject>C++</dc:Subject>
      <dc:Subject>Java</dc:Subject>
      <dc:Description>The author provides his perspective on why C++
is a better language than Java, with specific examples that illustrate
C++'s efficiencies in many different applications.</dc:Description>
      <dc:Publisher>Non-Existent Publishing, Inc.</dc:Publisher>
      <dc:Date>2001-11-26</dc:Date>
```

```
    <dc:Language>en-US</dc:Language>
    <dc:Format>HTML</dc:Format>
    <dc:Format>PDF</dc:Format>
    <dc:Format>text</dc:Format>
    <dc:Format>XML</dc:Format>
    <readerRating unit="stars">2</readerRating>
    <articleFile format="HTML">
        ./articles/2001/11/art00345.html
    </articleFile>
    <articleFile format="PDF">
        ./articles/2001/11/art00345.pdf
    </articleFile>
    <articleFile format="text">
        ./articles/2001/11/art00345.txt
    </articleFile>
    <articleFile format="XML">
        ./articles/2001/11/art00345.xml
    </articleFile>
</article>

<article>
    <dc:Identifier system="internal">20011027-00005</dc:Identifier>
    <dc:Title>Why XML?</dc:Title>
    <dc:Creator>Angela Martin</dc:Creator>
    <dc:Subject>Markup languages</dc:Subject>
    <dc:Subject>XML</dc:Subject>
    <dc:Description>In this enlightening article, author Angela
Martin discusses the rise of XML as a tool for structured data
exchange, and compares it to other mechanisms.</dc:Description>
    <dc:Publisher>Non-Existent Publishing, Inc.</dc:Publisher>
    <dc:Date>2001-10-27</dc:Date>
    <dc:Language>en-US</dc:Language>
    <dc:Format>HTML</dc:Format>
    <dc:Format>text</dc:Format>
    <dc:Format>XML</dc:Format>
    <readerRating unit="stars">4</readerRating>
    <articleFile format="HTML">
        ./articles/2001/10/art00005.html
    </articleFile>
    <articleFile format="text">
        ./articles/2001/10/art00005.txt
    </articleFile>
    <articleFile format="XML">
        ./articles/2001/10/art00005.xml
    </articleFile>
</article>
```

```
<article>
   <dc:Identifier system="internal">20011127-00314</dc:Identifier>
   <dc:Title>Wahoo for Yahoo!</dc:Title>
   <dc:Creator>Hugh Noble</dc:Creator>
   <dc:Subject>Web</dc:Subject>
   <dc:Subject>Search engines</dc:Subject>
   <dc:Subject>Yahoo!</dc:Subject>
   <dc:Description>While other search engine/portal sites such
as Excite and AltaVista have languished, Yahoo! manages to keep
chugging along. But does the future look rosy for this survivor?
   </dc:Description>
   <dc:Publisher>Non-Existent Publishing, Inc.</dc:Publisher>
   <dc:Date>2001-11-27</dc:Date>
   <dc:Language>en-US</dc:Language>
   <dc:Format>HTML</dc:Format>
   <readerRating unit="stars">4</readerRating>
   <articleFile format="HTML">
       ./articles/2001/11/art00314.html
   </articleFile>
</article>

<article>
   <dc:Identifier system="internal">20010914-00121</dc:Identifier>
   <dc:Title>The Superhighway to Nothing</dc:Title>
   <dc:Creator>Hugh Noble</dc:Creator>
   <dc:Subject>Web</dc:Subject>
   <dc:Description>Thanks to the ubiquity of Internet access in
most parts of the worldand the dearth of &quot;killer apps&quot;, Web
hype no longer has the effect on consumers it once did. For Web-based
companies, the question is, "Now what?".</dc:Description>
   <dc:Publisher>Non-Existent Publishing, Inc.</dc:Publisher>
   <dc:Date>2001-09-14</dc:Date>
   <dc:Language>en-US</dc:Language>
   <dc:Format>HTML</dc:Format>
   <dc:Format>text</dc:Format>
   <dc:Format>XML</dc:Format>
   <readerRating unit="stars">5</readerRating>
   <articleFile format="HTML">
       ./articles/2001/09/art00121.html
   </articleFile>
   <articleFile format="PDF">
       ./articles/2001/09/art00121.pdf
   </articleFile>
   <articleFile format="text">
       ./articles/2001/09/art00121.txt
   </articleFile>
   <articleFile format="XML">
```

```
              ./articles/2001/09/art00121.xml
        </articleFile>
    </article>

    <article>
        <dc:Identifier system="internal">2001001-00211</dc:Identifier>
        <dc:Title>The PGP vs Perl Shootout</dc:Title>
        <dc:Creator>Frank deFord</dc:Creator>
        <dc:Subject>Programming</dc:Subject>
        <dc:Subject>PGP</dc:Subject>
        <dc:Subject>Perl</dc:Subject>
        <dc:Description>Frank deFord offers his take on the relative
merits of these two workhorse scripting languages.</dc:Description>
        <dc:Publisher>Non-Existent Publishing, Inc.</dc:Publisher>
        <dc:Date>2001-10-01</dc:Date>
        <dc:Language>en-US</dc:Language>
        <dc:Format>HTML</dc:Format>
        <readerRating unit="stars">2</readerRating>
        <articleFile format="HTML">
            ./articles/2001/10/art00211.html
        </articleFile>
    </article>
</articleCatalog>
```

As you can see, this article index lists several articles, providing general
information about their content and format as well as links to the actual article files.
The metadata portion of the index (title, date published, subject, and so on) is provided
using the Dublin Core metadata element set; for more information on this element
set and what it can do, go to http://dublincore.org. The remaining elements (the reader
ratings and article file references) are proprietary to this particular application.

The requirements of the content provider are that all articles in the index:

▶ Be available in American English

▶ Be related to computer programming

▶ Be available in XML format (assume for simplicity's sake that the
    articles can be provided using the appropriate DTD)

The entries in the new index must be sorted in ascending publication date sequence.
Our proposed solution to the problem is shown in the next stylesheet. Comments
are provided after each template to explain the logic.

```
<xsl:stylesheet version="1.0"
                xmlns:xsl=http://www.w3.org/1999/XSL/Transform
```

```
                    xmlns:dc="http://purl.org/dc/elements/1.1/" >
<xsl:output method="xml" version="1.0" encoding="UTF-8"
indent="yes"/>

    <xsl:param name="lang1">default</xsl:param>
    <xsl:param name="subj1">default</xsl:param>
    <xsl:param name="form1">default</xsl:param>
```

Parameters are used to allow the language, subject, and format to vary without having to change the stylesheet. If in the future this content provider needs an index of articles on a different subject, in a different format, or in a different language, this same stylesheet can be used to generate that index.

```
<xsl:strip-space elements="articleCatalog" />
```

The xsl:strip-space element prevents extraneous whitespace from being included in the output document. While not strictly necessary, removing extraneous whitespace (combined with document indentation, as requested using the xsl:output indent="yes" attribute) makes the final document more easily readable by humans.

```
<xsl:template match="articleCatalog" >
   <xsl:copy>
      <xsl:for-each select="article" >
         <xsl:if test="dc:Language=$lang1">
            <xsl:if test="dc:Subject=$subj1">
               <xsl:if test="dc:Format=$form1">
                  <xsl:apply-templates select="." mode="mode1" >
                     <xsl:sort select="dc:Date" order="ascending" />
                  </xsl:apply-templates>
               </xsl:if>
            </xsl:if>
         </xsl:if>
      </xsl:for-each>
   </xsl:copy>
</xsl:template>
```

This template loops through each article node in the index, testing for each of the criteria requested by the customer. When a node makes it all the way through the checks, it is sorted (along with all other nodes matching the criteria) into date order and then passed to the next template for formatting. Because xsl:sort must be

called from (and must be the first element) within xsl:apply-templates
or xsl:for-each, the final output formatting needs to be applied in a separate
template; to do this, we use the mode attribute on xsl:apply-templates to
force the formatting template to be callable only from this xsl:apply-templates
element and to prevent all of the other article elements from matching on the
same template.

```
<xsl:template match="article" mode="model" >
<xsl:element name="article">
        <xsl:element name="dc:Title">
           <xsl:value-of select="dc:Title" /></xsl:element>
        <xsl:element name="dc:Creator">
           <xsl:value-of select="dc:Creator" /></xsl:element>
        <xsl:for-each select="dc:Subject">
           <xsl:element name="dc:Subject">
              <xsl:value-of select="." /></xsl:element>
        </xsl:for-each>
        <xsl:element name="dc:Date">
           <xsl:value-of select="dc:Date" /></xsl:element>
        <xsl:element name="dc:Language">
           <xsl:value-of select="dc:Language" /></xsl:element>
        <xsl:for-each select="articleFile" >
           <xsl:if test="@format=$form1">
              <xsl:element name="articleFile">
                 <xsl:attribute name="format">
                    <xsl:value-of select="@format" /></xsl:element>
                 <xsl:text>http://www.nonexistentpublishing.com/</xsl:text>
                 <xsl:value-of select="." />
              </xsl:element>
           </xsl:if>
        </xsl:for-each>
    </xsl:element>
  </xsl:template>

</xsl:stylesheet>
```

This template formats the output, removing elements we don't want the customer
to see (such as our internal dc:Identifier element) and including only the
article file reference appropriate for the requested data format. The mode attribute
value specified on xsl:template matches that specified on the xsl:apply-
templates element that invokes this template.

The resulting output document, shown here, is ready for customer consumption.

```
<?xml version="1.0" encoding="UTF-8"?>
<articleCatalog xmlns:dc="http://purl.org/dc/elements/1.1/">
    <article>
        <dc:Title>Java vs C++: Another Perspective</dc:Title>
        <dc:Creator>Frank deFord</dc:Creator>
        <dc:Subject>Programming</dc:Subject>
        <dc:Subject>C++</dc:Subject>
        <dc:Subject>Java</dc:Subject>
        <dc:Date>2001-11-26</dc:Date>
        <dc:Language>en-US</dc:Language>
        <articleFile format="XML">
http://www.nonexistentpublishing.com/./articles/2001/11/art00345.xml
        </articleFile>
    </article>
    <article>
        <dc:Title>Why XML?</dc:Title>
        <dc:Creator>Angela Martin</dc:Creator>
        <dc:Subject>Programming</dc:Subject>
        <dc:Subject>Markup languages</dc:Subject>
        <dc:Subject>XML</dc:Subject>
        <dc:Date>2001-10-27</dc:Date>
        <dc:Language>en-US</dc:Language>
        <articleFile format="XML">
http://www.nonexistentpublishing.com/./articles/2001/10/art00005.xml
        </articleFile>
    </article>
</articleCatalog>
```

In this stylesheet, we used a very simple technique—nested `xsl:if` elements—to select the nodes to be included in the customized article index. Another possible approach is to use multiple templates, each of which calls the next with a successively small number of nodes, until the desired subset is reached. Here's an example of this approach, with the single template and nested `xsl:if` statements replaced.

```
<xsl:template match="article" >
    <xsl:if test="dc:Language=$lang1">
       <xsl:apply-templates mode="mode1" />
    </xsl:if>
</xsl:template>

<xsl:template match="dc:Subject" mode="mode1">
```

```
        <xsl:if test="current()=$subj1">
           <xsl:apply-templates select="../dc:Format" mode="mode2" />
        </xsl:if>
   </xsl:template>

   <xsl:template match="dc:Format" mode="mode2" >
      <xsl:if test='current()=$form1'>
         <xsl:apply-templates select=".." mode="mode3">
            <xsl:sort select="dc:Date" order="ascending" />
         </xsl:apply-templates>
      </xsl:if>
   </xsl:template>
```

Each template here forwards processing on to the next, using the `mode` attributes of `xsl:apply-templates` and `xsl:template` to restrict the templates that can be called. The `mode` attribute allows us to control which templates get called in situations where the children of an element are to be processed, but there are multiple templates, called in different contexts, that might match those children. By using common `mode` attribute values on both `xsl:apply-templates` and `xsl:template`, we can control exactly which templates `xsl:apply-templates` can be executed.

The first template matches on the `article` element and checks for a match on the value of the `dc:Language` element; if it matches, then the next template is called. This template, in turn, checks the value of `dc:Subject` and forwards processing on to the next template if the desired value is specified. The third template sorts the set of nodes that matches all three templates and forwards them to the final template (shown next), which formats the output.

```
   <xsl:template match="article" mode="mode1" >
      <xsl:element name="article">
         <xsl:element name="dc:Title">
            <xsl:value-of select="dc:Title" /></xsl:element>
         <xsl:element name="dc:Creator">
            <xsl:value-of select="dc:Creator" /></xsl:element>
         <xsl:for-each select="dc:Subject">
            <xsl:element name="dc:Subject">
               <xsl:value-of select="." /></xsl:element>
         </xsl:for-each>
         <xsl:element name="dc:Date">
            <xsl:value-of select="dc:Date" /></xsl:element>
         <xsl:element name="dc:Language">
            <xsl:value-of select="dc:Language" /></xsl:element>
         <xsl:for-each select="articleFile" >
```

```
    <xsl:if test="@format=$form1">
        <xsl:element name="articleFile">
            <xsl:attribute name="format">
                <xsl:value-of select="@format" />
            </xsl:attribute>
            <xsl:text>http://www.nonexistentpublishing.com/</xsl:text>
            <xsl:value-of select="." />
        </xsl:element>
    </xsl:if>
    </xsl:for-each>
    </xsl:element>
    </xsl:template>

</xsl:stylesheet>
```

Generating Stylesheets

The situation described in the previous example represents an opportunity to leverage XSLT's ability to generate other stylesheets as well as XML documents. By using an external configuration file, we can write a stylesheet that will automatically generate all of the stylesheets required to correctly syndicate content to customers.

First, let's look at the external configuration file. The following example has three sections:

▶ The `selectParams` section represents selection criteria to be applied against the entries in the article index to determine whether they should be sent to the customer.

▶ The `sortby` section indicates how entries in the final document are to be sorted.

▶ The `includeData` section presents the article index entry content to be generated.

```
<?xml version="1.0" ?>
<ssgenerate>
    <selectParams>
        <param name="subj" match="dc:Subject">Programming</param>
        <param name="lang" match="dc:Language">en-US</param>
        <param name="fmt"  match="dc:Format">XML</param>
    </selectParams>
```

```
    <sortby match="dc:Date" order="ascending" />
    <includeData>
        <element name="dc:Title" />
        <element name="dc:Subject" />
        <element name="dc:Language" />
        <element name="dc:Creator" />
        <element name="dc:Description" />
        <element name="dc:Date" />
        <element name="dc:Format" />
        <element name="articleFile" />
    </includeData>
</ssgenerate>
```

We'll write a stylesheet that reads external configuration files such as the one shown here and generates stylesheets capable of selecting and writing entries from our article index that match the criteria specified. Because many of the elements in our output stylesheet will have attribute values and element content that comes from the input configuration file, we'll use xsl:element to generate all of the output stylesheet elements. In situations where the output stylesheet contains more static data, it may be more appropriate (and coding may be faster) to create the output stylesheet elements using a combination of literal elements and an alternate XSLT namespace. For information on how to use alternate XSLT namespaces, look at the description of the xsl:namespace-alias element in Chapter 7.

Our stylesheet-generator stylesheet is shown next. For readability, the elements responsible for generating the output stylesheet are highlighted, and comments are included after each template to explain what's going on.

```
<xsl:stylesheet version="1.0"
                xmlns:xsl=http://www.w3.org/1999/XSL/Transform
                xmlns:dc="http://purl.org/dc/elements/1.1/" >
<xsl:output method="xml" version="1.0" encoding="UTF-8" indent="yes"
                omit-xml-declaration="yes" />
```

Note that we've specified the omit-xml-declaration attribute on the xsl:output element. This suppresses the generation of the ?xml? prolog element in the stylesheet.

```
    <xsl:template match="ssgenerate">
        <xsl:element name="xsl:stylesheet">
            <xsl:attribute name="version">1.0</xsl:attribute>
            <xsl:element name="xsl:output">
```

```
        <xsl:attribute name="method">xml</xsl:attribute>
         <xsl:attribute name="version">1.0</xsl:attribute>
        <xsl:attribute name="encoding">UTF-8</xsl:attribute>
        <xsl:attribute name="indent">yes</xsl:attribute>
    </xsl:element>
    <xsl:comment> </xsl:comment>
    <xsl:element name="xsl:strip-space">
        <xsl:attribute name="elements">
            articleCatalog
        </xsl:attribute>
    </xsl:element>
    <xsl:comment> </xsl:comment>
    <xsl:element name="xsl:template">
        <xsl:attribute name="match">
            articleCatalog
        </xsl:attribute>
        <xsl:element name="xsl:copy">
            <xsl:element name="xsl:for-each">
                <xsl:attribute name="select">
                    article
                </xsl:attribute>
                <xsl:element name="xsl:apply-templates">
                    <xsl:attribute name="select">
                        <xsl:value-of
                            select="selectParams/param[1]/@match" />
                    </xsl:attribute>
                </xsl:element>
            </xsl:element>
        </xsl:element>
    </xsl:element>
    <xsl:comment> </xsl:comment>
    <xsl:apply-templates select="selectParams/param"
            mode="genCompare" />
    <xsl:comment> </xsl:comment>
    <xsl:call-template name="writeOutput" />
    <xsl:comment> </xsl:comment>
    </xsl:element>
 </xsl:template>
```

This template generates our output xsl:stylesheet element, an xsl:
output element, an xsl:strip-space element, and an xsl:template
element that matches on the articleCatalog element in our article index. The

template, in turn, includes an `xsl:copy` element to copy the `articleCatalog` element, an `xsl:for-each` element to iterate through the `article` children of `articleCatalog`, and an `xsl:apply-templates` element that calls the first of the three templates used to qualify the article index entries to be extracted.

You'll notice that the template contains two elements that don't directly generate elements but are critical to constructing the final stylesheet. The first, `xsl:apply-templates select="selectParams/param" mode= "genCompare" /`, tells the stylesheet to select each of the param elements that is a child of the `selectParams` element and call the template with the `genCompare` mode to process these elements. This template called in this manner generates templates in the output stylesheet that match on each of the elements that contains selection criteria and passes elements that have the correct values on to the next template. This is the same multiple-template technique described at the end of the earlier example that was used as a replacement for multiple nested `xsl:if` elements; in reality, you could also generate multiple `xsl:if` elements in this stylesheet by replacing the `xsl:apply-templates mode="genCompare"` element with the appropriate `xsl:element` elements.

Note that when we generated the `xsl:stylesheet` element, we didn't have to include elements for the `xmlns:xsl` and `xmlns:dc` namespaces. That's because when the elements are generated, the namespaces in effect are propagated to the generated elements; because these namespaces are in effect from this stylesheet's `xsl:stylesheet` element, they are added to the output stylesheet as well.

```
<xsl:template match="selectParams/param" mode="genCompare">
    <xsl:element name="xsl:template">
        <xsl:attribute name="match">
            <xsl:value-of select="@match" /></xsl:attribute>
        <xsl:element name="xsl:if">
            <xsl:attribute name="test">
                current()=&apos;<xsl:value-of select="." />&apos;
            </xsl:attribute>
            <xsl:if test="position()=last()">
                <xsl:element name="xsl:apply-templates">
                    <xsl:attribute name="select">..</xsl:attribute>
                    <xsl:attribute name="mode">genTmpl</xsl:attribute>
                    <xsl:element name="xsl:sort">
                        <xsl:attribute name="select">
                            <xsl:value-of
                                select="../../sortby/@match" />
                        </xsl:attribute>
                        <xsl:attribute name="order">
```

```
                <xsl:value-of
                    select="../../sortby/@order" />
            </xsl:attribute>
        </xsl:element>
    </xsl:element>
</xsl:if>
<xsl:if test="not(position()=last())">
    <xsl:element name="xsl:apply-templates">
        <xsl:attribute name="select">
        ../<xsl:value-of
        select="following-sibling::param[position()=1]/@match"
        /></xsl:attribute>
    </xsl:element>
</xsl:if>
        </xsl:element>
    </xsl:element>
    <xsl:comment> </xsl:comment>
</xsl:template>
```

For each `param` element in our configuration file, this template writes a template to the output stylesheet that contains an `xsl:if` element to test for the desired condition. In all of the templates but the last one, a positive test passes control to an `xsl:apply-templates` element, which calls the next template in line; in the last template, an `xsl:apply-templates` element is generated with an `xsl:sort` child to sort the output document according to the rules in the configuration file.

```
<xsl:template name="writeOutput">
    <xsl:element name="xsl:template">
        <xsl:attribute name="match">article</xsl:attribute>
        <xsl:attribute name="mode">genTmpl</xsl:attribute>
        <xsl:element name="xsl:element">
            <xsl:attribute name="name">article</xsl:attribute>
            <xsl:for-each select="/ssgenerate/includeData/element">
                <xsl:element name="xsl:element">
                    <xsl:attribute name="name">
                        <xsl:value-of select="@name" /></xsl:element>
                    <xsl:element name="xsl:value-of">
                        <xsl:attribute name="select">
                            <xsl:value-of select="@name" />
```

```
            </xsl:attribute>
          </xsl:element>
        </xsl:element>
      </xsl:for-each>
    </xsl:element>
  </xsl:element>
</xsl:template>

</xsl:stylesheet>
```

This final template writes a template to the output file that is responsible for generating the actual output. The generated template is called when an element that matches all of the required criteria is found.

The generated stylesheet looks like this:

```
<xsl:stylesheet xmlns:dc="http://purl.org/dc/elements/1.1/"
                xmlns:xsl="http://www.w3.org/1999/XSL/Transform" version="1.0">
<xsl:output method="xml" version="1.0" encoding="UTF-8" indent="yes"/>

<xsl:strip-space elements="articleCatalog"/>

<xsl:template match="articleCatalog">
<xsl:copy>
<xsl:for-each select="article">
<xsl:apply-templates select="dc:Subject"/>
</xsl:for-each>
</xsl:copy>
</xsl:template>

<xsl:template match="dc:Subject">
<xsl:if test="current()='Programming'">
<xsl:apply-templates select="../dc:Language"/>
</xsl:if>
</xsl:template>

<xsl:template match="dc:Language">
<xsl:if test="current()='en-US'">
<xsl:apply-templates select="../dc:Format"/>
</xsl:if>
</xsl:template>

<xsl:template match="dc:Format">
<xsl:if test="current()='XML'">
<xsl:apply-templates select=".." mode="genTmpl">
<xsl:sort select="dc:Date" order="ascending"/>
```

```
</xsl:apply-templates>
</xsl:if>
</xsl:template>

<xsl:template match="article" mode="genTmpl">
<xsl:element name="article">
<xsl:element name="dc:Title">
<xsl:value-of select="dc:Title"/>
</xsl:element>
<xsl:element name="dc:Subject">
<xsl:value-of select="dc:Subject"/>
</xsl:element>
<xsl:element name="dc:Language">
<xsl:value-of select="dc:Language"/>
</xsl:element>
<xsl:element name="dc:Creator">
<xsl:value-of select="dc:Creator"/>
</xsl:element>
<xsl:element name="dc:Description">
<xsl:value-of select="dc:Description"/>
</xsl:element>
<xsl:element name="dc:Date">
<xsl:value-of select="dc:Date"/>
</xsl:element>
<xsl:element name="dc:Format">
<xsl:value-of select="dc:Format"/>
</xsl:element>
<xsl:element name="articleFile">
<xsl:value-of select="articleFile"/>
</xsl:element>
</xsl:element>
</xsl:template>

</xsl:stylesheet>
```

Building References Between Generated Documents

When a single XML document is used to generate multiple output documents (HTML pages, for example), it's often necessary to build references between the different generated documents. These references can be created using any combination of attributes and content that forms a unique identifier for one or more elements in an XML document.

To illustrate the creation of these references, we'll build a table of contents for a fictitious book about Java programming. Our goal is to use a single XML document and some number of XSLT stylesheets to create both the display pages for the book itself (in HTML) and a table of contents (also in HTML) that can be used to link to various portions of the book's content. The following XML document shows the structure of the book.

```xml
<?xml version="1.0" encoding="UTF-8" ?>
<Book xmlns:dc="http://purl.org/dc/elements/1.1/" >
   <dc:Metadata>
      <dc:Identifier system="ISBN">9999999999</dc:Identifier>
      <dc:Title>Java in 15 Minutes or Less</dc:Title>
      <dc:Creator>Chris von See</dc:Creator>
      <dc:Creator>Nitin Keskar</dc:Creator>
      <dc:Subject>Java</dc:Subject>
      <dc:Description>A unique technique to learn Java in 15
minutes</dc:Description>
      <dc:Publisher>Non-Existent Publishing, Inc.</dc:Publisher>
      <dc:Date>2001</dc:Date>
      <dc:Language>en-US</dc:Language>
   </dc:Metadata>
   <body>
      <Part name="The Java Programming Language">
         <Unit name="Introduction to Java">
            <Chapter name="What is Java?">
               <Section name="What You Will Learn In This Chapter">
                  <!-- Content of section goes here -->
               </Section>
               <Section name="What Is Java?">
                  <!-- Content of section goes here -->
               </Section>
               <Section name="What Java Can Do For You">
                  <!-- Content of section goes here -->
               </Section>
            </Chapter>
            <Chapter name="Getting Started With Java">
               <Section name="What You Will Learn In This Chapter">
                  <!-- Content of section goes here -->
               </Section>
               <Section name="How Do I Get Started?">
                  <!-- Content of section goes here -->
               </Section>
               <Section
                 name="Coding Your First Java Application - Hello, World!">
                  <!-- Content of section goes here -->
               </Section>
               <Section name="What's Next?">
                  <!-- Content of section goes here -->
```

```
            </Section>
        </Chapter>
        <Chapter name="Introducing The Java Packages">
            <Section name="What You Will Learn In This Chapter">
                <!-- Content of section goes here -->
            </Section>
            <Section name="The Java Core API">
                <!-- Content of section goes here -->
            </Section>
            <Section name="java.lang">
                <!-- Content of section goes here -->
            </Section>
            <Section name="java.io">
                <!-- Content of section goes here -->
            </Section>
            <Section name="java.util">
                <!-- Content of section goes here -->
            </Section>
            <Section name="java.net">
                <!-- Content of section goes here -->
            </Section>
            <Section name="java.applet">
                <!-- Content of section goes here -->
            </Section>
            <Section name="java.awt And Related Classes">
                <!-- Content of section goes here -->
            </Section>
            <Section name="java.rmi And Related Classes">
                <!-- Content of section goes here -->
            </Section>
            <Section name="java.security">
                <!-- Content of section goes here -->
            </Section>
            <Section name="java.sql">
                <!-- Content of section goes here -->
            </Section>
            <Section name="java.text">
                <!-- Content of section goes here -->
            </Section>
            <Section name="What's Next?">
                <!-- Content of section goes here -->
            </Section>
        </Chapter>
    </Unit>
</Part>
<Part name="Java Tools">
    <Unit name="Java Development Tools">
```

```
      <Chapter name="The Java Development Kit (JDK)">
         <Section name="What You Will Learn In This Chapter">
            <!-- Content of section goes here -->
         </Section>
         <Section name="What&apos;s In The Java Development Kit?">
            <!-- Content of section goes here -->
         </Section>
         <Section name="How Do I Use the JDK?">
            <!-- Content of section goes here -->
         </Section>
      </Chapter>
      <Chapter name="Integrated Development Environments">
         <Section name="What You Will Learn In This Chapter">
            <!-- Content of section goes here -->
         </Section>
         <Section name="Microsoft Visual J++">
            <!-- Content of section goes here -->
         </Section>
         <Section name="WebGain Visual Cafe">
            <!-- Content of section goes here -->
         </Section>
         <Section name="Borland JBuilder">
            <!-- Content of section goes here -->
         </Section>
         <Section name="Oracle JDeveloper">
            <!-- Content of section goes here -->
         </Section>
      </Chapter>
   </Unit>
  </Part>
  <Part name="Appendices">
   <Unit name="Java Resources">
      <Chapter name="Java Resources On The Web">
         <Section name="What&apos;s Available On The Web?">
            <!-- Content of section goes here -->
         </Section>
      </Chapter>
   </Unit>
  </Part>
 </body>
</Book>
```

The key sections of the book that we're interested in showing in the table of contents are the part-, unit-, chapter-, and section-level headings, which are represented in the document by the Part, Unit, Chapter, and Section elements, respectively. Of course, had we wanted to represent other sections of the book in the table of contents (end-of-chapter questions, appendixes, or the book's index, for example), the technique used in this example would apply equally well.

Generate Unique IDs

To make the process of building the links between the table of contents and the actual content a little easier, we're going to assign unique IDs to each `Part`, `Unit`, `Chapter`, and `Section` element in the document. XSLT is a great way to do this; a stylesheet to accomplish this goal is shown here.

```
<xsl:stylesheet version="1.0"
                 xmlns:xsl="http://www.w3.org/1999/XSL/Transform" >

   <xsl:template match="@*|node()" >
     <xsl:copy >
     <xsl:if test="local-name(.)='Part'">
     <xsl:attribute name="id">
       part-<xsl:value-of select="generate-id()" />
     </xsl:attribute>
     </xsl:if>
     <xsl:if test="local-name(.)='Unit'">
     <xsl:attribute name="id">
       unit-<xsl:value-of select="generate-id()" />
     </xsl:attribute>
     </xsl:if>
     <xsl:if test="local-name(.)='Chapter'">
     <xsl:attribute name="id">
        chap-<xsl:value-of select="generate-id()" />
     </xsl:attribute>
     </xsl:if>
     <xsl:if test="local-name(.)='Section'">
     <xsl:attribute name="id">
        sect-<xsl:value-of select="generate-id()" />
     </xsl:attribute>
     </xsl:if>
     <xsl:apply-templates select="@*|node()" />
     </xsl:copy>
   </xsl:template>

</xsl:stylesheet>
```

This stylesheet provides an example of an identity transformation—a template that makes an exact copy of its input—with an extra twist. The template matches on any attribute or node in the input document, and the `xsl:copy` element tells XSLT to make a copy of the currently matched node. The little twist is that we've added `xsl:attribute` elements inside the `xsl:copy` element to add our `id` attributes; to determine which element we've matched on, the template uses the `local-name()` function to compare the names of the elements we're interested in. To generate an ID value for each matched element that is guaranteed to be unique across the entire document, we've used XSLT's very handy `generate-id()` function; because the IDs generated in this way are somewhat arbitrary, we have combined the generated value with prefixes that are specific to each type of element. If we had wanted to generate IDs that are somewhat less arbitrary (such as ascending numbers), we could have used `xsl:number level="any" count="Part|Unit|Chapter|Section"` / instead of using the `generate-id()` function.

Now every heading element has an additional attribute that we can use to create HTML anchors in the main document and links in the table of contents.

Generate the Master Document

To give the table of contents something to link to, we'll generate a simple HTML master document containing the headings and our content placeholders. Let's look at the following stylesheet to find out how this is done. The comments interspersed among the stylesheet templates explain what each portion of the stylesheet is doing, and key portions of the stylesheet are highlighted in bold.

```
<xsl:stylesheet version="1.0"
               xmlns:xsl=http://www.w3.org/1999/XSL/Transform
               xmlns:dc="http://purl.org/dc/elements/1.1/" >

  <xsl:template match="Book" >
    <html>
    <head>
      <title><xsl:value-of select="dc:Metadata/dc:Title" /></title>
    </head>
    <body>
    <xsl:apply-templates />
    </body>
    </html>
  </xsl:template>
```

This template opens the output page by generating the html, head, title, and body elements. The title of the page is taken from the dc:Title element inside the input document's metadata.

```
<xsl:template match="Part" >
   <xsl:element name="a">
      <xsl:attribute name="name">
        <xsl:value-of select="@id" />
      </xsl:attribute>
   </xsl:element>
   <h1>Part <xsl:number level="single" count="Part" />
      : <xsl:value-of select="@name" /></h1>
   <xsl:apply-templates />
</xsl:template>
<xsl:template match="Unit" >
   <xsl:element name="a">
      <xsl:attribute name="name">
         <xsl:value-of select="@id" />
      </xsl:attribute>
   </xsl:element>
   <h2>Unit <xsl:number level="single" count="Unit" />: <xsl:value-of
select="@name" /></h2>
   <xsl:apply-templates />
</xsl:template>
<xsl:template match="Chapter" >
   <xsl:element name="a">
      <xsl:attribute name="name">
         <xsl:value-of select="@id" />
      </xsl:attribute>
   </xsl:element>
   <h3>Chapter <xsl:number level="single" count="Chapter" />
      : <xsl:value-of select="@name" />
   </h3>
   <xsl:apply-templates />
</xsl:template>

<xsl:template match="Section" >
   <xsl:element name="a">
      <xsl:attribute name="name">
         <xsl:value-of select="@id" />
      </xsl:attribute>
```

```
    </xsl:element>
    <h4>Section <xsl:number level="single" count="Section" />
       : <xsl:value-of select="@name" /></h4>
    <xsl:apply-templates />
  </xsl:template>
```

These four templates generate the headings for the `Part`, `Unit`, `Chapter`, and `Section` elements, respectively. In addition to the title, each heading contains a number representing the position of that heading relative to the ones that precede it. Prior to each heading, an HTML named anchor is generated using the ID value of the matched node; this is the location to which each link in the table of contents will navigate when clicked.

```
  <xsl:template match="comment()" >
     <p>--- <xsl:value-of select="." /> ---</p>
  </xsl:template>
  <xsl:template match="text()" >
  </xsl:template>
```

```
</xsl:stylesheet>
```

The template matching on `comment()` is used to pick up the comments in the input document that serve as placeholders for book content, and the template matching on `text()` simply suppresses generation of any output that we don't want in our final document.

This is a very straightforward stylesheet; you've seen the techniques illustrated here used in many examples throughout this book. When we run it against our document, the resulting HTML looks like this:

```
<a name="part-N26"></a>
<h1>Part 1: The Java Programming Language</h1>
<a name="unit-N29"></a>
<h2>Unit 1: Introduction to Java</h2>
<a name="chap-N2C"></a>
<h3>Chapter 1: What is Java?</h3>
<a name="sect-N2F"></a>
<h4>Section 1: What You Will Learn In This Chapter</h4>
<p>---  Content of section goes here  ---</p>
<a name="sect-N35"></a>
<h4>Section 2: What Is Java?</h4>
<p>---  Content of section goes here  ---</p>
```

```
<a name="sect-N3B"></a>
<h4>Section 3: What Java Can Do For You</h4>
<p>---  Content of section goes here  ---</p>   .
```

Figure 11-1 shows the content page of the Java book.

Generate the Table of Contents

Finally, we need to generate the table of contents itself. The stylesheet for doing so looks very similar to that used to generate the actual book content, except that

Figure 11-1   *The content page for our Java book*

instead of generating named anchors, this stylesheet generates links to the anchors in the content document.

```
<xsl:stylesheet version="1.0"
                 xmlns:xsl=http://www.w3.org/1999/XSL/Transform
                 xmlns:dc="http://purl.org/dc/elements/1.1/" >

   <xsl:template match="Book" >
      <html>
      <head>
        <title><xsl:value-of select="dc:Metadata/dc:Title" /></title>
      </head>
      <body>
      <xsl:apply-templates />
      </body>
      </html>
   </xsl:template>

   <xsl:template match="dc:Metadata" >
      <p>&quot;<xsl:value-of select="dc:Title" />&quot;, by
         <xsl:for-each select="dc:Creator" >
            <xsl:value-of select="." />
            <xsl:if test="position() != last()" > and </xsl:if>
         </xsl:for-each>
      </p>
      <p>Copyright <xsl:value-of select="dc:Date" />. All Rights Reserved.</p>
<p><xsl:value-of select="dc:Identifier/@system" />: <xsl:value-of
select="dc:Identifier" /></p>
      <p>Subject: <xsl:value-of select="dc:Subject" /></p>
      <p>Description: <xsl:value-of select="dc:Description" /></p>
      <br /><br />
      <xsl:apply-templates />
   </xsl:template>
```

The metadata contained in the original input document is a short description of the book, placed preceding the table of contents.

```
<xsl:template match="Part" >
    <h1>Part <xsl:number level="single" count="Part" />:
        <xsl:element name="a">
            <xsl:attribute name="href">
                javabook-content.html#<xsl:value-of select="@id" />
            </xsl:attribute>
            <xsl:value-of select="@name" />
        </xsl:element>
    </h1>
    <xsl:apply-templates />
</xsl:template>

<xsl:template match="Unit" >
    <h2>Unit <xsl:number level="single" count="Unit" />:
        <xsl:element name="a">
            <xsl:attribute name="href">
                javabook-content.html#<xsl:value-of select="@id" />
            </xsl:attribute>
            <xsl:value-of select="@name" />
        </xsl:element>
    </h2>
    <xsl:apply-templates />
</xsl:template>

<xsl:template match="Chapter" >
    <h3>Chapter <xsl:number level="single" count="Chapter" />:
        <xsl:element name="a">
            <xsl:attribute name="href">
                javabook-content.html#<xsl:value-of select="@id" />
            </xsl:attribute>
            <xsl:value-of select="@name" />
        </xsl:element>
    </h3>
    <xsl:apply-templates />
</xsl:template>

<xsl:template match="Section" >
    <h4>Section <xsl:number level="single" count="Section" />:
        <xsl:element name="a">
            <xsl:attribute name="href">
```

```
            javabook-content.html#<xsl:value-of select="@id" />
          </xsl:attribute>
          <xsl:value-of select="@name" />
        </xsl:element>
      </h4>
      <xsl:apply-templates />
    </xsl:template>

    <xsl:template match="text()" >
    </xsl:template>

</xsl:stylesheet>
```

Note that each template matching on a `Part`, `Unit`, `Chapter`, or `Section`
element generates a hyperlink to the named anchor for the corresponding section on
the content page. Now (assuming that both the content page and table of contents are
in the same directory), a click on one of the headings in the table of contents will
take the reader to the corresponding section in the content document.

An example section of the HTML looks like this:

```
<h1>Part 1:
        <a href="javabook-content.html#part-N26">
          The Java Programming Language</a>
</h1>
<h2>Unit 1:
        <a href="javabook-content.html#unit-N29">
          Introduction to Java</a>
</h2>
<h3>Chapter 1:
        <a href="javabook-content.html#chap-N2C">
          What is Java?</a>
</h3>
<h4>Section 1:
        <a href="javabook-content.html#sect-N2F">
          What You Will Learn In This Chapter</a>
</h4>
<h4>Section 2:
        <a href="javabook-content.html#sect-N35">
          What Is Java?</a>
</h4>
```

```
<h4>Section 3:
        <a href="javabook-content.html#sect-N3B">
            What Java Can Do For You</a>
</h4>
```

When rendered by a browser, the page looks like Figure 11-2.

Creating Multiple Documents from One Source

After working through the prior example, you should start to understand how XSLT can be used to generate multiple documents from the same input source. Let's explore this in more detail now, with an example that illustrates how we can generate

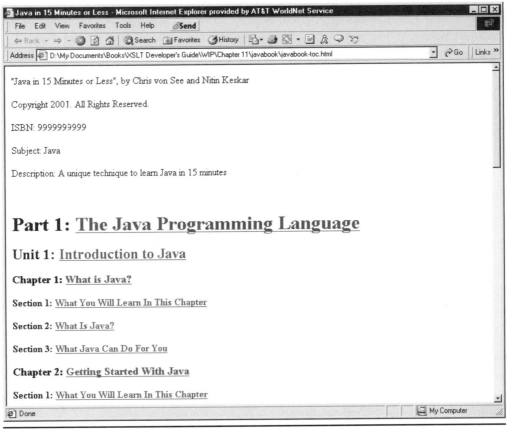

Figure 11-2 *Our table of contents*

different brandings for the same content and reuse that content across more than one site. As our input document, we'll use the HTML book used in the previous example.

Although this example generates an admittedly simplistic web site, the concepts illustrated are in use in many real-life applications.

Define the Presentation Characteristics

To start, we'll need to define our brands: the variable portions of our presentation. This example assumes that there are four different branding characteristics we'll want to manipulate: the header graphics, the navigation bar, the footer content, and the text styles used to control presentation of the content itself. These four branding characteristics are defined in an XML file, shown here.

```xml
<?xml version="1.0" ?>
<brandDefinition>
    <header>
        <headerImage>
            <name>myImage.gif</name>
            <height>100</height>
            <width>100%</width>
            <altText>This is my image</altText>
        </headerImage>
    </header>
    <navigation>
        <page name="Home">/index.html</page>
        <page name="About us">/aboutus.html</page>
        <page name="Products">/products/index.html</page>
        <page name="Contact us">/contactus.html</page>
        <page name="Support">/support/support.html</page>
    </navigation>
    <footer>
        <text>Copyright 2001 CompanyA, Inc.</text>
        <text>All rights reserved.</text>
    </footer>
<contentStyles>
        <contentStyle name="dfdf">
            font-family: Times New Roman, Times, serif; font-size: 20pt;
            background-color: #FF0000
        </contentStyle>
    </contentStyles>
</brandDefinition>
```

Isolating these presentation characteristics in a separate XML file makes it possible to refer to them from many different stylesheets, and for one stylesheet to refer to many different branding files.

Create a Content Presentation Frame

Next we'll create a frame for our content that uses the information in our branding file to render the HTML components surrounding the actual content. In this stylesheet, we make use of several features of XSLT:

▶ Parameters are used to declare information that is passed in to the stylesheet from the stylesheet processor. These could be command-line arguments, for example, or they could be arguments passed in from a Java or Perl program that invokes the processor.

▶ Variables are used to define data items that are used in many places.

▶ The xsl:include element is used to include a base content presentation stylesheet, which renders the actual content inside the framework defined in this stylesheet (more on this shortly).

▶ The XSLT document() function is used to open the branding file and extract information for use in creating the presentation.

▶ An HTML table is defined to contain the pages's content, and xsl:call-template is used to generate each variable (branding) portion of the page. This makes the presentation-related sections of the stylesheet (HTML tables and other tags) more readable.

▶ The xsl:element and xsl:attribute elements are used to generate HTML tags when the content of those tags is variable (such as the < img> tag in the BrandingHeader template).

The stylesheet used to define the presentation frame is shown here.

```
<xsl:stylesheet version="1.0"
                xmlns:xsl="http://www.w3.org/1999/XSL/Transform" >
  <xsl:output method="html" />

  <xsl:param name="brand">default</xsl:param>
```

This parameter is passed in from the command line and defines the brand to be used.

```
<xsl:variable name="brandDefinitionFile">
   <xsl:value-of select="$brand" />-branding.xml</xsl:variable>
<xsl:variable name="brandDefinitionPath"
   select="document($brandDefinitionFile)/brandDefinition" />
```

The brand name passed in to this stylesheet is used to construct the full file name of the XML file containing the branding information. Note that the `brandDefinition` node must be appended to the node set returned from the `document()` function; this is because `brandDefinition` is the root node of the branding file.

```
<xsl:include href="..\multibrand-base.xsl" />
```

The content presentation stylesheet is included. When `xsl:apply-templates` is called form the `BrandContent` template, the templates in this stylesheet will be used to render the content.

```
    <xsl:template match="/" >
       <html>
       <head>
          <title>Welcome to <xsl:value-of select="$brand" /></title>
          <style type="text/css">
          <![CDATA[<!--]]>
          <xsl:for-each
             select="$brandDefinitionPath/contentStyles/contentStyle">
             <xsl:text>.</xsl:text>
             <xsl:value-of select="@name" />
             <xsl:text> { </xsl:text>
<xsl:value-of select="." /><xsl:text> }</xsl:text>
          </xsl:for-each>
          <![CDATA[-->]]>
          </style>
       </head>
       <body>
          <table width="100%" border="2" cellspacing="0" cellpadding="0">
          <tr>
             <td colspan="3" valign="top">
                <xsl:call-template name="BrandHeader" /></td>
          </tr>
          <tr>
             <td width="150" valign="top">
                <xsl:call-template name="BrandNavigation" /></td>
             <td colspan="2">
                <xsl:call-template name="BrandContent" />
             </td>
          </tr>
```

```
        <tr>
          <td colspan="3" valign="top">
            <xsl:call-template name="BrandFooter" /></td>
        </tr>
        </table>
      </body>
      </html>
    </xsl:template>
```

The HTML page is defined containing a table into which the header, navigation bar, content, and footer will be placed. Note that the CSS styles are generated in a `style` element inside the HTML `head` element, and that the `BrandHeader`, `BrandNavigation`, `BrandContent`, and `BrandFooter` templates are called to generate the actual contents of the table.

```
    <xsl:template name="BrandHeader" >
      <xsl:element name="img">
        <xsl:attribute name="src"><xsl:value-of
select="$brandDefinitionPath/header/headerImage/name" /></xsl:attribute>
        <xsl:attribute name="height">
          <xsl:value-of
            select="$brandDefinitionPath/header/headerImage/height" />
        </xsl:attribute>
        <xsl:attribute name="width">
          <xsl:value-of
            select="$brandDefinitionPath/header/headerImage/width" />
        </xsl:attribute>
        <xsl:attribute name="alt">
          <xsl:value-of
            select="$brandDefinitionPath/header/headerImage/altText" />
        </xsl:attribute>
      </xsl:element>
    </xsl:template>
```

This template generates the header. The header contains an image whose characteristics are extracted from the branding file using the variable ($brandDefinitionPath) defined previously. Path elements appended to the $brandDefinitionPath variable refer to the various parts of the branding file.

```
<xsl:template name="BrandNavigation" >
  <table width="150" border="0" cellspacing="0" cellpadding="0">
  <xsl:for-each select="$brandDefinitionPath/navigation/page">
  <tr>
    <td>
      <xsl:element name="a">
```

```
            <xsl:attribute name="href">
             <xsl:value-of select="." /></xsl:attribute>
            <xsl:value-of select="@name" />
          </xsl:element>
        </td>
      </tr>
      </xsl:for-each>
      </table>
</xsl:template>
```

This template generates the navigation bar. It simply generates an HTML hyperlink for each navigation element defined in the branding file.

```
<xsl:template name="BrandContent" >
      <xsl:apply-templates />
    </xsl:template>
```

The input document is processed when `xsl:apply-templates` is called from this template, resulting in the formatted content.

```
    <xsl:template name="BrandFooter" >
      <p>
      <xsl:for-each select="$brandDefinitionPath/footer/text">
        <xsl:value-of select="." />
        <xsl:if test="position() != last()"> <br /> </xsl:if>
      </xsl:for-each>
      </p>
    </xsl:template>
</xsl:stylesheet>
```

The footer is generated from one or more text elements found in the branding file.

Create a Base Content Presentation Stylesheet

Next we'll create a stylesheet that will render our content. The only presentation-related items in this stylesheet are the HTML tags used to render the content; these, in turn, use the CSS styles defined in the branding file to describe how the content is to be presented. The CSS styles are available because they are generated as part of the content presentation frame.

This example uses the same stylesheet as was used to create the content page in the Java book example, so we won't reproduce it here.

Putting It All Together

Now that we have all the pieces in place, we can generate our first branded file. Running our stylesheet processor against our Java book document and using the content presentation frame stylesheet to generate our output, we end up with the output shown in Figure 11-3.

By creating more branding files and rerunning the transformation process with different parameters, we can generate as many versions of this page as we want.

Creating Internationalized Output

In our increasingly multinational economy, providing web sites and other systems that support multiple languages is increasingly critical. A key to providing this

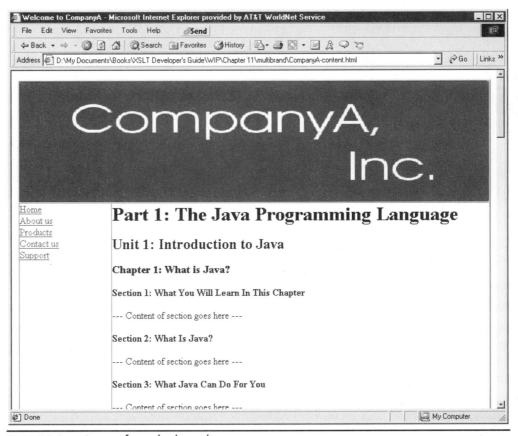

Figure 11-3   *Output from the branding process*

support is the ability to extract all static string data from a system so that it can be translated by a third party and substituted into the application with minimal disruption to code and interface design. While this in and of itself does not make a completely internationalized interface (there are still character set issues and requirements for localized dates and currency, as well as user interface color and layout considerations), the ability to easily add new languages through external files is critical. Java programmers can often address this problem using resource bundles, but in our XML-based system, we need to find another way.

Either of two similar approaches is usually used to provide internationalized output: a single file containing all of the necessary static strings in all supported languages can be created, or multiple files can be created, each containing the static strings for a given language. Although both approaches work, the latter approach is used more frequently because each translation can be managed separately, and it is more efficient to load and search smaller documents. The example here illustrates this approach, but many of the concepts presented apply equally when a single large file is used.

Design and Build the String Document

The first step is to design and build the XML document that will contain our translated strings. A major design consideration is search speed; if all strings are identified using a common element name under a single parent, the XSLT processor will often be required to search a very long chain of sibling elements to find the one requested. A preferable approach is to segment the strings into groups such that the parentage of a given string can be easily calculated programmatically. A sample document illustrating one possible approach is shown here.

```xml
<?xml version="1.0" encoding="UTF-8" ?>
<strings xml:lang="en-US">
   <stringGroup class="main-general">
      <string id="welcomeTitle">
         Welcome to Non-Existent Publishing, Inc.!
      </string>
      <string id="welcomeMessage">
         Welcome to Non-Existent Publishing, where you'll find the finest in
         computer science and electrical and chemical engineering texts.
         Please feel free to browse our catalog; if you don't find what you
         want, contact us!</string>
      <string id="copyright">
         Copyright (c) 2001 Non-Existent Publishing, Inc.
         All Rights Reserved.</string>
   </stringGroup>
```

```
    <stringGroup class="main-navigation">
        <string id="Home">Home</string>
        <string id="About us">About us</string>
        <string id="Management team">Management team</string>
        <string id="Board of Directors">Board of Directors</string>
        <string id="Our Catalog">Our Catalog</string>
        <string id="Computer science">Computer Science</string>
        <string id="Electrical Engineering">Electrical Engineering</string>
        <string id="Chemical Engineering">Chemical Engineering</string>
        <string id="Contact us">Contact us</string>
    </stringGroup>
    <stringGroup class="main-catalogSearch">
        <string id="enterSearch">
            Enter as many different search criteria as you can, then
            press the &quot;Search&quot; button.</string>
        <string id="Title">Title:</string>
        <string id="Author">Author:</string>
        <string id="Keywords">Keywords:</string>
        <string id="Search">Search</string>
    </stringGroup>
    <stringGroup class="errorMessages">
        <stringGroup class=" info">
            <string id="pleasewait">Please wait...</string>
            <string id="nomatch">
                There were no books matching your search criteria - please
                try again.</string>
            <string id="yesmatch">
                Your search results are displayed below:</string>
        </stringGroup>
        <stringGroup class=" warn">
            <string id="systemBudy">
                We&apos;re sorry... our catalog system is busy. Please try
                your search again.</string>
            <string id="toomanyresults">
                Your search returned a very large number of results - please
                provide additional qualifying information and try your search
                again.</string>
        </stringGroup>
        <stringGroup class=" error">
            <string id="notavail">
                We&apos;re sorry - our catalog system is
                temporarily unavailable. Please try again later.</string>
            <string id="internalerr">An internal error has occurred.</string>
        </stringGroup>
    </stringGroup>
</strings>
```

Note that the XML prolog specifies `encoding="UTF-8`, which is a good
general encoding that both supports internationalized characters and represents many
common English and European language characters as recognizable single bytes.
The `strings` element specifies `lang="en-US"`, which allows the programs that
use this file to easily identify the target language. The strings are grouped according
to their use, making searches for a particular string much faster overall.

Find Internationalized Strings

Now that we have our string file, let's explore the logic needed to retrieve
strings. We saw in our previous example how the XSLT `document()` function
can be used to open a document other than the processor's input; we'll use that
same technique to retrieve messages from our string file. Here's an example
stylesheet that illustrates the point:

```
<xsl:stylesheet version="1.0"
                xmlns:xsl="http://www.w3.org/1999/XSL/Transform">

   <xsl:param name="stringFile">strings-en-US.xml</xsl:param>
   <xsl:variable name="stringFilePath"
        select="document($stringFile)/strings" />

   <xsl:template match="/" >
      <html>
      <head>
         <title>
            <xsl:value-of select="$stringFilePath
/stringGroup[@class='general']/string[@id='welcomeTitle']" />      ]— Should be one line
         </title>
      </head>
      <body>
      <table width="100%" cellpadding="0" cellspacing="0" border="0">
         <tr>
            <td colspan="2">
               <p><xsl:value-of select="$stringFilePath
/stringGroup[@class='general']/string[@id='welcomeTitle']" /></p>      ]— Should be one line
               <p><xsl:value-of select="$stringFilePath
/stringGroup[@class='general']/string[@id='welcomeMessage']" /></p>    ]— Should be one line
            </td>
         </tr>
         <tr>
            <td valign="top">
               <br />
               <a href="/index.html"><xsl:value-of select="$stringFilePath
/stringGroup[@class='navigation']/string[@id='Home']" /></a><br />    ]— Should be
                                                                          one line
```

```
                    <a href="/aboutus.html"><xsl:value-of select="$stringFilePath
/stringGroup[@class='navigation']/string[@id='About us']" /></a><br />
                    <a href="/catalog.html"><xsl:value-of select="$stringFilePath
/stringGroup[@class='navigation']/string[@id='Our Catalog']" /></a><br />
                    <a href="/contact.html"><xsl:value-of select="$stringFilePath
/stringGroup[@class='navigation']/string[@id='Contact us']" /></a><br />
                </td>
                <td>
                    <p><br /><xsl:value-of select="$stringFilePath
/stringGroup[@class='catalogSearch']/string[@id='enterSearch']" /><br /></p>
                    <form action="/searchCat.jsp">
                        <p><xsl:value-of select="$stringFilePath
/stringGroup[@class='catalogSearch']/string[@id='Title']" /></p>
                        <input type="text" name="Title" />
                        <p><xsl:value-of select="$stringFilePath
/stringGroup[@class='catalogSearch']/string[@id='Author']" /></p>
                        <input type="text" name="Author" />
                        <p><xsl:value-of select="$stringFilePath
/stringGroup[@class='catalogSearch']/string[@id='Keywords']" /></p>
                        <input type="text" name="Keywords" />
                        <xsl:element name="input">
                            <xsl:attribute name="type">submit</xsl:attribute>
                            <xsl:attribute name="name">submit</xsl:attribute>
                            <xsl:attribute name="value"><xsl:value-of
select="$stringFilePath/stringGroup[@class='catalogSearch']
/string[@id='Search']" /></xsl:attribute>
                        </xsl:element>
                    </form>
                </td>
            </tr>
            <tr>
                <td colspan="2">
                <p><xsl:value-of select="$stringFilePath
/stringGroup[@class='general']/string[@id='copyright']" /></p>
                </td>
            </tr>
        </table>
        </body>
        </html>
    </xsl:template>
</xsl:stylesheet>
```

> *Should be one line* (×9, marking the wrapped XPath expressions above)

All of the highlighted portions of this stylesheet show how strings can be extracted from the language-specific static string file and inserted into the output document. In each case, we build the XPath expression that retrieves the appropriate string using a combination of the following:

▶ The global variable definition (`$stringFilePath`) that retrieves the message document.

▶ One or more nodes that select the `stringGroup` element with the appropriate `class` attribute value.

▶ A node that selects the appropriate string element from the children of the `stringGroup` element selected previously.

▶ In our example, the name of the static string file is stored in the `stringFile` parameter, with a default value of `strings-en-US.xml`; to substitute a different language file, simply pass a parameter of the same name to the stylesheet.

Figure 11-4 shows an English-language translation of the output document.

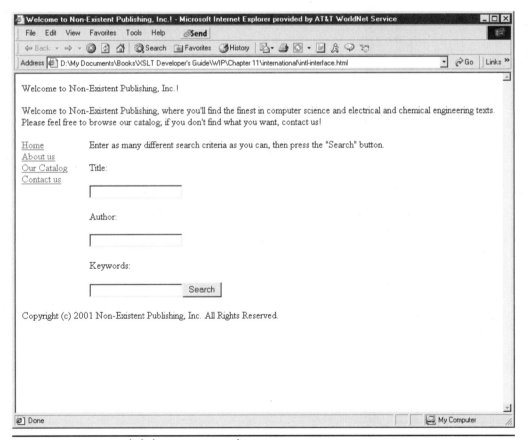

Figure 11-4   *An English-language translation*

Summary

This chapter showed you how XSLT can be used to solve real-life problems and offered some ideas on how it can be applied to your own data transformation and software development problems. Think of XSLT not as a solution to every problem, but rather as one tool among many in your development toolbox. The key to effective use of this powerful tool is realizing what XSLT is and is not, and thinking about the problems you need to solve with those capabilities (and constraints) in mind.

CHAPTER 2

XSLT in the Enterprise

U p to this point in the book, we have discussed the syntax and semantics of XSLT, as well as the strengths and limitations of XSLT. While it is true that XSLT is a Turing-complete language, and that, *given enough time and resources*, you could use it to solve any computing problem, it is equally true that the Turing completeness of XSLT is perhaps too theoretical a consideration for many who have to architect and develop enterprise applications within the familiar constraints of time, money, and resources, while ensuring good quality, code reusability, robustness, and ease of future maintenance. In this chapter, we discuss the use of XSLT at a different level of abstraction: that is, we discuss the practical considerations for deciding which areas of enterprise-level applications are most appropriate for the use of XSLT. We will start by discussing the XSLT support provided by the major web browsers. Then we will use this knowledge as the foundation for discussing the important topics of content syndication and the creation of applications in which content is separated from presentation. Then we will discuss application integration, both within the enterprise boundaries (EAI) and across them (B2B). Finally, we will put all these pieces together to formulate a framework of deployment issues to consider in building useful XSLT applications.

Client-Side XSLT

Client is a broad term that may mean different things to different people. It may refer to a presentation conduit such as a web browser or a WAP microbrowser embedded in a PDA or a cell phone. In a different context, it may refer to a hardware device such as a PC, PDA, or cell phone. In the EAI or B2B realm, it might refer to a client application that subscribes to data published by another application. For the purpose of the present discussion, we will use the term *client* to refer to a web browser or microbrowser.

In the same vein, using XSLT on the client side means pushing the stylesheet along with the source XML document to the client and giving the client the freedom to interpret it. Of course, this also means delegating the responsibility of parsing the source file and the stylesheet to the client as well, and therein lies the crux of the discussion.

There are two questions to be reckoned with here. The first is whether the client is *capable* of processing XSLT, which is what we will discuss in this section. The second question is whether you *should* architect an application so that XSLT processing becomes the client's responsibility. We will defer the second question until the next section.

Clients Capable of XSLT Processing

Until recently, the question as to whether you should use client-side XSLT was really a nonquestion since the browsers used by a large fraction of the population—that is, Internet Explorer (IE) and Netscape Navigator (NN)—could not process XSLT, at least not without specialized DLLs or plug-ins. To be sure, XSLT-compliant browsers have been available for some time (for example, the VSMS Jumbo, W3C Amaya, InDelv XML, and MultiDoc Pro 2.1 browsers), although their users have been mainly serious technophiles.

Even now, one of the hotly debated questions in the XML world is whether client-side XSLT is ready for widespread use. From what we have seen in many of these spirited debates, it appears that a definitive and absolute answer is unlikely to emerge any time soon. However, one thing is clear: the major browsers have been steadily improving their support for XSLT. We are at a point where many, if not all, key XSLT features are supported by the browsers. Thus, we can argue that as a computing community, we are moving in the right direction, and sooner or later we may expect near-complete compliance with the XSLT specifications within the web clients.

Thus, for the rest of the discussion in this chapter, we will consider a browser to be XSLT compliant for all practical purposes if it adheres to *most* of the XSLT specification.

Using Client-Side XSLT Processing

Delegating the XSLT processing responsibility to a client is a rather simple matter. When the source XML file (say, `auth.xml`) and the corresponding XSLT stylesheet (say, `auth.xsl`) are pushed from the server to the client, the connection between them is established in the preamble to the source tree document, as shown in the following example. Note the use of the MIME media type `text/xml`, which we will discuss shortly.

```
<?xml version="1.0"?>
<?xml-stylesheet type="text/xml" href="auth.xsl"?>
 <!-- data specifications begin -->
<All_authors>
  <Author AuthID="77">
  <Name>
    <First_name>
     ...
  </Author>
</All_authors>
<!-- data specifications end -->
```

Thus, in an n-tier application, when the browser makes a request to the web server that requires access to `auth.xml`, the server will send out to the web browser both the source tree document `auth.xml` and the stylesheet to which it makes a reference: that is, `auth.xsl`. Then it is the browser's responsibility to render the data on the web page by *interpreting* the XSLT stylesheet. For those of you familiar with cascading style sheets (CSS), this is not much different from the use of the MIME media type `text/css`, as shown in the following code sample:

```
<?xml-stylesheet type="text/css" href="auth.css"?>
```

Browser Support for XSLT

Although the XSLT 1.0 specification has been around for over two years as of this writing, the browsers took a while to catch up with the specification. The standard installation of Internet Explorer prior to version 6.*x* did not support XSLT 1.0.

Starting with Internet Explorer (IE) 5.0, Microsoft provided support for its own set of nonstandard, *XSLT-like* elements using the MSXML parser. We say XSLT-like to distinguish the Microsoft specification from the true W3C specification of XSLT. To be fair to Microsoft, IE5.0 was shipped in 1998 with the built-in MSXML parser version 1.0 prior to the finalization of the W3C specification, which happened in November 1999. So in this circumstance, we will give Microsoft the benefit of the doubt and say that the company did its best to support a truly emerging standard that was in a state of flux. In that case, however, it is mildly perplexing that even with the release of IE5.5, Microsoft still had not implemented W3C's specification in its parser. Only with release 3.0 of the MSXML parser did IE come closer to supporting standard XSLT. This MSXML3 implementation was released in November 2000, a year after W3C released the final 1.0 specification, and even then, it was the end user's responsibility to download the new version of the XSLT parser from Microsoft's XML Development Center and install it in *replace* mode before testing the use of client-side XSLT. Naturally, developers could not assume that all end users would use IE, or even that all IE users would upgrade to MSXML3, and hence hesitated to use client-side XSLT.

Microsoft's first release of the MSXML parser embedded in IE5.0 made reference to the old XSLT namespace as shown in the following code sample:

```
xmlns:xsl="http://www.w3.org/TR/WD-xsl
```

This was corrected later when MSXML 3.0 supported the correct XSLT namespace:

```
http://www.w3.org/1999/XSL/Transform
```

IE6.0 comes bundled with a parser that supports XSLT. Of course, as is the case with most other Microsoft products, IE6.0 supports several nonstandard XSLT-like tags that you would be well advised to stay away from. This suggestion is not simply for the purists, but for other XSLT practitioners as well since your potential user community will generally use a variety of different types of browsers, and it will be in your interest to stick to the standard XSLT specification.

Netscape Navigator (NN), despite all its other strengths, did not fare much better in providing support for client-side XSLT in version 4.7*x*, which is probably the most widely installed version of NN as of this writing. XSLT plug-ins have been available as third-party products, but to our knowledge, NN 4.7*x* did not have a production-release browser plug-in that came from Netscape itself. Only with NN6.*x* was the client-side support for XSLT provided. The examples in the previous chapters were also tested using Netscape 6.1, and they all seemed to work well.

The Correct MIME Type?

W3C's XSLT 1.0 specification states that the MIME media types `text/xml` and `application/xml` *should* be used. This makes sense since an XSLT document itself is an XML document. The specification further says that a separate media type (then unspecified) will be registered specifically for XSLT stylesheets, in which case the new media type may *also* be used. Alas, as of early 2002 neither of the major browsers will work if you use `text/xml`. You must use the `text/xsl` MIME media type to take advantage of the client-side XSLT support.

IE6.0 does support XSLT, albeit two years after the XSLT 1.0 specification was finalized. The browser recognizes `application/xml` as a valid application type. However, it still incorrectly assumes that the mime of `text/xsl` is valid and does not recognize the valid mime type `text/xml`. Interestingly, NN6.1 does not differ much from IE6.0 in the implementation of these mime types, either. We must say here that W3C's XSLT specification states that the MIME types `text/xml` and `application/xml` should be used for XSLT stylesheets. The specification further states that a media type will be registered specifically for XSLT stylesheets, and that new media type may *also* be used at that time. Since the name of the new MIME type for XSLT stylesheets is not finalized yet, we are not surprised that the browser vendors have provided support for the media type with the possible name `text/xsl`, although we would have expected support for the media type `text/xml` as well.

Processing Syndicated Content

Since XML has its roots in the area of electronic publishing, it naturally has an important role to play in content syndication. Since content syndication involves distributing and reusing information, the benefits of the use of a common vocabulary among the business partners are self-evident. Toward this end, the publisher and the subscriber of the information should ideally use a common protocol and information management model. With this in mind, an industry consortium designed the Information and Content Exchange (ICE) protocol around XML and submitted it as a W3C note in October 1998. When using ICE, you can keep the structured content in XML form independent from the protocol itself and use the standard HTTP POST request/response model for content transport. ICE supports the use of both "push" and "pull" models for distribution of the content. ICE is slowly being adopted by software vendors and large companies such as Reuterspace Media Group (Reuters).

The name Reuters is practically synonymous with content syndication, providing news and information feeds to over 900 web sites. Reuters has been publishing electronic content to such web sites since 1994, and in April 2000 the group launched its Internet delivery system (IDS), which leverages ICE. This is probably the strongest endorsement of XML and ICE in the area of content syndication. Since we have already discussed an example of XSLT use in the area of content syndication, let us move on to the next topic.

Building Presentation-Independent Applications

As we have progressed from monolithic, stand-alone applications to client-server systems to n-tier web applications, the advantages of separating data from presentation has become increasingly apparent. In building enterprise web applications, we must pay close attention to the types of client that will access these applications. Particularly important are thin clients such as web browsers and wireless devices such as ones that support WAP. Thus, we should aim at having common tiers to support data management and application logic and provide separate presentation schemes for each of the clients that the application must support.

Since its development began in 1996, XML has been on the fast track to becoming the de facto standard for structuring platform-independent portable data and thus facilitating information interchange. SGML, a superset of XML, is an international standard (ISO standard since 1986), which further adds to XML's strength in building a new breed of n-tier applications that may be used globally. XML does not put any restrictions on how the client may interpret and present this data. In fact, this ability to delegate the transformation and presentation aspects to another tool gives XML its true power.

Content publishing in multiple output formats, syndication of the content, data delivery to diverse channels of presentation, and a powerful way to provide rich metadata (that is, data about data) are where the combination of XML, XSL-FO, and XSLT could play particularly well.

As an example, let us consider an n-tier application that has customer data stored in the back end. Since we are concerned primarily with understanding XSLT application, we will assume that the customer data has been extracted and is available in the form of the following source XML file, `customers.xml`:

```xml
<?xml version="1.0"?>
<?xml-stylesheet type="text/xsl" href="Present2HTML.xsl"?>
<Customers>
  <Company CompanyID="7001" >
    <Name>Powergadgets, Inc.</Name>
    <SalesRep EmpID="20556" Region="Southcentral">
      <First_name>Mark</First_name>
      <Last_name>McCarthy</Last_name>
    </SalesRep>
    <Contact>
      <First_name>John</First_name>
      <Last_name>Doe</Last_name>
    </Contact>
    <Phone>972-777-1111</Phone>
    <Address>
      <Address_line1>111 Corporate Boulevard</Address_line1>
      <Address_line2></Address_line2>
      <City>Addison</City>
      <State>TX</State>
      <ZIP>75001</ZIP>
    </Address>
    <About> Powergadgets is a Fortune 222 company and has been doing
    business with us for 20 years. Roughly 40 % of our revenue come
    from Powergadgets. This customer should be treated very well. Should
    any problem arise at all with this customer, make sure that you bring
    the matter to the attention of the VP of Sales, Jerry Salinger.
    </About>
  </Company>
  <Company CompanyID="8002" >
    <Name>Ultimate Tools, Inc.</Name>
    <SalesRep EmpID="88157" Region="East">
      <First_name>Jane</First_name>
      <Last_name>Appleton</Last_name>
    </SalesRep>
    <Contact>
      <First_name>Jane</First_name>
      <Last_name>Doe</Last_name>
    </Contact>
```

```
    <Phone>212-888-2222</Phone>
    <Address>
      <Address_line1>222 57th Street</Address_line1>
      <Address_line2>Suite 990</Address_line2>
      <City>New York</City>
      <State>NY</State>
      <ZIP>10021</ZIP>
    </Address>
    <About> Small, but very innovative, Ultimate Tools has received a lot of
    media attention of late. We know that they purchase more material from
    our largest competitor. Also, the volume of their orders tends to be
    relatively small. But given how fast they are growing, we expect that
    they will be one of our top 10 customers in the next 5 years.
    </About>
  </Company>
  <Company CompanyID="9889" >
    <Name>Ultra Machines Corporation</Name>
    <SalesRep EmpID="22222" Region="Midwest">
      <First_name>Rocky</First_name>
      <Last_name>Asimov</Last_name>
    </SalesRep>
    <Contact>
      <First_name>Roxy</First_name>
      <Last_name>Surfer</Last_name>
    </Contact>
    <Phone>312-666-2222</Phone>
    <Address>
      <Address_line1>333 Lake Shore Boulevard</Address_line1>
      <Address_line2>Suite 12001</Address_line2>
      <City>Chicago</City>
      <State>IL</State>
      <ZIP>300225</ZIP>
    </Address>
    <About> Ultra Machines was spun-off from Robotics Corporation about 4
    years ago. Like many other very successful spin-offs, this company has
    shown unfailing growth quarter after quarter. Even in the most difficult
    economic times they have never incurred a loss, and their cash flow is
    very solid.
    </About>
  </Company>
</Customers>
```

Our task is to build a presentation-independent application, so we will work with the same data that is to be presented to either of the two clients: a web browser and a WAP microbrowser. We will accomplish this by writing two separate XSLT stylesheets.

Let us start with the first stylesheet, `Present2HTML.xsl`:

```
<?xml version="1.0"?>

<xsl:stylesheet
  xmlns:xsl="http://www.w3.org/1999/XSL/Transform"
  xmlns="http://www.w3.org/TR/REC-html40"
  version="1.0">

<xsl:output method="html"/>

<xsl:template match="/">
<html>
  <head>
    <title>Customer Info</title>
  </head>
  <body>
  <h1>Results of customer query</h1>
  <h2><A NAME="toc">Key customers of Big Company Inc.:</A></h2>
    <xsl:for-each select="Customers/Company">
      <p><a href="#{generate-id(.)}">
          <b><xsl:value-of select="./Name"/></b>
        </a>
      </p>
  </xsl:for-each>
  <br/><br/>

  <h2>Customer Details</h2>
  <xsl:for-each select="//Company">
    <h3><a name="{generate-id(.)}"><xsl:value-of select="Customer/Company"/></a></h3>
        <b>Company name: </b><xsl:value-of select="./Name"/><br/>
        <b>Company ID: </b><xsl:value-of select="@CompanyID"/>)<br/>
        <b>Customer contact: </b><xsl:value-of select="Contact"/><br/>
        <b>Phone: </b><xsl:value-of select="Phone"/><br/>
        <b>Sales representative: </b><xsl:value-of select="SalesRep"/><br/>
        <b>Address: </b><xsl:value-of select="Address/Address_line1"/>
        <xsl:value-of select="Address/Address_line2"/>,
        <xsl:value-of select="Address/City"/>,
        <xsl:value-of select="Address/State"/>,
        <xsl:value-of select="Address/ZIP"/> <br/>
        <p><u>About the company:</u> <xsl:value-of select="./About"/></p>
        <a href="#toc"><small>Back to customer list</small></a>
        <br/><br/><br/>
  </xsl:for-each>
  </body>
</html>
</xsl:template>

</xsl:stylesheet>
```

Figure 12-1 shows the output resulting from the application of Present 2HTML.xsl to customers.xml. Note the use of generated IDs in the code to generate the links seen in the figure. If you click one of the links, say Ultra Machines Corporation, you will be taken to the screen shown in Figure 12-2.

Here all the details regarding a particular customer are provided. All these details can be displayed in a web browser window since plenty of space is available to show them. However, how would you condense the information if the size of the display were very limited, as in the case of a WAP device? To solve this problem, we will show the use of a separate stylesheet called Present2WML.xsl. We will display the same information as before, although we will organize it differently to accommodate the much smaller form factor of WAP-enabled devices. In WML, the concept of *cards* is used for such organization, and we can code for navigation from one card to another.

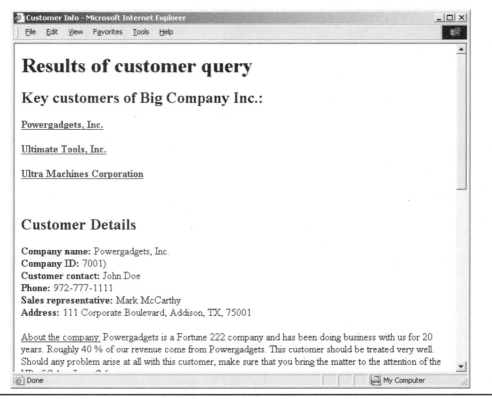

Figure 12-1   *HTML output from the application of* Present2HTML.xsl *to* customers.xml *rendered using IE6.0. We have used generated IDs to create links necessary for navigation from the list of companies to details about the companies. See also Figure 12-2.*

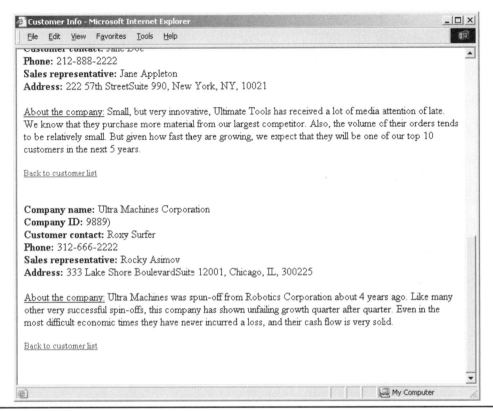

Figure 12-2   *HTML output from the application of* `Present2HTML.xsl` *to* `customers.xml` *rendered using IE6.0. When you click on the link for Ultra Machines Corporation shown in Figure 12-1, the details about that company are displayed as depicted in this figure.*

Even if you have not programmed in WML before, the following XSLT code should be fairly straightforward to follow:

```
<?xml version="1.0"?>
<!-- Stylesheet Present2WML.xsl -->
<xsl:stylesheet
  xmlns:xsl="http://www.w3.org/1999/XSL/Transform"
  version="1.0">

<xsl:output
  method="xml"
  doctype-public="-//WAPFORUM//DTD WML 1.1//EN"
  doctype-system="http://www.wapforum.org/DTD/wml_1.1.xml"/>

<xsl:template match="/">
```

```
<wml>
  <!-- Card showing the customer list -->
  <card id="toc" title="Customer List">
    <p align="center"><b>Results</b></p>
    <xsl:for-each select="Customers/Company">
     <p>
       <b><anchor>
         <xsl:value-of select="./Name"/>
         <go href="#{generate-id(.)}"/>
       </anchor></b>
     </p>
    </xsl:for-each>
  </card>

  <xsl:for-each select="Customers/Company">
    <card id="{generate-id(.)}" title="Customer info">
      <p align="center">
        <b><xsl:value-of select="./Name"/></b>
      </p>

      <p>
        <small>
          <b>ID: </b> <xsl:value-of select="@CompanyID"/><br/>
          <b>Contact: </b><xsl:value-of select="Contact"/><br/>
          <b>Phone: </b><xsl:value-of select="Phone"/><br/>
          <!--
            Give the user the option to go back to the list,
            or view more details about the customer.
          -->
          <anchor>Back to list<go href="#toc"/></anchor><br/>
          ... or Down for more ...<br/>

          <b>Sales Rep: </b><xsl:value-of select="SalesRep"/><br/>
          <b>Address: </b>
            <xsl:value-of select="Address/Address_line1"/>
            <xsl:value-of select="Address/Address_line2"/>,
            <xsl:value-of select="Address/City"/>,
            <xsl:value-of select="Address/State"/>,
            <xsl:value-of select="Address/Zip"/><br/>
          <!--
            Give the user the option to go back to the list,
            or view more details about the customer.
          -->
          <anchor>Back to list<go href="#toc"/></anchor><br/>
          ... or Down for more ...<br/>
```

```
        <b>About:</b>
         <!--
          All info about the customer has been shown.
          Show the user a link to go back to the list.
         -->
          <xsl:value-of select="./About"/><br/>
        <anchor>Back to list<go href="#toc"/></anchor><br/>
       </small>
      </p>
     </card>
   </xsl:for-each>
 </wml>

</xsl:template>

</xsl:stylesheet>
```

An excerpt from the output resulting from the application of `Present2WML.xsl` to the source tree from `customers.xml` is shown here. For the sake of brevity, we have shown the detailed card only for the first customer, Powergadgets, Inc.:

```
<?xml version="1.0" encoding="utf-8"?>
<!DOCTYPE wml
  PUBLIC "-//WAPFORUM//DTD WML 1.1//EN"
  "http://www.wapforum.org/DTD/wml_1.1.xml">
<wml>
<card id="toc" title="Customer List">
  <p align="center"><b>Results</b></p>

  <p><b><anchor>Powergadgets, Inc.<go href="#d1e4"/></anchor></b></p>
  <p><b><anchor>Ultimate Tools, Inc.<go href="#d1e51"/></anchor></b></p>
  <p><b><anchor>Ultra Machines Corporation<go href="#d1e99"/></anchor></b></p>
</card>

<card id="d1e4" title="Customer info">
  <p align="center"><b>Powergadgets, Inc.</b></p>
  <p><small><b>ID: </b>7001<br/><b>Contact: </b>
     John Doe<br/>
     <b>Phone: </b>972-777-1111<br/>

     <anchor>Back to list<go href="#toc"/></anchor><br/>
       ... or Down for more ...<br/>
     <b>Sales Rep: </b>Mark McCarthy<br/>
     <b>Address: </b>111 Corporate Boulevard,
        Addison, TX, 75001<br/>

     <anchor>Back to list<go href="#toc"/></anchor><br/>
```

```
    ... or Down for more ...<br/>
  <b>About:</b> Powergadgets is a Fortune 222 company and has
     been doing business with us for 20 years. Roughly 40 % of
     our revenue come from Powergadgets. This customer should be
     treated very well. Should any problem arise at all with
     this customer, make sure that you bring the matter to the
     attention of the VP of Sales, Jerry Salinger.<br/>

  <anchor>Back to list<go href="#toc"/></anchor><br/>
  </small></p>
  </card>

<!-- Detailed cards for the other two customers look similar to the
     one shown above. Therefore, they have been omitted from this
     listing for the sake of brevity -->
...
<wml>
```

We rendered the WML output using the WAP emulator from Nokia's Mobile Internet Kit 3.0. The first screen of the output is shown in Figure 12-3.

Figure 12-3 *WML output from the application of* `Present2WML.xsl` *to* `customers.xml` *rendered using Nokia's WAP emulator. The actual display will automatically adjust depending on the actual form factor of the particular WAP client device much as the HTML display is automatically adjusted depending on the size of a web browser client.*

When the user clicks the selected link, say the one for Powergadgets, Inc., the next card (see Figure 12-4) will be shown to the user.

If the user scrolls down to view further details about the customer, the display will change to the one shown in Figure 12-5. From there, the user can navigate back to the original list or scroll up to go back to the view in Figure 12-4.

Hopefully, you will get an idea about how you can build presentation-independent n-tier applications aimed at a variety of clients. Given the scope of this book, we focused on demonstrating the use of XSLT to transform the output for different clients such as a web browser or a WAP microbrowser. Be aware, thought, that designing applications for WAP clients requires careful consideration, and for a detailed treatment of this topic you should consult a book specializing in WAP applications. Here, however, are a few key considerations.

First, the form factors are much smaller than for PCs, so you have to decide carefully what to display to the user target audience. Second, the form factors vary widely across WAP devices, so you will have to test the application extensively to ensure that your user population using a multiplicity of the devices can see what you intended for them to see. Last, the data transfer rate to the WAP-enabled device is

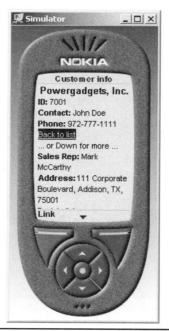

Figure 12-4   *The WML card with details about the customer is displayed using Nokia's WAP emulator. The user is given the options of going back to the customer list that is shown in Figure 12-3 or viewing further details about the customer by scrolling down.*

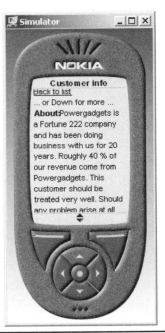

Figure 12-5   *The WML card with further details about the customer is displayed using Nokia's WAP emulator. The user can scroll back to the display shown in Figure 12-4 or click a link to go back to the customer list that is shown in Figure 12-3.*

quite restrictive today, so you will have to organize the information to be sent in small packets. Developers' kits may provide some help in this regard: for example, Nokia's Mobile Internet Kit 3.0 used for the examples here will display a warning if the compiled byte code of the resulting WML file exceeds the suggested size of 1,397 bytes, since a large output may not be displayed correctly on some WAP devices available on the market.

B2B Integration and EAI Using XSLT

Many companies have built disparate systems over time without paying a great deal of attention to how these applications may share data with each other, and the need for integration among these applications has likewise grown over time. That is why enterprise application integration (EAI) has enjoyed a great deal of attention for nearly a couple of decades. EAI is a very broad topic, and entire volumes have been devoted to it, and a detailed discussion of EAI is outside the scope of this book. In connection with XSLT, what is relevant to us here is that in any EAI undertaking, *information interchange* and *rules-based data transformations* appear to be dominant needs.

Even when companies have streamlined their internal business processes and executed successful application integration initiatives, they have generally done so within the confines of the enterprise. However, for companies to be successful in the larger scheme of things, the automation of B2B commerce is needed. The potential benefits of B2B electronic commerce include:

▶ Reduction of excessive paperwork

▶ Elimination of manual data-entry errors inherent in the rekeying of data at the recipient's end

▶ Quicker transfer of business information between trading partners that could lead to faster response times

▶ Supply-chain efficiency improvement and just-in-time inventory management

▶ Cost savings for all trading partners

Companies have been aware of these benefits for a long time, and business-to-business electronic commerce itself is not new. What has changed over the years is the way it is conducted and the cost of conducting it, and consequently the size of the companies that have access to it now.

A Brief History of B2B Electronic Commerce

Although the B2B buzzword seemed to appear out of nowhere just a few years ago, business-to-business electronic commerce has been going on for over 40 years now. In the earliest incarnation of B2B, trading partners communicated with each other over telephone lines using a proprietary data format that they agreed upon. This method of doing business was revolutionary at that time, and it did help reduce the paperwork and minimize data transcription errors. Its obvious downside was that it was not very efficient for scale-up since data formats varied widely across trading partners. The advent of EDI in the 1960s was the first attempt at providing a standardized way of exchanging data between trading partners. Initially, these formats could be used only within a given industry. Only about a decade later did EDI become a widespread standard that was hardware independent and allowed the originator of the transaction to track the data payload and find out if and when the transmission was received by the recipient. Although several formats of EDI messages were developed and even survive today, two enjoy particularly wide adoption: X12 and the Electronic Data Interchange for Administration, Commerce, and Transport (EDIFACT).

Even in the early days of EDI, it was quickly realized that point-to-point communication between trading partners would be difficult to manage, not to mention expensive. This gave rise to the emergence of value-added networks (VANs) that provided a single channel to facilitate the B2B communication. The major benefit of this approach was that a company had to worry only about managing its link to the network, and the responsibility of secure delivery of the message and maintenance of the message's audit trail was delegated to the VAN. Of course, since individual VANs were not interconnected, all trading partners within any given industry had to flock around a particular VAN. With the development of interconnections between the VANs, trading partners exchanging data can now be connected to different VANs, although this does mean sacrificing a rigorous end-to-end audit trail of the data. Historically, EDI has been expensive to implement and, out of necessity, has involved the use of proprietary VANs.

The emergence of XML promised significant advances in B2B integration. This is because users can store or transmit structured data using this highly flexible open standard. Moreover, the use of XML requires no special infrastructure for data transport other than Internet connectivity. Also, with database vendors providing built-in tools for extracting data from and inserting data into RDBMS, it is easier than ever to use XML in B2B commerce transactions.

How XML and XSLT Fit into EAI and B2B Integration

As e-business has passed through several phases of maturity, B2B integration has steadily gathered momentum and is now being taken seriously by a vast majority of companies. B2B integration has the potential to streamline the business processes across the enterprise's boundaries, and therefore often offers a rapid ROI. You will probably agree that B2B is a natural extension of EAI: that is, *information interchange* between companies and *rules-based data transformations* between the disparate data formats that these companies may support. Hence, we will treat B2B and EAI in a similar way in the following discussion.

In the areas of EAI and B2B, there is a need for a common message broker architecture that can support, in addition to message persistence and routing, commonly used services such as rules processing and data transformation. Software vendors have made admirable advances in providing robust implementations of these services to solve complex business problems. However, in the absence of common industry standards, all too frequently they have come up with solutions that do not necessarily work well with each other. It is clear that there is a very real need for standards for data interchange, rules processing, and data transformation. Emerging standards such as RosettaNet, ebXML, and BizTalk have an important role to play in the realm of data interchange, and XSLT has the potential to be a standard tool for processing rules and performing data transformation.

A Sample B2B Problem

Let us consider an example that highlights the important aspects of B2B application integration. Consider a retailer that receives products from a large number of suppliers. Currently, the retailer manages the inventory of these goods using an ERP system and places orders for products using the phone, fax machines, and so forth. The suppliers, in turn, receive the orders and enter the data manually in their back-end systems. The retailer wants to streamline the B2B interactions with its suppliers and gain efficiencies by eliminating paperwork to the extent possible. This is expected to improve the response time of the suppliers and help the retailer manage a just-in-time inventory. For this to happen, the retailer wants to build a web-based B2B application that will enable its purchasers to enter orders using a browser. These orders will be electronically placed, and the suppliers will receive the relevant data almost instantly. The suppliers, in turn, prevent costly errors in data entry through the automation of that process and can store the order data in their back-end systems. For a given supplier, orders can then be viewed by the employees of the shipping department using a web browser, who can respond to the orders and accept or reject them. If they accept an order, they enter information such as the delivery date, terms of the invoice, and so forth and submit the response. From that point on, the order is processed following the existing business processes. The supplier's response goes back to the retailer electronically, and the relevant data is then entered into the retailer's back-end systems.

The key steps in the new B2B interaction are listed here:

▶ An internal web-based application is built by the retailer that enables its purchasers to view the inventory data using a web browser.

▶ For items with low inventories, the purchasers are able to place orders using the web browser. This data is pushed to a particular supplier electronically over the Internet. This data is formatted according to the retailer's internal specifications.

▶ The supplier receives the order data that is to be entered in its back-end systems using an automated process. For this to happen correctly, the data must be formatted according to the supplier's internal specifications.

The key hurdle in this scenario is that the supplier and the retailer use their own data formats to store the same information, which may very well be incompatible. Hence, a data transformation must occur at the retailer's end (or the supplier's end) to ensure that the transformed data follows the specifications of the supplier. This scenario presents an excellent opportunity for the use of XML and XSLT. The supplier as well as the retailer can use a mechanism to extract data from (or insert data into) their respective back-end systems as XML trees. Each of them can (and generally will) follow their own internal specifications to determine the structure of the XML trees. XSLT can then be used to transform one source tree into another.

For example, let us say that the retailer wants to send the order in the form of the following source tree, `RetailerOrder.xml`:

```xml
<?xml version="1.0"?>
  <Order OrderID=1001>
  <Product ProductID="2001">
    <Name>Widget1</Name>
    <Department>Ceramic processing</Department>
    <Buyer>
      <First_name>Jean-luc</First_name>
      <Last_name>Picard<Last_name>
    </Buyer>
    <NegotiatedPrice Currency="US Dollar">2005</NegotiatedPrice>
    <Quantity>5000</Quantity>
    <Description>
      Our retail company describes the product in its own terms.
    </Description>
    <Comments>A very important widget in our production process. Orders
      will get installed without this product. Therefore, at least a
      one-month supply of this product should be held in reserve.
    </Comments>
  </Company>
</Order>
```

Let us say that the supplier in question uses an XML tree (here, a result tree), `SupplierOrder.xml`, that looks like this:

```xml
<?xml version="1.0" encoding="utf-8"?>
  <Order>
    <Company>The Big Retailer</Company>
    <OrderID>1001</OrderID>
    <Product ProductID="2001">
      <Name>Widget1</Name>
      <Description>
          Our retail company describes the product in its own terms.
      </Description>
    </Product>
    <Department>Ceramic processing</Department>
    <BuyerName>Picard,Jean-luc</BuyerName>
    <NegctiatedPrice Currency="US Dollar">2005</NegotiatedPrice>
```

```
   <Quantity>5000</Quantity>
   <DateNeeded>22-DEC-2002</DateNeeded>
</Order>
```

Thus, our task is to write a stylesheet that will support the B2B integration between the retailer and the supplier by transforming the source tree RetailerOrder.xml into the result tree SupplierOrder.xml. Notice that the result tree differs from the source tree in the following respects:

▶ The root element is Order, and the CompanyName attribute (that is, the retailer's name) is stored as a child element of the Order element.

▶ The order ID is stored as a child element of Order rather that its attribute.

▶ The name of the buyer is stored simply as Buyer_name, which is of the form Last_name, First_name.

▶ The retailer's comments are not of any particular relevance to the supplier; therefore, they are ignored.

The stylesheet Retailer2Supplier.xsl required for this B2B integration is shown here:

```
<?xml version="1.0"?>

<!-- stylesheet specifications begin -->
<xsl:stylesheet version="1.0"
    xmlns:xsl="http://www.w3.org/1999/XSL/Transform">

  <xsl:template match="Company">
    <Order>
    <Company>
      <xsl:value-of select="@CompanyName"/>
    </Company>
     <xsl:apply-templates/>
    </Order>
  </xsl:template>

  <xsl:template match="Order">
     <OrderID>
     <xsl:value-of select="@OrderID"/>
     </OrderID>
     <xsl:apply-templates/>
  </xsl:template>

  <xsl:template match="Product">
```

```xsl
  <!-- Output the Product node exactly as it is in the source tree -->
  <xsl:text disable-output-escaping="yes">
    &lt;Product ProductID="
  </xsl:text>
  <xsl:value-of select="@ProductID"/>
  <xsl:text disable-output-escaping="yes">"&gt;</xsl:text>

  <Name>
    <xsl:value-of select="./Name"/>
  </Name>
  <Description>
    <xsl:value-of select="./Description"/>
  </Description>
  <xsl:text disable-output-escaping="yes">&lt;/Product&gt;</xsl:text>
</xsl:template>

<xsl:template match="Department">
  <Department>
    <xsl:value-of select="."/>
  </Department>
</xsl:template>

<xsl:template match="Buyer">
  <BuyerName>
    <xsl:value-of select="./Last_name"/>,
    <xsl:value-of select="./First_name"/>
  </BuyerName>
</xsl:template>

<xsl:template match="NegotiatedPrice">
  <!-- Output the Product node exactly as it is in the source tree -->
  <xsl:text disable-output-escaping="yes">
    &lt;NegotiatedPrice Currency="
  </xsl:text>
  <xsl:value-of select="@Currency"/>
  <xsl:text disable-output-escaping="yes">"&gt;</xsl:text>
  <xsl:value-of select="."/>
  <xsl:text disable-output-escaping="yes">
    &lt;/NegotiatedPrice&gt;
  </xsl:text>
</xsl:template>

<xsl:template match="Quantity">
  <Quantity>
    <xsl:value-of select="."/>
  </Quantity>
</xsl:template>

<xsl:template match="DateNeeded">
```

```
   <DateNeeded>
     <xsl:value-of select="."/>
   </DateNeeded>
 </xsl:template>

</xsl:stylesheet>
```

More often than not, the form of the result tree will differ from one supplier to the next—hence the need to write multiple stylesheets. Of course, the result trees will share some commonalities, and therefore you will be able to find efficiencies by having the common transformations in one stylesheet and importing that into another that contains the rest of the transformations required to support the business needs of that supplier.

Deployment Issues

We conclude this topic by considering the key deployment issues that you are likely to come across while using XSLT to solve enterprise-level problems. To accomplish this, we provide a checklist of questions that you will want to go over to solve the XSLT-related problem at hand effectively and optimally.

► *What is the business problem that needs to be solved?*   Perhaps to you are learning XSLT just for the fun of learning to program in a new declarative language. That is fine, and hopefully the discussion in this book has helped you in this regard. However, chances are that you will be wanting to use XSLT to solve real-life technical problems, which generally have the end goal of supporting a business need within an enterprise. Therefore, ask further questions to determine whether this problem belongs in one of the well-defined domains such as B2C, B2B, EAI, content syndication and management, and the like. To the extent that you define the problem at hand clearly, your design and development approach will be that much more efficient.

► *Is XSLT appropriate for my business problem, or will some other language be better to solve the current problem?*   This is not always an easy question to answer, partly because we as developers try to solve problems using the tools that we are most comfortable with. Moreover, we have our own biases toward and against certain programming languages. You will be well served by revisiting the sections that address the strengths and limitations of XSLT before deciding to use it for your project. XSLT appears to be a bit verbose at first glance: certain tasks that take only a couple of lines of code in certain programming languages take perhaps a page of XSLT coding. However, as long as there is a pattern within the input and output, you can automate repetitive tasks by writing templates, and this is where XSLT's primary strength lies. If you then decide that XSLT is the right approach for the problem at hand, there are more questions to be asked before jumping into programming.

▶ *Is it best for me to wait until XSLT is more widely adopted by the business community, or should I take a more proactive approach to stay ahead of the pack?* You have probably come across spirited discussions about whether XSLT is ready for a wider use, particularly on the client side. We believe so, and we believe you should seriously consider it in building enterprise strength applications. Support for XSLT shown by major software vendors such as Oracle, Vignette, and Interwoven and organizations such as Reuters in solving real-life problems are strong endorsements of the strength of XSLT. With the XSLT 2.0 specification just around the corner, further enhancements are clearly in the works and are likely to bode well for the future of XSLT.

▶ *What, if any, is my organization's XML strategy?* Ever since XML became a buzzword, most companies have been at least somewhat curious about what it can do for them. There is no question that there is plenty of hype about how XML (and XSLT) can help a company's ROI. You will want to decide if XML fits within the larger context of your company's IT strategy. We believe that this is one of the most important questions to be answered before starting a project that involves extensive use of XML/XSLT, although few people think about this point carefully—so if you are one of them, give yourself a pat on the back!

▶ *Who is my intended audience, and which clients do I need to support?* Perhaps XSLT is a very good fit to solve your current problem. However, you will need to consider whether your intended audience is ready for its use. For example, if you decide to use client-side XSLT extensively for your application, you will want to make sure that your audience uses XSLT-enabled browsers. This issue gets particularly tricky if you decide to build presentation-independent applications that will be accessed from channels such as wireless phones and PDAs. As far as we know, none of the widely deployed WAP microbrowsers currently support XSLT. In such a case, you will want to use server-side XSLT, generate WML, and provide it for the benefit of the WAP clients. Hence, think carefully about using XSLT client side versus server side, and think about whether this decision can be made conditional within your application logic. Also consider performance issues. For example, if you are carrying out extensive XSLT transformations, does it make sense to defer the transformation load to the client side, or will you serve your audience better by performing the transformations on the server side.

▶ *Which other technologies will be a part of the solution: for example, RDBMS, Java, and so on?* Large RDBMS vendors such as Oracle, IBM, and Microsoft provide very good support for XML: that is, the process for extracting the data in an XML form or inserting data from XML files into a database is quite straightforward. Languages such as Java and Perl also work very well with XSLT, and entire volumes have been devoted to address such use of XSLT.

▶   *Is someone in my industry, either an individual company or a consortium, already addressing this problem?*   Before embarking on an extensive (and expensive!) XML/XSLT undertaking, you will be well-advised to do research around this question. Perhaps a trade magazine has published an article related to a similar business problem that you could learn from. Perhaps your competitors have addressed similar problems and have published case studies or discussed their undertakings at a conference. You could learn valuable lessons from any difficulties that they may have came across and any workarounds that they may have found, and certainly you can avoid any mistakes they may have made. Perhaps a consortium is working on finalizing a standard specific to your industry. If this is the case, you might be better off waiting until this standard is finalized and then leveraging it for a quicker implementation that will also work better when interfacing with your customers and suppliers. Such research could help you avoid costly and time-consuming mistakes in your implementation. It will also help you create a more robust and longer-lasting implementation.

By no means is the list of issues provided here exhaustive. However, we ourselves have come across such issues over and over again, and therefore we hope that addressing these questions will be a good starting point for you.

Summary

In this chapter, we considered practical issues related to the development of applications that use XSLT. We discussed how XSLT is useful in solving problems related to content syndication, B2B, and EAI. We also discussed the state of the art of client-side support for XSLT and ways to build presentation-independent applications that can be accessed by clients of differing types.

Armed with this knowledge, you should now be well-prepared to benefit from the next chapter, which discusses a variety of XML and XSLT tools, as well as the technologies that complement XSLT.

Programming Tools and Technologies

IN THIS CHAPTER:

Programming with XSLT

Programming Languages and XSLT

XSLT Programming Models

Summary

One of the benefits to programmers of accepted standards is the fact that software vendors large and small flock to create tools that use, leverage, or extend the standard. This is true for XML and XSLT, too, and over the relatively short life of these standards vendors have come out in substantial numbers to support these technologies. Some vendors arrived on the scene with tools that strictly adhere to the letter of the standards; some have extended the standards in useful, albeit often proprietary, ways; and some have supported only those portions of the standards that apply to or complement their particular platforms, operating environments, or product suites.

This chapter explores the most popular of the XSLT programming tools (and, by association, the most popular XML tools as well) and explains how the tools can facilitate your XSLT development efforts. There are a number of programming languages for which vendors have provided some level of XSLT support, and this chapter also touches on what's been done with the most common of these languages: Java, C++, and Perl.

Programming with XSLT

Before we dive into the programmatic use of XSLT, we need to lay a little groundwork by briefly examining the two main application programming interfaces used to process XML documents. These APIs are called the Document Object Model and the Simple API for XML, and if you've done any work with XML or HTML documents, you've probably already heard of (and maybe even used) one or both of these interfaces.

The Document Object Model

The Document Object Model, or DOM, describes an in-memory, hierarchical representation of an XML document. In Chapter 2, we discussed the XSLT processor's view of an XML document as a hierarchy, composed of nodes of various types: elements, attributes, text, processing instructions, and so on. This is essentially the same view of an XML document that the DOM gives you, and along with its ability to structure the document as a hierarchy, the DOM also gives you powerful ways to manipulate nodes, traverse the document hierarchy, and perform other programming tasks.

When an XML document is read by an XML parser that supports the DOM, each part of the input document (elements, attributes, text, comments, processing instructions, and so on) is converted to a node in an in-memory tree. The root node of the tree is the document's root element, and every other part of the document becomes a child node of that root. For example, if we convert the following simple document into a DOM hierarchy, we end up with the tree shown in Figure 13-1.

```
<?xml version="1.0" ?>
<rootElement>
<child1>This is the text of child 1</child1>
<child2 name="foo">This is the text of child 2</child2>
</rootElement>
```

Because of their straightforward, familiar structure, DOM trees have the advantage of being very easy for applications to process. If the task at hand requires extensive processing of the document or many traversals of parent-child relationships between elements, the DOM is easily the most effective tool. However, for some applications there are two substantial downsides to using the DOM:

▶ Because the document hierarchy is held in memory, very large XML documents can be nearly impossible to handle. The largest document that can be handled effectively by a given program depends on the amount of memory available and on the particular parser's implementation. Depending on the application, developers may be able to design around this limitation by breaking their documents into multiple pieces (chapters in a book, for example), but in many cases the documents are composed of an arbitrary number of data items over which the developer has little or no control.

▶ The entire document must be read before any of the nodes it contains can be processed. If the application will be performing substantial work on the in-memory document, the amount of time required to read and convert the document into a hierarchy may be negligible; however, if only a portion of the document needs to be processed, or if the task at hand is small or time critical, the overhead of creating the entire tree in memory may be prohibitive and unnecessary.

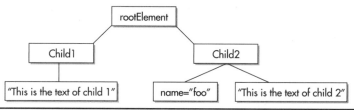

Figure 13-1   *A sample DOM hierarchy*

For more information on the Document Object Model, take a look at the World Wide Web Consortium (W3C) DOM pages at http://www.w3.org/DOM/.

Simple API for XML

An alternative application programming interface that can address some of the problems associated with the DOM is the Simple API for XML, or SAX. This API was collaboratively developed by the members of the XML-DEV mailing list, led by Peter Murray-Rust, Tim Bray, and David Megginson. SAX is a fine example of the power of remote, collaborative design: the SAX 1.0 Java package was developed and deployed in less than five months.

XML parsers that support SAX allow applications to process an input XML document as a series of events, each of which represents the parser's encounter with some portion of the input document. By registering a content handler to receive and process each of these events, a program can quickly find and process only those portions of the input document it really needs.

To illustrate this further, let's say that we have a document that looks like this:

```
<?xml version="1.0" ?>
<rootElement>
<child1>This is the text of child 1</child1>
<child2 name="foo">This is the text of child 2</child2>
</rootElement>
```

A program using a SAX-compliant parser can process each part of this document as the XML parser reads it instead of having to wait until the entire document has been read, as would be the case with the DOM. As the parser reads our sample document, it sends events to the program's SAX content handler for each node in the document:

▶   startDocument

▶   startElement (`rootElement`)

▶   startElement (`child1`)

▶   characters ("`This is the text of child 1`")

▶   endElement (`child1`)

▶   startElement (`child2`)—includes attributes

▶   characters ("`This is the text of child 2`")

▶   endElement (`child2`)

- ▶ endElement (`rootElement`)
- ▶ endDocument

SAX is meant primarily for applications that create their own data structures based on the contents of an XML document. By allowing a very rapid document-order traversal of the input, SAX allows applications to maintain state in their content handlers and to create output based on content that may come from a single element or a range of elements without necessarily having to know the structure of the input document. Because the document is processed as it is read, documents of any size can be processed, even with limited memory; this makes SAX parsers great for memory-restricted applications or those attempting to handle arbitrarily large documents. Of course, SAX, like DOM, has its downsides as well:

- ▶ Because the input document is processed by the SAX application as it is read, SAX doesn't allow you to process an input document backward or to perform any traversal of relationships among the portions of the document.

- ▶ SAX requires applications to handle each part of an XML document separately—that is, the application must, for example, provide functions to handle the start and end of an element different from those that handle the element's content. This means that your SAX application has to maintain some sort of state in order to remember which element it's processing at the time, which can increase the application's complexity.

More information on SAX's capabilities can be found at http://www.saxproject.org/.

Programming Languages and XSLT

There are many situations in which it's possible to use XSLT without ever writing a line of code. The most popular tools provide command-line utilities that allow you to invoke the XSLT processor, specify the input and output file names, and provide any special processing options or stylesheet parameters. Using a command-line tool allows you to integrate XSLT into many applications—especially those driven by batch files, shell scripts, or Perl scripts.

With more complex applications—and especially those that combine XSLT transformations with substantial processing of the input or output, either before or after processing—it's often necessary to write code in order to meet your applications needs. Fortunately, there are many tools and application programming interfaces available that can make this task easier; in the sections that follow, we'll explore the facilities that are available for the three most popular XSLT programming languages.

Java

If you listen to the Java and XML marketing hype, you might come to the conclusion that Java and XML are a match made in heaven: a combination of a portable, structured, object-oriented programming language and a portable, structured, but highly flexible and type-independent data representation format. In this particular case, the objects of the marketing team's affection actually resemble the hype generated; although one might argue with the enthusiasm with which Java and XML are touted by vendors and the press, there's no denying that, individually and together, the two are powerful technologies indeed.

Recently, the relationship between Java and XML has been strengthened further with the introduction of a standard application programming interface: the Java API for XML Parsing (JAXP). Prior to JAXP, each Java parser or transformation engine had its own programming interface, which provided varied flexibility to programmers and limited programmers' ability to swap the underlying engines. The creators of JAXP have produced a highly flexible interface that allows applications to use XML and XSLT in almost any way imaginable.

Java API for XML Parsing

The JAXP specification includes five Java packages:

▶ `javax.xml.parsers`, which provides the ability for a JAXP-compliant XSLT transformation engine to readily switch to any SAX- or DOM-compliant XML parser.

▶ `javax.xml.transform`, which is the package that contains the core transformation classes.

▶ `javax.xml.transform.dom`, which supplies helper classes that work in conjunction with those in `java.xml.transform` to provide the ability to read and write DOM hierarchies.

▶ `javax.xml.transform.sax`, which contains helper classes that allow transformation engines to read and write SAX event streams.

▶ `javax.xml.transform.streams`, which contains helper classes that support the use of standard files or Java streams, readers, and writers as input to or output from a transformation engine.

The general process for performing transformations using JAXP is very straightforward. The `javax.xml.transform.Transformer` class represents the core XSLT transformation engine; `Transformer` uses classes that implement the `javax.xml.transform.Source` interface to represent the XSLT stylesheet used to transform documents as well as the input XML document and the destination for the transformation output. The `Source` interface is implemented by the `DOMSource` (for DOM hierarchies), `SAXSource` (for SAX event streams), and `StreamSource` (for Java streams, readers, and writers) classes.

To perform a transformation, the application creates a new Transformer object and provides a Source object representing the XSLT stylesheet. Any number of XML documents can then be transformed using this stylesheet by calling the `transform()` method on the Transformer object; the input and output can be files, DOM hierarchies, or SAX event streams, providing maximum flexibility to the application.

We'll explore the use of JAXP further in the section "XSLT Programming Models" later in this chapter.

J2EE and XML

In addition to serving as a solid general-purpose programming language, Java has emerged as an excellent tool for developing enterprise-class applications. The key to Java's success in the enterprise is the Java 2 Enterprise Edition (J2EE) set of specifications, which provide interface and behavioral blueprints, design patterns, and practices that best govern how J2EE-compliant applications should be developed and how they will be supported by the underlying application servers and related infrastructure systems. Many vendors deliver J2EE support in their products, which include application servers from BEA, IBM, and iPlanet; databases from Oracle and Sun; enterprise application integration tools from IBM and webMethods; and a host of other products.

As you've seen in the application examples in this book, XML and XSLT have broad applicability in enterprise applications. In particular, XML and XSLT are used extensively to generate user interfaces, transforming structured XML data representing a page or screen's content into HTML, WML, or text. XML is also a great solution to the problem of storage and manipulation of complex data and the exchange of this data among dissimilar systems inside and outside the organization, and XSLT is often used to transform standardized enterprise data into formats appropriate for consumption by customers and business partners.

Although many of the leading J2EE application servers provide XML parsers and XSLT processors, you usually also can use any third-party Java tools you may be familiar with. The only major downside of using a third-party tool is that you must ensure that the tool is packaged with your applications (and licensed appropriately!). Fortunately, this is a very straightforward process when using the J2EE's deployment model.

XSLT Processors for Java

There are many excellent XML and XSLT (and free!) processors for Java. Perhaps the best-known and most widely used tool is the Xalan-J XSLT processor from The Apache Group (http://xml.apache.org/xalan-j/). Xalan-J is a full-featured processor that supports the JAXP transformation APIs and allows the exchange of the bundled Apache Xerces parser for any other parser that supports JAXP's pluggable parser architecture. The Apache Group XML products have received support and contributions from some large commercial software companies, such as IBM and Sun; in fact, although Sun continues to be very involved in the evolution of XML and related standards, it has donated its XSLT processor to Apache and now recommends Xalan-J as the processor of choice.

A close second on the list of Java XSLT processors is Michael Kay's SAXON (available at http://saxon.sourceforge.net). SAXON comes in two different packages: a "full" version and an "instant" version, which differ only in the bundling of tools and examples beyond the base XSLT processor. The full SAXON package includes not only the XSLT processor, but also a suite of extension elements and functions and a set of sample applications, while the Instant SAXON package includes only the XSLT processor. SAXON supports its own full-featured but proprietary API in addition to the standard JAXP interface.

Rounding out the top three free products is James Clark's XT Java processor. James Clark has been involved in the evolution of both SGML and XML for some time and is either the author of or a contributor to many of the most widely used SGML products. The XP XML parser and XT XSLT transformation engine are distributed as individual products as well as being embedded in many commercial and open-source development tools; their popularity is due in no small part to their flexibility and extremely good performance. While these tools are not maintained on the cutting edge of development, they do have a wide and devoted following; recently, a site called 4xt.org (http://www.4xt.org) has sprung up to take over maintenance and enhancement of the XT processor.

Of course, there are many commercial products available as well from companies such as Microsoft, IBM, and Oracle. Because of the high level of competition from the open-source XSLT tool community and the functional parity and excellent support that open-source vendors provide, these commercial vendors almost always provide their XML and XSLT tools free or for a very minimal charge.

C++

Although the Java-XML combination receives the overwhelming majority of attention in the developer community, the needs of C++ developers are also represented. XML and XSLT processors written in C++ have not progressed quite as far down the standardization path as their Java brethren, but almost all of the C++ products do have solid support for both SAX and DOM.

Apache provides a version of its Xalan XSLT engine for C++, with distributions providing support for the Microsoft Win32, Red Hat Linux, AIX, HP-UX, and Solaris environments. Because there are no standardized applications programming interfaces for C++ XSLT processors, Xalan C++ implements its own full-featured API for both its XSLT and XPath functions. It comes with a set of sample applications that can help you understand how to use this API effectively.

The Ginger Alliance has produced an XSLT processor called Sablotron, which is written entirely in C++ (although it does use James Clark's expat XML processor, which is written in C). In recent benchmarks available at XML.com (http://www.xml.com), Sablotron performed well on many of the tests. Sablotron is available in source and binary form for Win32 platforms, Linux, and Solaris; more information can be found at http://www.gingerall.com/charlie/ga/xml/p_sab.xml.

Microsoft also provides an XSLT processor that can be used as a Component Object Model (COM) object, enabling its use from any language supporting COM (including C++). Because this processor is implemented as a COM object, its use is restricted to Windows platforms.

Perl

Early in the life of the Web, Perl was the programming language of choice for Common Gateway Interface (CGI) scripts, which were used for forms processing, database retrieval, and many other applications. It was only the advent of Java servlets and JSP, with their substantially lower startup overhead and greater overall scalability, that pushed Perl to second place as the tool of choice for Web applications. However, Perl's powerful text processing capabilities and active, devoted user base—not to mention its honored place as *the* language for rapid development of many types of Unix applications—have kept it at the forefront for low- to medium-volume Web applications and quick application development and prototyping.

Perl devotees have ensured that XML and XSLT tools are available to support the revolution in Web application development that these technologies started. Interestingly, the most popular Perl modules for processing XML documents are not written entirely in Perl; rather, they call existing processors written in C or C++, such as James Clark's expat XML parser or the Sablotron C++ parser. This hasn't kept the Perl community from wholeheartedly embracing these tools, but it does force users to think a little harder if code portability is an issue in their applications.

The available Perl modules take one of two approaches to providing support for XSLT. Some modules do most of the grunt work themselves and call other modules only to perform functions that are inordinately difficult to program in Perl, such as XML parsing (a task for which James Clark's expat parser seems to be the odds-on favorite with Perl programmers). Others (such as the XML::LibXSLT module by Matt Sergeant) simply provide a Perl wrapper for a full-function XSLT processor such as the Gnome LibXSLT engine or the Ginger Alliance's Sablotron. It's important to know which type of module you have, as the performance characteristics can vary widely between the two types. As with C++, Perl modules don't provide a consistent programming interface, so it's worth reviewing both the functionality list and the programming interface when selecting modules for your application.

Perhaps the best repository for information about XML and Perl is the XMLPerl web site (http://www.xmlperl.com), which provides both extensive information on XML-related developments in the Perl community and an extract of interesting news from other XML-related web sites. Most of the Perl modules for XML and XSLT processing are available on the Comprehensive Perl Archive Network (CPAN); a simple search for XML and XSLT turned up dozens of entries.

Resources for Other Programming Languages

XSLT support is available, to varying degrees, for a slew of other programming and scripting languages. Aside from the languages discussed in this chapter, the Python scripting language has the greatest (and, arguably, the fastest-growing) support for XML, but there are also XML tools available for PHP, TCL, and other languages.

For more information, visit the XML Cover Pages site (http://xml.coverpages.org), an excellent resource maintained by Robin Cover. Everything you could ever want to know about SGML, XML, XSL, and related standards can be found somewhere in this collection, including references to just about every software package ever developed that supports these technologies. Perhaps the biggest challenge in using the XML Cover Pages is knowing what *not* to read; this site makes an excellent historical reference for SGML and XML, but its depth also makes it difficult to determine which products have strong support in the developer community.

There are also many other XML-related web sites and mailing lists that provide general XML and XSLT information along with pointers to language-related materials, benchmarks, and so on. The best known of these is the aptly named XML.com (http://www.xml.com), which is hosted by O'Reilly and Associates and contains regular contributions from many of the major contributors in the XML world. Another major resource is the <?xmlhack?> Web site (http://www.xmlhack.com), which provides information slanted more toward developers of XML applications rather than general information and contains a great cross-reference by category (including Perl, Java, and C++) and by date.

James Tauber's XML software site (http://www.xmlsoftware.com) is a great repository for information about XML and XSLT products. The site covers not only parsers and processors, but authoring tools, document management systems, stylesheet development tools, and many other useful items.

Microsoft Windows developers can visit the company's MSDN web site (http://www.microsoft.com/xml) to find a host of resources related to the use of XML, XSLT, and other XML-related technologies with Microsoft's presentation technologies (ASP, Visual Basic) and server-side technologies (COM+, MTS, SQL Server, and others).

XSLT Programming Models

You'll typically find three general programming models when working with XSLT. All of the myriad ways in which a transformation can be performed derive in some way from one of these three models; in fact, as you review and understand the models, you'll see that they can be combined in various ways to meet the unique needs of your particular application.

If you want more extensive examples of any of these models, download the Apache Xalan-J XSLT processor or the full SAXON package; both provide many examples of the use of their respective processors. The Xalan-J package, in particular, has great examples of the various ways in which the JAXP API can be used for various programming tasks.

Batch Programming Model

The first model we'll look at, which we'll call the *batch model*, is also the simplest: invoking an XSLT transformer to read a file as input and write a file as output. The program has very little involvement in the transformation process except to create the transformer and pass it the names of the files to be processed (or, alternately, to pass it the input stream from which to read input and the output stream to which to write output). This model is appropriate when the goal is simply to automate the transformation process, possibly as an isolated step in a larger automated process.

As an example, let's look at one mechanism for invoking an XSLT processor using the batch processing model. We'll assume that the transformation step is part of a larger process, and that the entire process is driven by a Java program that accepts the names of the files to be transformed as command-line arguments. Our illustration uses the Apache Xalan XSLT processor, which is one of the more popular processors in use today, but other XSLT processors are capable of performing this task in essentially the same way.

```java
import javax.xml.transform.TransformerFactory;
import javax.xml.transform.Transformer;
import javax.xml.transform.stream.StreamSource;
import javax.xml.transform.stream.StreamResult;
import javax.xml.transform.TransformerException;
import javax.xml.transform.TransformerConfigurationException;
import javax.xml.transform.TransformerFactoryConfigurationError;

import java.io.FileInputStream;
import java.io.FileOutputStream;
import java.io.FileNotFoundException;
import java.io.IOException;
public class BatchXsltTransformer
{
    Transformer  m_transformer;

    public BatchXsltTransformer( String stylesheetName )
        throws TransformerFactoryConfigurationError,
               TransformerConfigurationException
    {
      TransformerFactory theFactory =
TransformerFactory.newInstance();
        m_transformer = theFactory.newTransformer(
                        new StreamSource( stylesheetName ) );
    }
```

In the constructor for our sample class, we'll create a new instance of the `javax.xml.transform.TransformerFactory` class using its static newInstance() method. Different transformer implementations might create different types of transformers, and by using a Factory pattern, the vendor set the configuration for this particular transformer appropriately.

After the transformer factory is created, we can use it to create a javax.xml.transform.Transformer object that will be used to actually perform the transformations. In this case, we're passing the name of our stylesheet to the TransformerFactory.newInstance() method when we create the Transformer object, but JAXP allows us to set this attribute on the transformer later if desired.

```
public void transform( String inputFileName,
                       String outputFileName )
    throws TransformerException, FileNotFoundException,
           IOException
{
m_transformer.transform(
    new StreamSource( new FileInputStream( inputFileName ) ),
    new StreamResult( new FileOutputStream( outputFileName ) ) );
}
```

Now that we've created a Transformer object, we can use it to transform any files we want using the stylesheet we provided when the transformer was created. Note that the transformation process accepts a javax.xml.transform.stream.StreamSource object to represent the input source and a javax.xml.transform.stream.StreamResult object to represent the output; abstracting the actual input and output using these classes allows the Transformer object to accept any input and output that can be extended from the StreamSource and StreamResult classes. For special situations, the programmer can also create subclasses of StreamSource and StreamResult to handle unusual or proprietary input and output formats.

An interesting note: StreamSource and StreamResult both come with constructors that accept Java File objects, streams, character readers/writers, and URLs. Because it's important to allow the XML parser to handle the document's encoding, it's more appropriate to use stream-oriented input and output methods, which allow the parser to interpret bytes rather than Java characters and to handle the input encoding and generate the output encoding itself rather than allowing Java to convert the data.

```
    public static void main( String[] args )
    {
```

```
    try  {
      BatchXsltTransformer  batchTransformer =
                  new BatchXsltTransformer( args[0] );
      batchTransformer.transform( args[1], args[2] );
    }
    catch( TransformerFactoryConfigurationError e ) {
      System.out.println( e.getMessage() );
    }
    catch( TransformerConfigurationException e ) {
      System.out.println( e.getMessage() );
    }
    catch( TransformerException e ) {
      System.out.println( e.getMessage() );
    }
    catch( FileNotFoundException e ) {
      System.out.println( e.getMessage() );
    }
    catch( IOException e ) {
      System.out.println( e.getMessage() );
    }
  }
}
```

The `main()` method in our example simply constructs a `BatchXsltTransformer`
object, passes it the stylesheet name and input/output file names from the command-
line arguments, and handles any exceptions that are generated.

Tree-Based Processing Model

In the *tree-based model*, the XML document to be processed is converted to a DOM
hierarchy before being processed by the XSLT processor. As mentioned previously,
DOM allows the greatest flexibility to applications that must traverse the document
hierarchy in order to perform their work; because the XSLT processor accepts a DOM
hierarchy as input and creates a DOM hierarchy as output, the application is able to
perform extensive navigation on the document both before and after transformation.

Let's recode our batch model example to use a tree-based approach, again using
the Apache Xalan processor. Because we need to transform the document into a
DOM hierarchy prior to running it through the XSLT processor, we'll add a step
that calls the Apache Xerces parser to perform that conversion prior to invoking
the transformation step.

```
import org.apache.xerces.parsers.DOMParser;
import org.apache.xerces.dom.DocumentImpl;
import org.xml.sax.SAXException;
import org.xml.sax.InputSource;
import org.w3c.dom.Document;
import org.w3c.dom.Node;
import org.w3c.dom.DOMException;
import org.apache.xml.serialize.XMLSerializer;
import org.apache.xml.serialize.OutputFormat;
import javax.xml.transform.TransformerFactory;
import javax.xml.transform.Transformer;
import javax.xml.transform.stream.StreamSource;
import javax.xml.transform.stream.StreamResult;
import javax.xml.transform.TransformerException;
import javax.xml.transform.TransformerConfigurationException;
import javax.xml.transform.TransformerFactoryConfigurationError;
import javax.xml.transform.dom.DOMSource;
import javax.xml.transform.dom.DOMResult;
import java.io.FileInputStream;
import java.io.FileOutputStream;
import java.io.FileNotFoundException;
import java.io.IOException;
public class TreeXsltTransformer
{
  Transformer  m_transformer;
public static void main( String[] args )
  {
    try {
      // Create an instance of the Xerces DOM parser and parse the
      // input document
      DOMParser theParser = new DOMParser();
      theParser.parse( new InputSource(
                   new FileInputStream( args[1] ) ) );
      Document  inputDoc = theParser.getDocument();
      // perform some processing on the tree
      // Call the XSLT processor to read the DOM tree and produce a
      // new tree
      TreeXsltTransformer  treeTransformer =
                new TreeXsltTransformer( args[0] );
      Document outputDoc = treeTransformer.transform( inputDoc );
      // perform processing on output tree
      // write output tree
      XMLSerializer theSerializer =
```

```
                new XMLSerializer( new FileOutputStream( args[2] ),
                new OutputFormat( "xml", "UTF-8", true ) );
      theSerializer.serialize( outputDoc );
    }
    catch( SAXException e ) {
      System.out.println( e.getMessage() );
    }
    catch( TransformerFactoryConfigurationError e ) {
      System.out.println( e.getMessage() );
    }
    catch( TransformerConfigurationException e ) {
      System.out.println( e.getMessage() );
    }
    catch( TransformerException e ) {
      System.out.println( e.getMessage() );
    }
    catch( FileNotFoundException e ) {
      System.out.println( e.getMessage() );
    }
    catch( IOException e ) {
      System.out.println( e.getMessage() );
    }
  }
}
```

Our example's `main()` method handles the creation and manipulation of the DOM trees used as input to the transformation process. Using the Xerces-J parser, this method creates a `DOMParser` object and uses it to parse our input file and create an object that conforms to the `org.w3c.dom.Document` interface (that is, a DOM document hierarchy). If we choose, we can preprocess this input document—to add nodes, rearrange nodes, or update text or attribute data, for example—prior to using it as input for the transformation process.

Once the input document is ready for transformation, we create an instance of our example `TreeXsltTransformer` class and call its `transform()` method. The method accepts our input document and returns a transformed document as output. After the output document is created, we can manipulate it further or (as shown in this example) use the Apache `XMLSerializer` class to write the document as a text XML document.

```
public TreeXsltTransformer( String stylesheetName )
    throws TransformerFactoryConfigurationError,
           TransformerConfigurationException
  {
```

```
TransformerFactory theFactory = TransformerFactory.newInstance();
m_transformer = theFactory.newTransformer(
                   new StreamSource( stylesheetName ) );
}
```

As with our prior example, we create an instance of the `Transformer` object using the JAXP `TransformerFactory` class and pass it the name of the stylesheet to be used for future transformations.

```
public Document transform( Document inputDoc )
    throws TransformerException
{
  DOMSource   theSource =
              new DOMSource( inputDoc.getDocumentElement() );
  DOMResult   theResult = new DOMResult( new DocumentImpl() );
  m_transformer.transform( theSource, theResult );
  return (Document)theResult.getNode();
}
}
```

Our new `transform()` method accepts an input object conforming to the `org.w3c.dom.Document` interface (that is, the DOM hierarchy we create in our `main()` method) and returns the result of the transformation process as another `Document` object as well. Note the use of the `javax.xml.transform.dom.DOMSource` and `javax.xml.transform.dom.DOMResult` classes to encapsulate the input and output DOM documents, respectively; these classes derive from the corresponding `Stream` classes we saw in our batch example, making them usable as input for the transformation process.

Note that some of what you see in this example is specific to the XML parser we used. All of the classes that come from the org.w3c.*, org.xml.sax.*, and org.apache.* packages are part of Xerces-J; but although other parsers may have different mechanisms for handling DOM documents, the basic pattern will be the same. It's also important to understand that it's not necessary in this programming model to use DOM hierarchies for both input *and* output; the program could easily have used a `StreamSource` object to read the input document directly from a file and still have used a `DOMResult` object to capture the output.

Event-Based Processing Model

The *event-based model* leverages SAX's capabilities to allow applications to work with the input and output documents in an event-oriented fashion rather than a tree-oriented fashion. Using SAX events as input to and output from the transformation process is somewhat more difficult, but substantial benefits can be gained in decreased memory use and improved processing speed.

The general process for using SAX as input for the transformation process is as follows:

1. Create a SAXTransformerFactory object by calling TransformerFactory.newInstance(), just as we did in our prior examples. SAXTransformerFactory is a special subclass of TransformerFactory that implements methods to allow the creation of objects that process SAX events, and it's created by any JAXP implementation that supports SAX input and output. Before using it in your program, you'll have to cast the TransformerFactory object returned by the newInstance() method to a SAXTransformerFactory object.

2. Use your new SAXTransformerFactory newTransformerHandler() method to create an instance of a class that implements the TransformerHandler interface. The TransformerHandler interface is implemented by SAX content handlers that can perform XSLT transformations; when you call newTransformerHandler(), you can pass in the name of an XSLT stylesheet for use by the transformation processor.

3. Call the static createXMLReader() method of the org.xml.sax. helpers.XMLReaderFactory class to create an object that implements the org.xml.sax.XMLReader interface. This interface is implemented by all SAX-compliant parsers, so calling createXMLReader() in essence creates an XML parser to create SAX events as input for the transformation process.

4. Set your TransformerHandler object to be the content handler for your XMLReader by calling XMLReader.setContentHandler(). This sets your transformation processor to process SAX events generated by the SAX-compliant parser.

5. Create a javax.xml.transform.sax.SAXResult object to accept the output from the transformation process, and associate it with the transformation processor by using TransformerHandler.setResult(). The SAXResult constructor accepts your application's content handler as an argument, so when the transformation processor calls the SAXResult object with the SAX events resulting from the transformation process, your content handler will get called, and you can execute your application's logic.

In essence, what you've done by following these steps is developed a processing pipeline composed of XMLReader, TransformerHandler, SAXResult, and the application's content handler, as shown in Figure 13-2.

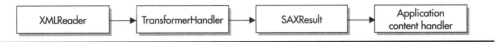

Figure 13-2   *The SAX event processing pipeline*

Sample code that shows how all of this works is shown here:

```
import org.xml.sax.ContentHandler;
import org.xml.sax.SAXException;
import org.xml.sax.Locator;
import org.xml.sax.Attributes;
import org.xml.sax.XMLReader;
import org.xml.sax.helpers.XMLReaderFactory;

import javax.xml.transform.TransformerFactory;
import javax.xml.transform.Transformer;
import javax.xml.transform.Templates;
import javax.xml.transform.stream.StreamSource;
import javax.xml.transform.stream.StreamResult;
import javax.xml.transform.TransformerException;
import javax.xml.transform.TransformerFactoryConfigurationError;
import javax.xml.transform.TransformerConfigurationException;
import javax.xml.transform.Result;
import javax.xml.transform.sax.SAXResult;
import javax.xml.transform.sax.SAXSource;
import javax.xml.transform.sax.SAXTransformerFactory;
import javax.xml.transform.sax.TemplatesHandler;
import javax.xml.transform.sax.TransformerHandler;
import java.io.FileInputStream;
import java.io.FileOutputStream;
import java.io.FileNotFoundException;
import java.io.IOException;
public class EventXsltTransformer implements ContentHandler
{
  SAXTransformerFactory  m_transformerFactory;
  TransformerHandler     m_transformerHandler;
  XMLReader              m_reader;

  public EventXsltTransformer( String stylesheetName )
      throws TransformerFactoryConfigurationError,
            TransformerConfigurationException, SAXException,
            FileNotFoundException
```

```
  {
    m_transformerFactory =
              SAXTransformerFactory)TransformerFactory.newInstance();
    m_transformerHandler =
m_transformerFactory.newTransformerHandler(
              new StreamSource(
              new FileInputStream( stylesheetName ) ) );
    m_reader = XMLReaderFactory.createXMLReader();
    m_reader.setContentHandler( m_transformerHandler );
  }
```

The constructor creates a SAXTransformerFactory object and then uses it to create its TransformerHandler (the actual transformation engine), passing it a StreamSource object that provides access to the stylesheet to be used to perform transformations. An XMLReader object (the SAX-compliant parser) is created, and the transformation engine is associated with XMLReader as its content handler. At this point, all our sample code needs to perform transformations is an input document and the application's content handler.

```
public void transform( String documentName,
                       ContentHandler appHandler )
     throws SAXException, IOException
{
  SAXResult  theResult = new SAXResult( appHandler );
  m_transformerHandler.setResult( theResult );
  m_reader.parse( documentName );
}
```

When the application is ready to process a document, it calls this transform() method, passing in the name of the document to be processed and the application's content handler. A SAXResult object, created to hold the content handler, is provided to our TransformerHandler object so that it can call our application code as SAX events from the transformation are generated. When XMLReader.parse() is called, the document is parsed into SAX events, which are given to the TransformerHandler to be transformed and then passed through the SAXResult to our application code.

```
public static void main( String[] args )
{
  try {
    EventXsltTransformer  eventTransformer =
              new EventXsltTransformer( args[0] );
```

```
    eventTransformer.transform( args[1], eventTransformer );
  }
  catch( SAXException e ) {
    System.out.println( e.getMessage() );
  }
  catch( TransformerFactoryConfigurationError e ) {
    System.out.println( e.getMessage() );
  }
  catch( TransformerConfigurationException e ) {
    System.out.println( e.getMessage() );
  }
  catch( TransformerException e ) {
    System.out.println( e.getMessage() );
  }
  catch( FileNotFoundException e ) {
    System.out.println( e.getMessage() );
  }
  catch( IOException e ) {
    System.out.println( e.getMessage() );
  }
}
```

Our example `main()` method simply creates an instance of our example class
and asks it to perform a transformation using the stylesheet, input file name, and
output file name passed in as arguments. Note that `main()` passes in its copy of
our example class as the content handler (we indicated that the class implemented
the `ContentHandler` interface in the class declaration).

```
/*
   The following methods are from the ContentHandler interface
*/
public void setDocumentLocator (Locator locator)
{
  System.out.println( "Received setDocumentLocator event" );
}
public void startDocument () throws SAXException
{
  System.out.println( "Received startDocumetn event" );
}
public void endDocument() throws SAXException
{
  System.out.println( "Received endDocument event" );
```

```
      }
      public void startPrefixMapping (String prefix, String uri)
           throws SAXException
      {
        System.out.println( "Received startPrefixMapping event - prefix "
             + prefix + ", uri " + uri );
      }
      public void endPrefixMapping (String prefix) throws SAXException
      {
        System.out.println( "Received endPrefixMapping event - prefix "
                  + prefix );
      }
      public void startElement (String namespaceURI, String localName,
                String qName, Attributes atts) throws SAXException
      {
        System.out.println( "Received startElement event - namespaceURI "
                  + namespaceURI + ", localName " + localName
                  + ", qName " + qName );
      }
      public void endElement (String namespaceURI, String localName,
                String qName) throws SAXException
      {
        System.out.println( "Received endElement event - namespaceURI " +
             namespaceURI + ", localName " + localName +
             ", qName " + qName );
      }
      public void characters (char ch[], int start, int length)
           throws SAXException
      {
        System.out.println( "Received characters event - characters "
             + ch + ", start " + start + ", length " + length );
      }
      public void ignorableWhitespace (char ch[], int start, int length)
           throws SAXException
      {
        System.out.println(
             "Received ignorableWhitespace event - characters "
             + ch + ", start " + start + ", length " + length );
      }
      public void processingInstruction (String target, String data)
         throws SAXException
      {
        System.out.println(
```

```
                "Received processingInstruction event - target " +
                    target + ", data " + data );
    }
    public void skippedEntity (String name) throws SAXException
    {
        System.out.println( "Received skippedEntity event - name "
                + name );
    }
}
```

The remaining methods in our example all come from the `ContentHandler` interface and simply register the fact that they were called.

One of the great benefits of using SAX events as input for a transformation process is that this allows your application to perform multiple transformations on the same document simultaneously, using one or more `XMLFilter` objects. Each `XMLFilter` object can accept a stylesheet to give it a set of transformation instructions, and `XMLFilter` objects can be chained together to create a processing pipeline for events read by the XML parser. A code snippet that shows how this is done appears here:.

```
SAXTransformerFactory m_transformerFactory =
        ((SAXTransformerFactory)TransformerFactory.newInstance());
XMLFilter xmlFilter1 =
    m_transformerFactory.newXMLFilter(new StreamSource("ssheet1.xsl"));
XMLFilter xmlFilter2 =
    m_transformerFactory.newXMLFilter(new StreamSource("ssheet2.xsl"));
XMLFilter xmlFilter3 =
    m_transformerFactory.newXMLFilter(new StreamSource("ssheet3.xsl"));
XMLReader reader = XMLReaderFactory.createXMLReader();

xmlFilter1.setParent(reader);
xmlFilter2.setParent(xmlFilter1);
xmlFilter3.setParent(xmlFilter2);
xmlFilter3.setContentHandler( myContentHandler );

xmlFilter3.parse(new InputSource("foo.xml"));
```

Each `XMLFilter` object is created with its own XSLT stylesheet, which it will use to perform its part of the transformation process. The `XMLReader` object is created and used as input to the first filter; this first filter is used as input to the second filter, and the second filter is used as input to the third. The pipeline is completed by setting our application's content handler as the handler for the last filter in line.

When `xmlfilter3.parse()` is called, the following happens:

▶ `xmlfilter3.parse()` calls `xmlfilter2.parse()` with the input document passed as an argument.

▶ `xmlfilter2.parse()` calls `xmlfilter1.parse()`, again with the input document passed as an argument.

▶ `xmlfilter1.parse()` calls `reader.parse()`, again with the input document passed as an argument.

▶ The reader parses the input document and generates SAX events, which it sends to `xmlfilter1` (its content handler).

▶ `xmlfilter1` processes each event and then forwards it to `xmlfilter2`.

▶ `xmlfilter2` processes each event and then forwards it to `xmlfilter3`.

▶ `xmlfilter3` processes each event and then forwards it to the application's content handler for final processing.

Summary

A wealth of information and technology is available to help with just about any XML and XSLT programming task. As you might expect, the "big three" web-related programming languages—Java, Perl, and C++—have the largest base of tools, sample code, and mindshare; however, other languages, such as Python, also have many resources and a growing base of users to drive future development.

For the primary XML and XSLT programming language—Java—there is an applications interface called the Java API for XML Parsing (JAXP), which provides very strong capabilities for integrating XSLT transformations into applications. This integration can be tailored to the needs of each individual application using a combination of files, DOM hierarchies, and SAX event streams for input and output.

APPENDIX

A

XSLT2 and XPath2: The Evolving Standards

As of this writing, XSLT 1.0 and XPath 1.0 are the only finalized W3C recommendations related to XSLT. These recommendations were released November 16, 1999, but even before that final release date, the developer community has been thinking of improvements that could be made to XSLT. This led to the publication of the XSLT 1.1 working draft on December 10, 2000. The working group stopped any further work on XSLT 1.1 on August 24, 2001 (interestingly, there is no working draft of XPath1.1). After much deliberation, the XSL Working Group decided to use the XSLT 1.1 working draft as the foundation to directly leapfrog to XSLT 2.0 instead of publishing an intermediate XSLT 1.1 recommendation. Working drafts 2.0 of XSLT and XPath were then released by the W3C on December 20, 2001. Less than a month after this working draft was published, Michael Kay released SAXON 7.0, which implements the XSLT2.0 specification on an experimental basis! This is clearly an indication of the widespread acceptance of XSLT, as well the frantic pace at which XSLT and XPath are evolving. This is great news for developers who have been waiting for "bigger and better" XSLT since the initial 1.0 release. Of course, that also means that to stay abreast of these latest developments, your work is clearly cut out for you.

This appendix summarizes the new developments related to XSLT and XPath that you should find useful. It is our earnest hope that this helps you stay ahead of the curve and gives you a glimpse into what is yet to come in the realm of XSLT. Since no further work is expected on the XSLT 1.1 working draft, we have used the XSLT 2.0 working draft as the basis for the following discussion.

How XSLT 1.1 Differs from XSLT 1.0

The working group seems to have made a sincere attempt to ensure backward compatibility with the 1.0 specification. However, backward compatibility was not used as a guiding principle, and you will notice major differences, some of which may take you by surprise. As expected, errors reported in the 1.0 specification have also been fixed.

▶ **Elimination of the result tree fragment data type**   As explained in Chapter 8, the result tree fragment data type is used to bind a portion of the result tree to a variable name. The result tree fragment is the only data type in XSLT 1.0 for which content is specified in the `xsl:variable` element. The principle limitation of using a result tree fragment is that the operations allowed for this data type are a subset of those for a node set. XSLT 1.1 makes a provision for a node-set data type with content within the `xsl:variable` element. Thus, as far as we can see, this change will be transparent to most users: you can continue specifying and using variables with content, although the XSLT 1.1 processor will construct node sets where you would have expected a result tree fragment. In a nutshell, you will have access to an enhanced node-set data type.

▶ **Namespace Fixup**   In XSLT 1.0, there is practically no restriction on the way namespace nodes may be added to the result tree when using the output method. In XSLT 1.1, you need to follow certain constraints while constructing the result tree. These constraints may not be satisfied by elements such as `xsl:element` and `xsl:attribute`, which do not use any instructions that create any namespace nodes. Hence, the XSLT processor is required to have a `namespace Fixup` process that corrects such deviations. This change is probably more important to you if you write XSLT parsers.

▶ **Support for XML Base**   XSLT 1.1 provides support for XML Base, which is a W3C specification that details how XML resources may be linked to each other. It is reminiscent of the `<base href="...>` tag in HTML. It is used in conjunction with `xlink`. In the following example, the absolute URI will be resolved to the value `http://www.mywebsite.com/index.html`.

```
<doc xml:base="http://www.mywebsite.com/"
     xmlns:xlink="http://www.w3.org/1999/xlink">
...
        <link xlink:type="simple" xlink:href="index.html">Main home page
        </link>
...
```

▶ **Multiple result trees**   XSLT 1.1 allows for the transformation of the source tree into multiple XML trees. This book discussed this topic in further detail when discussing XSLT 2.0, since that specification significantly amends what was stated in the XSLT 1.1 specification.

▶ **Support for language bindings**   XSLT 1.1 made provisions for extension functions to be written in commonly used web development languages such as Java and JavaScript via language bindings. However, XSLT 2.0 does not address language bindings since the XSL Working Group considered it best to handle this topic separately from the core XSLT specification. On a related but separate note, XSLT 1.1 allows extension functions can now return external objects, which do not have a corresponding XPath data type associated with them. This facility has clearly been provided for interaction with code written in other programming languages.

Major Changes from XSLT 1.1 to 2.0

In the 2.0 specification, changes from XSLT 1.1 to 2.0 are categorized as major or minor. Since the 2.0 specification is still in a state of flux, the minor changes are more likely to change a lot before the final recommendation emerges. Therefore, we will review only the major changes here.

▶ **Node grouping**   Output nodes may be grouped using the element `xsl:for-each-group` and the corresponding function `current-group()`. If you are familiar with SQL, such facilities will sound very familiar. In XSLT 2.0 nodes may be grouped based on common string values, common names, and common values, and even allow the selection of distinct values via the identification and subsequent elimination of duplicate values. Such grouping is nestable to multiple levels.

▶ **Support for user-defined functions**   XSLT 2.0 allows definition of user-specified functions and their use in XPath expressions within the stylesheet. In keeping with the namespace philosophy to avoid collision between resources sharing similar names, each user-defined function is required to have a prefixed name. It has not yet been specified whether user-defined functions with the same names as vendor-specified ones will be allowed to override the latter. However, it is likely that some sort of function *overloading* will be permitted in the final 2.0 specification.

▶ **Multiple result trees and multiple output documents**   This facility has been significantly modified from the 1.1 working draft stage and is supported via the use of the element `xsl:result-document`. Contained within this element is a *content constructor* that is evaluated to create a series of nodes that are the children of a secondary result tree.

▶ **New XHTML output method**   In this book we have extensively used the HTML output method to write XSLT 1.0 stylesheets. XSLT 2.0 also supports XHTML output. Although a large base of web sites use HTML, it appears that XHTML will likely dominate future web implementations. Hence, we see the support for XHTML as a very prudent step to take at this juncture.

▶ **A new `xsl:sort-key` element**   The support for sorting is now provided within an XPath expression. This is done using the element `xsl:sort-key` that is used to define named sort specifications.

B

Review of the W3C XSL Working Group

Ｔhe World Wide Web Consortium (W3C) supports several working groups (WGs) that work on interrelated technologies such as XSL/XSLT, XML Protocol, HTML, DOM, HTTP, and encryption. Among other things, these working groups develop the specifications and recommendations for those web technologies. W3C's XSL Working Group was formed on January 23, 1998, with participants from W3C's member organizations such as IBM, Sun, Adobe, Arbortext, CNGroup, and so on. Here we will discuss the highlights of the group's charter. You can view the complete charter of the XSL WG at http://www.w3.org/Style/2000/xsl-charter.html.

Initially, the principal charge of the XSL working group is to define a practical style and transformational language to handle XML documents on either clients (such as browsers) or servers, and to support the following operations on the XML content: browsing, printing, interactive editing, and translation among different XML dialects. Since the working group's inception, XSL has been subdivided into three components: XSL-FO for formatting and styling of content; XSLT for data transformations; and XPath, an expression language for addressing parts of XML documents. The XSL Working Group now publishes the specifications for each of these components separately.

Since W3C supports several interrelated technologies, the XSL WG maintains communication with W3C working groups responsible for CSS, WAI, I18N, XML Query, MathML, and XForms. Moreover, the XSL WG participates in W3C's coordination groups (CGs) for hypertext and XML. The purpose of interaction between XSL WG and the other working groups is summarized here:

▶ **Web Accessibility Initiative (WAI) WG**   The goal of this WG is to ensure that XSL meets W3C's web accessibility goals.

▶ **I18N WG**   This WG serves two purposes related to internationalization of XSLT: to provide the expertise needed to ensure the extension of XSL-FO to support non-Western languages, and to determine whether XSLT can be used to transform documents written in any language. That is why the XSL WG maintains a liaison with I18N WG.

▶ **XML Query WG**   Since XSLT is so closely linked with XML, the XSL WG interacts with the XML Query WG to ensure the compatibility of XML Query with XPath and XSLT.

▶ **Math WG**   A part of MathML, this WG developed a presentation language for mathematical expressions. The goal of its interaction with the XSL WG is to ensure that XSLT addresses the requirements of mathematical text formatting.

▶ **XForms WG**   Interaction between XSL WG and XForms WG is required to ensure that the elements from extended forms (XForms) work well with XSL-FO.

The XSL WG has principal and alternate members, who are required by the W3C to be experts in composition, typography, computer display rendering, or computer language design. Members' expertise was defined by Sharon Adler (IBM) and Steve Zilles (Adobe) who were co-chairs of the WG when it was formed. W3C specified a list of deliverables and a schedule for their delivery. W3C also laid out structured rules about the level of involvement of the members, communication within the WG (meetings, teleconferences), and communication with the public. In particular, W3C holds the XSL WG responsible for maintaining active communication with national and international standards bodies and the industry consortia whose scope of work overlaps that of the WG, such as ISO/IEC JTC1/WG4, the national bodies corresponding to WG4, Oasis, and IETF.

W3C established completion of the 1.0 Recommendation as the major criterion of success of the XSL WG, soon to be followed by the next version of XSL. At the time of its formation, the XSL WG was expected to start its work in June 2000 and continue until February 2002 to complete the official W3C Recommendation (2.0) for XSL-FO, XSLT, and XPath. As of early 2002, the group had successfully completed several of its deliverables, including the 1.0 Recommendation and requirements documents and working drafts of the 2.0 specifications. It seems only a matter of time before the 2.0 Recommendation is finalized by the XSL Working Group.

XSL and XSLT Resources

This appendix lists XSLT resources that the authors use frequently in their work. Since the latest information about web-related developments is found on the Web itself, you should visit the web sites mentioned here periodically to check for any useful updates.

- ▶ W3C's official web site at http://www.w3.org.
- ▶ The web site at http://www.xslt.com, for general information and news about XSLT.
- ▶ The XML cover pages at http://www.oasis-open.org/cover/sgml-xml.html, hosted by the Organization for the Advancement of Structured Information Standards (OASIS). This web site provides a comprehensive online reference for XML and SGML. OASIS is a nonprofit, international consortium that creates interoperable industry specifications based on public standards such as XML and SGML. The information related to XSL and XSLT is on the XSL page at http://www.oasis-open.org/cover/xsl.html.
- ▶ James Clark's web page about XML resources at http://www.jclark.com/xml/. Information about the XT XSLT processor can be found at http://www.jclark.com/xml/xt.html.
- ▶ An open forum for XSL is provided by Mulberry Technologies, Inc., at http://www.mulberrytech.com/xsl/xsl-list/. There is also an associated mailing list at XSL-List@lists.mulberrytech.com.
- ▶ *XSLT Programmer's Reference, 2nd edition,* by Michael Kay (Wrox Publishers, 2001).
- ▶ *XSLT* by Doug Tidwell (O'Reilly & Associates, 2001).
- ▶ *XML Bible, 2nd edition,* by Elliote Rusty Harold (Hungry Minds, 2001).
- ▶ The resources mentioned on XSLT.com's web page at http://www.xslt.com/xslt_resources.htm.
- ▶ The web site http://www.xslinfo.com authored by James Tauber, Jamie Rice, and Daniel Krech.
- ▶ An XSLT tutorial, "XSLT by Example," at http://www.objectsbydesign.com/projects/xslt/xslt_by_example.html, provided by Objects by Design.
- ▶ The Zvon tutorials at http://www.zvon.org. These provide useful information about a range of web-related technologies. The XSLT tutorial is located at http://www.zvon.org/xxl/XSLTutorial/Output/index.html.
- ▶ The web site of *XML Magazine* at http://www.xmlmag.com/.

▶ O'Reilly's XML web site at http://www.xml.com.

▶ The web site http://www.xml.org also provides a comprehensive list of XML-related resources, news, and other general information.

▶ The web site at http://www.xmlhack.com provides important news, opinions, tips and issues related to XML development.

▶ The web site http://www.xmlsoftware.com provides a good general resource for information about XML and XSLT tools, as well as other XML-related software.

▶ Information on the Simple API for XML can be found on David Megginson's web site, http://www.megginson.com.

Glossary

absolute path   Points to the location of a node within the XML tree starting at the root node. By definition, it does not depend on the context node—for example, `//All_authors/Author/Name/First_name`.

ancestor   A node that occurs above the context node in the XML tree—that is, somewhere between the current node and the root node. Of course, the root node is a descendant of every other node in the XML tree.

CSS   Cascading Style Sheets, an official W3C specification used to describe style rules for document formatting elements such as font type, font size, color, positioning, paragraphs, and background.

descendant   A node that occurs below the current node in the XML tree—that is, all nodes between the current node up to and including the leaf nodes that can be reached from the current node. By definition, the leaf nodes do not have any descendants.

document element   The element in the XML tree that contains the entire XML document. It is also known as the root element, not to be confused with the root node, which is actually the parent of the node that represents the root element.

DOM   Document Object Model, a W3C specification. It is a platform- and language-neutral interface used to represent HTML and XML documents, and it allows scripts and programs to access and update dynamically the content, structure, and style of these documents. DOM provides a standard set of objects for representing marked-up documents, and a model of how these objects can be accessed, manipulated, and combined. *See also* SAX.

DTD   Document Type Definition, which is used to define the set of rules that the components (elements, attributes, and the like) of a source XML file must follow. Unlike an XML Schema, a DTD is not an XML document. *See also* XML Schema.

EDI   Electronic Data Interchange, a standard used for the communication of business transaction information between organizations.

entity   Specialized character strings that can be used in an XML document to point to special characters or to MIME types such as audio or video files, static graphic files, and so on. *See also* internal entities; external entities.

extensions   XSLT extensions, which include extension functions and extension elements. These are the elements or functions that are defined outside the W3C specification. Such extensions may either be user defined or provided by a specific XSLT processor vendor as an additional capability. XSLT specification 1.0 does not mention how such extensions may be defined, but it does provide support for using them within an XSLT stylesheet.

external entities   Specialized character strings that reference external resources via a URI. External entities may be either parsed or unparsed. *See also* unparsed entities.

fallback processing   A type of exception handling capability provided by an XSLT processor that uses the `xsl:fallback` element. The `xsl:fallback` element is activated only if the instruction element surrounding it cannot be processed by the current XSLT implementation.

forwards-compatible mode   The processing mode initiated by an XSLT processor when the version attribute of a stylesheet element is higher than the current implemented version of XSLT. In this case, the forwards-compatible mode is enabled for the current element and all of its descendants.

GML   Generalized Markup Language. This language can be considered a *protolanguage* of the SGML. It was invented at IBM by Charles Goldfarb along with Ed Losher and Ray Lorie in 1969.

ICE   Information and Content Exchange, a protocol for defining the format and method of information exchange between organizations. It is a W3C specification application that is aimed at promoting content exchange and reuse. In content syndication, ICE is used to describe the roles and responsibilities of the syndicators and their subscribers.

internal entities   Five prebuilt entities that are provided in XML to represent special characters such as <, >, &, ", and '.

literal result element   An element in the XSLT stylesheet that is not a part of any defined namespace—neither the default W3C namespace nor a namespace provided by the user or the software vendor providing the XSLT processor. Such elements are copied literally from the source tree to the result tree without any specialized processing.

metadata   Data about data. For example, a DTD defines the metadata related to source XML documents. *See also* DTD.

metalanguage   A language used to define other languages. SGML and XML are examples of metalanguages in that they are used to construct other markup languages.

MIME   Multipurpose Internet Mail Extensions, a web standard used to specify the way that e-mail messages must be formatted so they can be exchanged between heterogeneous systems. It is a very flexible standard and allows practically any type of document (audio, video, static images, plain text, or other application-specific data) to be embedded in an e-mail message. MIME uses base-64 encoding to represent nontextual information as text within an e-mail message.

namespace   Provides a way of avoiding collision between elements that have identical names but that refer to different URIs. Namespaces allow users to use multiple XML dialects in the same XML document (such as an XSLT stylesheet) without leaving any room for ambiguity.

OASIS   Organization for the Advancement of Structured Information Standards, a nonprofit, international consortium of companies and individuals that creates interoperable industry specifications based on public standards such as XML and SGML. The OASIS web site provides a comprehensive online reference for XML, SGML, and other related standards.

parameter   A means of creating a name-value binding in XSLT. The value specified in the parameter definition is just a default value that can be overridden when the template of the stylesheet containing the parameter is invoked. Once set, the value of the parameter cannot be changed. *See also* variable.

parent   A node that is the immediately ancestor of the current node. In an XML tree, any node other than the root node can have only one parent.

relative path   Points to the location of a node within the XML tree in relation to the current node. By definition, it depends on the context node. For example, if `Author` is the context node, `./Name/First_name is equivalent` to the node with absolute path `//All_authors/Author/Name/First_name`.

SAX Simple API for XML, an interface provided by XML parsers and used by event-based applications. *See also* DOM.

SGML Standard Generalized Markup Language. The roots of all modern markup languages can be traced back to SGML. It is a metalanguage used to construct other markup language. According to the W3C XML specification, XML is "an extremely simplified dialect of SGML." *See also* GML.

sibling All nodes that have the same parent are termed each other's siblings.

tag The unit of markup that serves as the delimiter for an element's definition. For example, `<Author AuthID="77">` is a start tag and `</Author>` is the corresponding end tag. Empty tags are ones that do not have any content—for example, `<Author AuthID="77"/>`. In XML, every tag other than empty tags must be closed.

unparsed entities Entities that are not processed by the XML parser. They are meant to be handled by an external application mentioned in the entity declaration.

URI Uniform Resource Identifier. The URI provides a way to access resources on the web. Uniform Resource Locators (URLs) are a particular type of URI.

valid document An XML document that conforms to all of the rules associated with the version declared in its XML declaration element *and* that adheres to all rules described in its DTD. Thus, a valid document is a well-formed document, but a well-formed XML document may not necessarily be a valid document.

variable A means of creating a name-value binding in XSLT using the `xsl:variable` element. Once set, the value of a variable cannot be changed within its context. A variable that is defined using a top-level `xsl:variable` element is a global variable, and its definition holds everywhere within the stylesheet. A local variable, by contrast, has a limited context since it is defined within a certain template. *See also* parameter.

well-formed document An XML document that conforms to all the rules associated with the version declared in its XML declaration element. These rules include having a single document element, properly nested tags, proper closure of all tags, and so on.

XHTML   Extensible Hypertext Markup Language. This language combines the best of HTML and XML capabilities. XHTML is an emerging W3C specification that builds on HTML 4.01.

XML Schema   Provides a way of representing the data model of an XML document similar to a DTD, including the elements, the relationships between elements, and any attributes that the elements may have. *See also* DTD.

Index

Page numbers in *italics* refer to illustrations or charts.

INTERNATIONAL CONTACT INFORMATION

AUSTRALIA
McGraw-Hill Book Company Australia Pty. Ltd.
TEL +61-2-9417-9899
FAX +61-2-9417-5687
http://www.mcgraw-hill.com.au
books-it_sydney@mcgraw-hill.com

CANADA
McGraw-Hill Ryerson Ltd.
TEL +905-430-5000
FAX +905-430-5020
http://www.mcgrawhill.ca

**GREECE, MIDDLE EAST,
NORTHERN AFRICA**
McGraw-Hill Hellas
TEL +30-1-656-0990-3-4
FAX +30-1-654-5525

MEXICO (Also serving Latin America)
McGraw-Hill Interamericana Editores S.A. de C.V.
TEL +525-117-1583
FAX +525-117-1589
http://www.mcgraw-hill.com.mx
fernando_castellanos@mcgraw-hill.com

SINGAPORE (Serving Asia)
McGraw-Hill Book Company
TEL +65-863-1580
FAX +65-862-3354
http://www.mcgraw-hill.com.sg
mghasia@mcgraw-hill.com

SOUTH AFRICA
McGraw-Hill South Africa
TEL +27-11-622-7512
FAX +27-11-622-9045
robyn_swanepoel@mcgraw-hill.com

**UNITED KINGDOM & EUROPE
(Excluding Southern Europe)**
McGraw-Hill Education Europe
TEL +44-1-628-502500
FAX +44-1-628-770224
http://www.mcgraw-hill.co.uk
computing_neurope@mcgraw-hill.com

ALL OTHER INQUIRIES Contact:
Osborne/McGraw-Hill
TEL +1-510-549-6600
FAX +1-510-883-7600
http://www.osborne.com
omg_international@mcgraw-hill.com